Adobe
XD
2020 release

CLASSROOM IN A BOOK®
The official training workbook from Adobe

Brian Wood

ISBN-13: 978-0-13-658380-6

ISBN-10: 0-13-658380-6

1 2020

WHERE ARE THE LESSON FILES?

Purchase of this Classroom in a Book in any format gives you access to the lesson files you'll need to complete the exercises in the book.

1   Go to www.adobepress.com/XDCIB2020.

2   Sign in or create a new account.

3   Click Submit.

● **Note:** If you encounter problems registering your product or accessing the lesson files or web edition, go to www.adobepress.com/support for assistance.

4   Answer the questions as proof of purchase.

5   The lesson files can be accessed through the Registered Products tab on your Account page.

6   Click the Access Bonus Content link below the title of your product to proceed to the download page. Click the lesson file links to download them to your computer.

● **Note:** If you purchased a digital product directly from www.adobepress.com or www.peachpit.com, your product will already be registered. However, you still need to follow the registration steps and answer the proof of purchase question before the Access Bonus Content link will appear under the product on your Registered Products tab.

CONTENTS

5 ORGANIZING CONTENT   124

GETTING STARTED

Adobe® XD® is an all-in-one cross-platform tool for designing and prototyping websites and mobile apps, creating presentations, and much more. Whether you are a general designer, web designer, User Experience (UX) designer, or User Interface (UI) designer, Adobe XD® offers you the tools you need to get professional-quality results.

About Classroom in a Book

Adobe XD Classroom in a Book® (2020 release) is part of the official training series for Adobe graphics and publishing software developed with the support of Adobe product experts. The features and exercises in this book are based on the February 2020 Adobe XD release.

The lessons are designed so that you can learn at your own pace. If you're new to Adobe XD, you'll learn the fundamentals you need to master to put the application to work. If you are an experienced user, you'll find that Classroom in a Book teaches many advanced features, including tips and techniques for using Adobe XD.

Although each lesson provides step-by-step instructions for creating a specific project, there's room for exploration and experimentation. You can follow the book from start to finish or do only the lessons that correspond to your interests and needs. Each lesson concludes with a review section summarizing what you've covered.

● **Note:** When instructions differ by platform, macOS commands appear first and then the Windows commands, with the platform noted in parentheses. For example, "press Option (macOS) or Alt (Windows) and click away from the artwork."

Prerequisites

Before beginning to use *Adobe XD Classroom in a Book (2020 release)*, you should have working knowledge of your computer and its operating system. Make sure that you know how to use the mouse and standard menus and commands and also how to open, save, and close files. If you need to review these techniques, see the printed or online documentation for macOS or Windows.

Installing the program

Before you begin using *Adobe XD Classroom in a Book (2020 release)*, make sure that your system is set up correctly and that you've installed the required software and hardware.

You must purchase the Adobe XD software separately. For complete instructions on installing the software, visit helpx.adobe.com/support/xd.html. You must install XD from Adobe Creative Cloud onto your hard disk. Follow the onscreen instructions.

● **Note:** In order to see the system requirements for Adobe XD, you can visit helpx.adobe.com/xd/system-requirements.html.

Minimum system requirements

macOS—macOS X v10.13 or later with the following minimum configuration:

- Intel® or AMD processor with 64-bit support
- Memory: 4GB of RAM
- Display: Non-retina display (Retina recommended)
- Internet connection and registration are necessary for required software activation, validation of subscriptions, and access to online services. Voice capabilities require users to be connected to the Internet to preview their prototypes.

Windows—Windows 10 Fall Creators Update (64-bit) – Version 1709 (build 10.0.16299) or later with the following minimum configuration:

- Intel® or AMD processor with 64-bit support
- Memory: 4 GB of RAM
- Display: 1280 x 800
- Minimum Direct 3D DDI Feature Set: 10. For Intel GPU, drivers released in 2014 or later are necessary.
- Internet connection and registration are necessary for required software activation, validation of subscriptions, and access to online services. Voice capabilities require users to be connected to the Internet to preview their prototypes.
- XD on Windows 10 supports Windows' native pen and touch features. You can use touch input to interact with XD tools, create artwork on canvas, navigate through layers, interact with components, wire prototypes, change shape properties in the Property Inspector, scroll through the preview window, drag images to the canvas, create repeat grids, and so on.

Online content

Your purchase of this Classroom in a Book includes online materials provided by way of your Account page on peachpit.com. These include:

Lesson files

To work through the projects in this book, you will need to download the lesson files from peachpit.com. You can download the files for individual lessons or it may be possible to download them all in a single file.

Web Edition

The Web Edition is an online interactive version of the book providing an enhanced learning experience. Your Web Edition can be accessed from any device with a connection to the Internet and it contains:

- The complete text of the book
- Hours of instructional video keyed to the text
- Interactive quizzes

In addition, the Web Edition may be updated when Adobe adds significant feature updates between major Creative Cloud releases. To accommodate the changes, sections of the online book may be updated or new sections may be added.

> **Note:** Adobe XD is evolving quickly, with frequent updates. We will evaluate the changes against the book and, if needed, supply a PDF of those changes where you access your lesson files.

Accessing the lesson files and Web Edition

If you purchased an eBook from peachpit.com or adobepress.com, your Web Edition will automatically appear under the Digital Purchases tab on your Account page. Click the Launch link to access the product. Continue reading to learn how to register your product to get access to the lesson files.

If you purchased an eBook from a different vendor or you bought a print book, you must register your purchase on peachpit.com in order to access the online content:

1 Go to www.adobepress.com/XDCIB2020.

2 Sign in or create a new account.

3 Click Submit.

4 Answer the questions as proof of purchase.

5 The lesson files can be accessed through the Registered Products tab on your Account page. Click the Access Bonus Content link below the title of your product to proceed to the download page. Click the lesson file links to download them to your computer. The Web Edition will appear under the Digital Purchases tab on your Account page. Click the Launch link to access the product.

Recommended lesson order

Adobe XD Classroom in a Book (2020 release) is designed to take you from A to Z in basic to intermediate app and website design. Each new lesson builds on previous exercises, using the files and assets you create to design and prototype an app. To achieve a successful result and the most complete understanding of all aspects of design in Adobe XD, the ideal training scenario is to start in Lesson 1 and perform each lesson in sequential order through the entire book to Lesson 11. Because each lesson builds essential files and content for the next, you shouldn't skip any lessons or even individual exercises. While ideal, this method may not be a practicable scenario for everyone.

Jumpstart

If you don't have the time or inclination to perform each lesson in the book in order, or if you're having difficulty with a particular lesson, you can work through individual lessons using the jumpstart method. Each lesson folder (when necessary) includes finished files and staged files (files that are completed to that point in the lessons).

To jumpstart a lesson, follow these steps:

1 The lesson files can be accessed through the Registered Products tab on your Account page. Click the Access Bonus Content link below the title of your product to proceed to the download page. Click the lesson file links to download them to your computer.

2 Open Adobe XD.

3 With no files open in Adobe XD, choose File > Open From Your Computer (macOS) or press Ctrl+O (Windows) and navigate to the Lessons folder on your hard drive, then to the specific lesson folder you are starting from. For instance, if you are jumpstarting Lesson 7, navigate to the Lessons > Lesson07 folder and open the file named L7_start.xd. All of the jumpstart lesson files include "_start" in their names.

   These simple steps will have to be repeated for each lesson you wish to jumpstart. If you choose the jumpstart method once, however, you do not have to continue using it for all subsequent lessons. For example, if you want to jumpstart Lesson 6, you can simply continue on to Lesson 7, and so on.

4 If the Assets panel shows missing or activating fonts, you can close the panel.

● **Note:** The lesson files were set up using the default font on macOS (Helvetica Neue). Windows users will see a missing fonts message and can close it, since the default font on Windows will be used in place of Helvetica Neue. For most of the lesson files, the Apple San Francisco Pro font is also used.

Additional resources

Adobe XD Classroom in a Book (2020 release) is not meant to replace documentation that comes with the program or to be a comprehensive reference for every feature. Only the commands and options used in the lessons are explained in this book. For comprehensive information about program features and tutorials, please refer to these resources:

Adobe XD Learn & Support: *helpx.adobe.com/support/xd.html* (accessible in Adobe XD by choosing Help > Learn & Support) is where you can find and browse tutorials, help, and support on *Adobe.com*.

Adobe Forums: *community.adobe.com* lets you tap into peer-to-peer discussions, questions, and answers on Adobe products.

Adobe Create Magazine: *create.adobe.com* offers thoughtful articles on design and design issues, a gallery showcasing the work of top-notch designers, tutorials, and more.

Resources for educators: *www.adobe.com/education* and *edex.adobe.com* offer valuable information for instructors who teach classes on Adobe software. Find solutions for education at all levels, including free curricula that can be used to prepare for the Adobe Certified Associate exams.

Also check out these useful links:

Adobe XD product home page: See *adobe.com/products/xd.html*.

Adobe Authorized Training Centers

Adobe Authorized Training Centers offer instructor-led courses and training on Adobe products. A directory of AATCs is available at *learning.adobe.com/partner-finder.html*.

1 AN INTRODUCTION TO ADOBE XD

Lesson overview

In this lesson, you'll explore the workspace and learn the following:

- What Adobe XD is.
- A typical Adobe XD workflow.
- How to open an Adobe XD file.
- How to work with the tools and panels.
- How to zoom, pan, and navigate multiple artboards.
- How to preview your projects.
- How to share your projects.

This lesson will take about 30 minutes to complete. To get the lesson files used in this chapter, download them from the web page for this book at www.adobepress.com/XDCIB2020. For more information, see "Accessing the lesson files and Web Edition" in the Getting Started section at the beginning of this book.

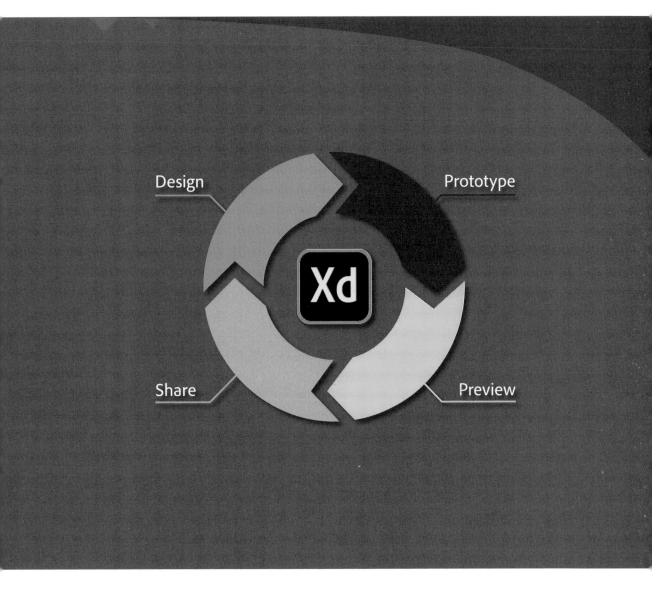

In this first lesson, you'll be introduced to a typical Adobe XD design workflow and explore the workspace.

Introducing Adobe XD

Adobe XD is a complete end-to-end solution for designing user experiences for mobile apps, websites, presentations, and more. You can design, prototype, preview, and share using this one tool.

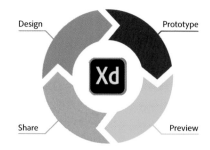

XD allows you to create the visual appearance of an app, website, or whatever you need—the behavior it exhibits is there merely to illustrate how the "real" app works. The prototype of the user experience you create in XD is not the actual app, website, or other, even though it can mimic much of the interactivity of the final product.

You design all the screens or pages of your project in a single Adobe XD file. Each page in Adobe XD is called an artboard, and you can add different sized artboards depending on the required screen sizes. You can then define interactivity between them to visualize how users navigate through the screens or pages. You can test the prototype you create locally or on a device and easily share prototypes with others to gather feedback via commenting and annotations. That feedback can then be incorporated into the design. Finally, you can send design specs and exported production-ready assets to a developer to create the app or website outside of Adobe XD.

A typical UX design workflow

In the early days of the web, designers created the user experience (UX) for websites on desktops, making sure to optimize that experience across different browsers, browser versions, and operating systems.

Since the rise of touchscreen devices, like the Apple iPhone, designers have had to consider the overall user experience of apps and websites on those different devices. These days, with the multitude of screen sizes and devices, operating systems, screen pixel densities (think Retina or hiDPI), and other factors, creating a consistent and pleasurable user experience is an integral part of the web or app design process. To get our products to market on time and budget, and to gain and retain users, we need to work quickly and efficiently.

In a typical web or app design workflow today, we follow the general process shown in the following figure:

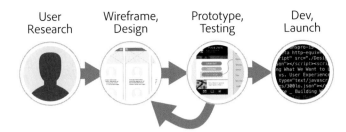

User Research → Wireframe, Design → Prototype, Testing → Dev, Launch

Your design process may be different, depending on the project scope, budget, size, and type, but this is generally how the process works.

First, we gather information through research. You can ask questions of clients and your potential target audience, work with focus groups, check existing analytics, and more. We then start a design. Your designs can be a hand-drawn sketch— also called a low-fidelity (low-fi) wireframe—or a fully designed, high-fidelity (hi-fi) design. Early in the days of the mobile web, we would sketch, wireframe, and design. Today we typically design, prototype, and collaborate (share).

Low-fidelity wireframe   High-fidelity design

To test the user experience, we create an interactive prototype at some point in the design process. A prototype is a tool for gathering feedback on the feasibility and usability of our designs. In the following figure, you'll see an example of prototyping interactivity in a high-fidelity design.

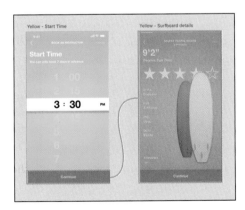

● **Note:** The smaller blue area at the bottom of the artboard on the left (covering the Continue button) represents a hotspot, or interactive area that users will tap or click. The larger blue area on the right represents the resulting screen that shows. The blue connector (also called a wire) indicates the connection between the hotspot and the resulting screen.

Adobe XD was born out of the need for a single all-in-one cross-platform tool for designing and prototyping websites and mobile apps.

Starting Adobe XD and opening a file

To start working in Adobe XD, you'll open a document and explore the XD workspace. You'll create and manipulate your design content using elements such as panels, bars, and windows, all of which make up the *workspace*.

● **Note:** If you have not already downloaded the project files for this lesson to your computer from your Account page at peachpit.com, make sure to do so now. See the "Getting Started" section at the beginning of the book.

The Home screen

When you first launch Adobe XD, the Home screen appears. The Home screen gives you easy access to presets, a list of recent files (if available), a list of add-ons, resources, a jumpstart tutorial, and more. The Home screen appears when you create a new file, regardless of whether a file is already open, or when you click the Home button (♠) in the upper-left corner of the application window with a document open.

1 Start Adobe XD.

● **Note:** The Home screen you see may look different, depending on your version of XD and whether you've opened files previously.

2 Click Your Computer on the left side of the Home screen. Navigate to the Lessons > Lesson01 folder and open the L1_start.xd file.

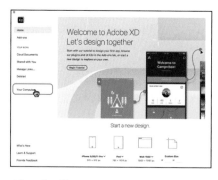

After the file opens in XD, the Assets panel may open on the left side of the workspace. In the panel, you may see a message about missing fonts. You can close the Assets panel for now by clicking the Assets panel icon (⊟) in the lower-left corner of the application. To learn more about missing fonts, see the sidebar titled, "Fixing missing fonts" in Lesson 3.

● **Note:** To maximize the Adobe XD application and give yourself more room to work, you may want to Option-click the green maximize button in the upper-left corner of the application window (macOS) or click Maximize in the upper-right corner (Windows).

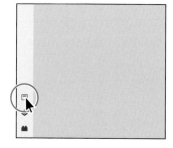

You will use the L1_start.xd file to practice navigating, zooming, and investigating an Adobe XD document and the workspace.

Exploring the workspace (macOS)

With the L1_start.xd project file open on macOS, you'll see the default XD workspace. If you are on Windows, proceed to the next section.

Choose View > Zoom To Fit All to see everything.

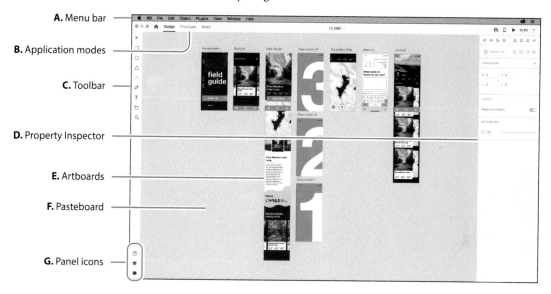

A. Menu bar
B. Application modes
C. Toolbar
D. Property Inspector
E. Artboards
F. Pasteboard
G. Panel icons

A. The **menu bar** at the top of the application window provides access to commands available in Adobe XD (macOS).

B. The **application modes** (Design, Prototype, and Share) provide a way to switch between Design mode, Prototype mode, and Share mode.

C. The **toolbar** contains tools for selecting, drawing, and editing shapes, paths, and artboards.

D. The **Property Inspector** is docked on the right side of the application window. Adobe XD consolidates many of the most frequently accessed options in the Property Inspector. The properties shown in the Property Inspector are contextual, which means that they are based on the content selected in the document.

E. Adobe XD uses **artboards** to represent the screens in your app or website.

F. The **pasteboard** is the gray area around the artboards; it's where you can place content that you don't want to associate with an existing artboard. The pasteboard and artboards are contained within the document window.

G. Access the **Layers**, **Assets**, and **Plugins** panels by clicking the appropriate button in the lower-left corner of the application window.

macOS users can skip the next section, "Exploring the workspace (Windows)," and proceed to the section "Working in Design mode."

Exploring the workspace (Windows)

With the L1_start.xd project file open on Windows, you'll see the default XD workspace.

Press Ctrl+0 (zero) to see everything.

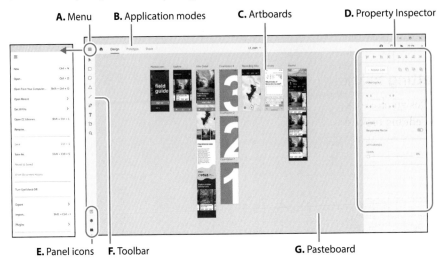

A. Menu **B.** Application modes **C.** Artboards **D.** Property Inspector

E. Panel icons **F.** Toolbar **G.** Pasteboard

A. On Windows, there is no top-level menu bar. Right-click an object and use the context menu instead. XD on Windows has a "hamburger" menu (≡) in the upper-left corner that allows you to create or open files, save, export assets, and more.

B. The **application modes** (Design, Prototype, and Share) provide a way to switch between Design mode, Prototype mode, and Share mode.

C. Adobe XD uses **artboards** to represent the screens in your app or website.

D. The **Property Inspector** is docked on the right side of the application window. Adobe XD consolidates many of the most frequently accessed options in the Property Inspector. The properties shown in the Property Inspector are contextual, which means they are based on the content selected in the document.

E. Access the **Layers**, **Assets**, and **Plugins** panels by clicking the appropriate button in the lower-left corner of the application window.

F. The **toolbar** contains tools for selecting, drawing, and editing shapes, paths, and artboards.

G. The **pasteboard** is the gray area around the artboards; it's where you can place content that you don't want to associate with an existing artboard. The pasteboard and artboards are contained within the document window.

Working in Design mode

On both macOS and Windows, when working on your project in Adobe XD, there are three modes you will be using: Design, Prototype, and Share. When you select a mode, certain features and tools specific to that mode become available in the application window. Each mode represents a stage in the design process.

When you open a file in Adobe XD, the program starts out in Design mode. In Design mode, you create and edit artboards and add your design content to them.

Getting to know the tools

In Design mode, the toolbar on the left side of the workspace contains selection and editing tools, drawing tools, a text tool, an artboard tool, and a zoom tool. As you progress through the lessons, you'll work with all of these tools.

- Move the pointer over the Select tool (▶) in the toolbar. Notice that the name (Select) and keyboard shortcut (V) are displayed in a tooltip.

Adobe XD was built for speed. To work faster, you can switch between tools using the keyboard command associated with each of the tools. For instance, pressing the letter Z will switch to the Zoom tool, and pressing the letter V will switch back to the Select tool.

Working with the Property Inspector

The Property Inspector is the docked panel on the right side of the workspace. It offers quick access to options and commands relevant to the currently selected content. It's also where you'll set appearance properties for most of your content.

1 Select the Select tool (▶) in the toolbar, and click the image at the top of the artboard named Hike Detail.

The options for the selected content appear in the Property Inspector on the right, including options for colors, border, effects, and more.

2 In the Property Inspector, click the checkmark to the left of the Fill option to deselect that option for the selected content (turn the fill off). The image disappears. Select the same Fill option to show the image again.

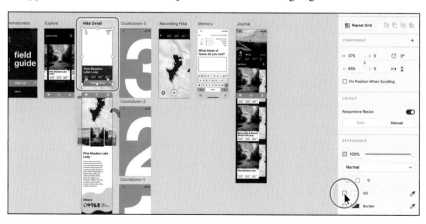

▶ **Tip:** To deselect all, you can also press Command+Shift+A (macOS) or Ctrl+Shift+A (Windows).

Most of the content in the Property Inspector changes depending on what is selected. If there is nothing selected, the Property Inspector is dimmed.

3 Click in the gray pasteboard area, away from the artboards, or choose Edit > Deselect All (macOS), so that the content on the artboard is no longer selected.

Working with panels

There are three main panels in Adobe XD, aside from the Property Inspector on the right, that give you quick access to layers, assets, and plugins. They are each opened by clicking a button in the lower-left corner of the workspace or pressing a keyboard command. Next, you'll experiment with closing and opening these panels.

▶ **Tip:** You can also press Command+Y (macOS) or Ctrl+Y (Windows) to toggle the Layers panel open and closed, or choose View > Layers (macOS).

1 Click the Layers panel button (◆) in the lower-left corner of the application window to open the Layers panel, if it isn't already open.

The Layers panel lists all of the artboards in the document when nothing in the document window is selected. You can think of an artboard as a page in a web design or a screen in an app design. Later in this lesson, you'll learn more about artboards and how to navigate them.

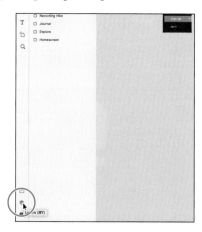

2 With the Select tool (▶) selected in the toolbar, click the same image on the Hike Detail artboard you selected earlier.

 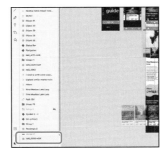

When you select content on an artboard, all of the content of that artboard is listed in the Layers panel. The Layers panel is contextual, which means it shows different content depending on what is (or isn't) selected.

3 Click the Layers panel button (≋) in the lower-left corner of the workspace to hide the Layers panel.

Prototype mode

As a step in the design process, you may wish to connect artboards (screens) to each other to visualize how users navigate your app, website, or presentation. With Adobe XD, you can create interactive prototypes to visualize the interactions between screens or wireframes in Prototype mode. You can preview the interaction to validate the user experience and iterate on your design to save time on development. You can also record the interactions and share them with stakeholders to get their feedback. Next, you'll briefly explore Prototype mode. You'll learn more about Prototype mode in Lesson 8, "Creating a Prototype."

1 Press Command+0 (macOS) or Ctrl+0 (Windows) to make sure you can see all of the design content.

2 Choose Edit > Deselect All (macOS) or click in a blank part of the gray pasteboard area to deselect all.

3 Click Prototype in the upper-left corner of the application window to enter Prototype mode.

▶ **Tip:** In Design mode on macOS, you can choose View > Switch Workspace to switch between modes. You can also press Control+Tab (macOS) or Ctrl+Tab (Windows) to toggle between Design, Prototype, and Share modes.

In Prototype mode, notice that the only tools available in the toolbar are the Select tool and Zoom tool, and the Property Inspector now contains settings for interactions. The main purpose of Prototype mode is to add interactivity to your designs. So for the purpose of visualizing how a transition from one screen to another might look, for instance, you can add the interactivity between those screens here.

4   To select all of the content in the document, press Command+A (macOS) or Ctrl+A (Windows).

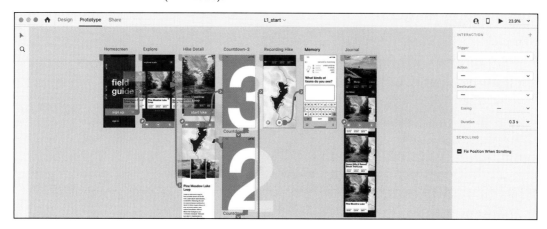

In the lesson file you currently have open, L1_start.xd, the artboards have interactivity added. The interaction between content appears as blue connector lines (also called "wires"). There will be no interactivity by default when you create a design. You can select an artboard or object and create a connection between it and another artboard. In Lesson 8, you'll learn all about how to create an interactive prototype.

As you add interactivity to your designs, you can test that interactivity either within the desktop version of Adobe XD or on a mobile device using the Adobe XD mobile app.

5   To deselect the artwork, choose Edit > Deselect All (macOS) or press Command+Shift+A (macOS) or Ctrl+Shift+A (Windows).

Changing the view of artwork

When you're working in files, it's likely that you'll need to change the zoom level and navigate among artboards. The magnification level, which can range from 2.5% to 6400%, is displayed near the upper-right corner of the application window.

There are a lot of ways to change the zoom level in Adobe XD, and in this section you'll explore several of the most common methods.

Using view commands

Next you'll familiarize yourself with enlarging or reducing the view of artwork using the View menu.

1   Click Design in the upper-left corner of the application window to enter Design mode.

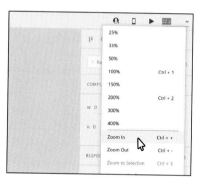

▶ **Tip:** You can zoom in using the keyboard shortcut Command and + (macOS) or Ctrl and + (Windows). You can zoom out using the keyboard shortcut Command and – (macOS) or Ctrl and – (Windows).

● **Note:** Using any of the viewing tools and commands affects only the display of the artwork, not the actual size of the artwork.

2   Choose View > Zoom In (macOS), or open the Zoom menu in the upper-right corner of the application window and choose Zoom In (Windows), to enlarge the display of the artwork.

3   Choose View > Zoom Out (macOS), or click the Zoom menu in the upper-right corner of the application window and choose Zoom Out (Windows), to reduce the view of the artwork.

The zoom level appears in a menu in the upper-right corner of the application window, identified by a down arrow next to a percentage.

4   Choose 150% from the Zoom menu in the upper-right corner of the application window.

macOS

Windows

On Windows in the Zoom menu, you'll see more options, like Zoom In and Zoom Out. On either platform, you can also type a value into the Zoom field and press Return or Enter to view your document content at different sizes.

▶ **Tip:** You can also press Command+0 (macOS) or Ctrl+0 (Windows) to fit all.

5   Choose View > Zoom To Fit All (macOS), or choose Zoom To Fit All from the Zoom menu (Windows).

Because the gray pasteboard (the area outside the artboards) extends to 50,000 pixels in both directions, you can easily lose sight of your design content. By choosing Zoom To Fit All, you make sure that all content is fit (and centered) in the document window.

6   With the Select tool (▶) selected in the toolbar on the left, click the image you selected earlier on the Hike Detail artboard.

▶ **Tip:** You can also press Command+3 (macOS) or Ctrl+3 (Windows) to zoom in to the selected content.

7   Choose View > Zoom To Selection (macOS), or choose Zoom To Selection from the Zoom menu in the upper-right corner of the application window (Windows), to zoom in to the selected content, centering it in the document window.

This zoom command is very useful, and one you will most likely use a lot. Learning the keyboard shortcut for this command, Command+3 (macOS) or Ctrl+3 (Windows), will allow you to work even faster.

8   Press Command+0 (macOS) or Ctrl+0 (Windows) to fit all of the artboards in the window before continuing.

Using the Zoom tool

In addition to the Zoom menu options, you can use the Zoom tool (Q) to magnify and reduce the view of artwork to predefined magnification levels. If you're familiar with the Zoom tool in other Adobe applications, you'll be familiar with the Zoom tool in XD.

1 Select the Zoom tool (Q) in the toolbar on the left, and then move the pointer into the document window.

   Notice that a plus sign (+) appears at the center of the Zoom tool pointer.

2 Move the Zoom tool over the large white number 3, and click a few times to zoom in.

   The Zoom tool performs an animated zoom, and the artwork is displayed at a higher magnification.

3 Move the pointer over another part of the document and click a few more times. Notice that the area where you clicked is magnified.

4 With the Zoom tool still selected, move the pointer over another part of the document and press the Option (macOS) or Alt (Windows) key. A minus sign (–) appears at the center of the Zoom tool pointer. With the Option or Alt key pressed, click twice in the document window to reduce the view of the artwork.

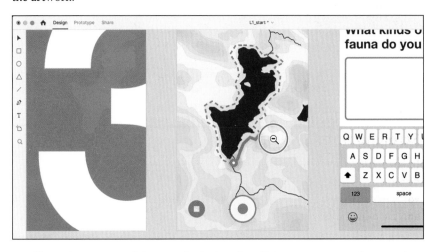

You'll use the Zoom tool frequently during the editing process to enlarge and reduce the view of artwork. Because of this, Adobe XD allows you to select it using the keyboard at any time without first deselecting any other tool you may be using. With any other tool selected, try the following:

- To access the Zoom tool using your keyboard, press spacebar *and then* Command (macOS), or press Ctrl+spacebar (Windows), and either click or drag to zoom in.

● **Note:** Dragging with the Zoom tool selected while pressing the Option (macOS) or Alt (Windows) key will zoom out, but it won't be an animated zoom. The effect is the same as Option-clicking (macOS) or Alt-clicking (Windows) with the Zoom tool selected.

- To zoom out, press spacebar+Option+Command (macOS) or Ctrl+Alt+spacebar (Windows) and click.

5 Press Command+0 (macOS) or Ctrl+0 (Windows) to see all of the design content again.

6 With the Zoom tool selected, drag from left to right across the content to zoom in.

This creates a marquee that indicates the area to be zoomed in to. You can drag in any direction to create a zoom box to zoom in to.

Scrolling through a document

In Adobe XD, you can use the Hand tool (✋) to pan to different areas of a document. Using the Hand tool allows you to push the document around much like you would a piece of paper on your desk. In this section, you'll access the Hand tool and see how it works.

1 Click to select any tool in the toolbar, and move the pointer into the document window.

2 Press and hold the spacebar to temporarily select the Hand tool, and then drag in any direction in the document window. When finished, release the spacebar.

● **Note:** The spacebar shortcut for the Hand tool (✋) does not work when the Text tool (T) is active and the cursor is in text. If the cursor is in text, you can press the Esc key (possibly a few times) to select the text object, not the text. You can then press the spacebar to access the Hand tool.

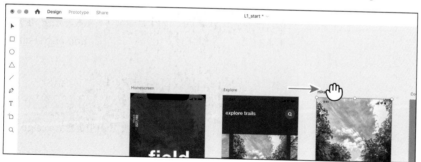

Instead of panning with the Hand tool, you can also drag on a trackpad with two fingers to pan in the document window.

● **Note:** To use the Hand tool, Windows users may need to press and hold the spacebar and, while pressing, press and let go of another key (like the Alt key). Then, while still pressing the spacebar, pan in the document window.

Navigating artboards

Artboards represent the screens in your app design or the pages in your web design or presentation (they're similar to artboards in Adobe Illustrator or Adobe Photoshop) and are found in the gray pasteboard area. You can have as many artboards in a single Adobe XD document as you like, and most documents you create in Adobe XD start with a single artboard. You can easily add, remove, and edit artboards after the document is created.

In Lesson 2, "Setting Up a Project," you'll learn how to work with artboards. In this section, you'll learn how to efficiently navigate a currently open document that contains multiple artboards.

1   Choose View > Zoom To Fit All (macOS), or choose Zoom To Fit All from the Zoom menu (Windows), to see all of the design content again.

The artboards in a document can be arranged in any order or orientation and can be different sizes—they can even overlap. Suppose that you want to create a simple app with four screens or design a website showing the screen sizes that represent different devices. You can create different artboards for every screen, all with the same (or a different) size and orientation.

2   With the Select tool (▶) selected, click in the gray pasteboard area around the artboards to ensure that all artwork is deselected.

3   Click the Layers panel button (≜) in the lower-left corner of the application window to show the Layers panel.

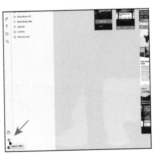 

The content you see in the Layers panel is contextual, which means it changes depending on what is selected in the document. If nothing is selected, you'll see a listing of all of the *artboards* in the open document. When you select artwork, the artboard that the artwork is on becomes the active artboard. The active artboard is listed at the top of the Layers panel. It's also indicated on the pasteboard by a subtle outline around the artboard. In the Layers panel, you can navigate between artboards, rename artboards, duplicate or delete artboards, and more.

4 Click each of the artboards in the Layers panel list, and notice that doing so selects that artboard in the document window.

▶ **Tip:** You can also click an artboard name in the document window to select an artboard. You'll learn all about selecting artboards in Lesson 2.

You can tell which artboard is selected because the name above the artboard is highlighted in blue and there is a blue highlight around the artboard.

5 Double-click the artboard icon (⬚) that appears to the left of the artboard name "Explore" in the Layers panel.

● **Note:** Double-clicking the artboard name (not the artboard icon [⬚]) in the Layers panel or above the artboard in the document allows you to change the name of the artboard.

The artboard named Explore is now centered in the document window. The Layers panel no longer lists all of the artboards and instead shows the content on the Explore artboard.

● **Note:** Simply clicking content on an artboard also shows the content for that artboard in the Layers panel.

6 Press Command+Y (macOS) or Ctrl+Y (Windows) to collapse the Layers panel.

Previewing your designs

You can test your prototype within Adobe XD using the desktop preview or the Adobe XD app on your iOS or Android device. Next, you'll take a look at previewing your designs within XD.

1 Press Command+0 (macOS) or Ctrl+0 (Windows) to see all of the design content again.

2 Click in the gray pasteboard area outside of the artboards to deselect all.

Tip: You can also choose Window > Preview (macOS) to open the Preview window, or press Command+Return (macOS) or Ctrl+Enter (Windows).

3 With nothing selected, click Desktop Preview (▶) in the upper-right corner of the application window to open the Preview window.

Note: On a Windows touch device such as a Microsoft Surface Pro, the Preview window may appear as a split screen. You can drag the divider between the screens to hide the Preview window.

In the Preview window, you should see the home artboard (named Homescreen), since nothing is selected. Normally, the artboard that is in focus (selected) shows in the Preview window. The Preview window opens at the size of either the selected artboard or the first artboard (with nothing selected).

4 Click the Sign Up button in the Preview window to show the next artboard that contains an image carousel.

Clicking interactive elements allows you to easily test the navigation between screens as you build your prototype.

5 Click the red button (macOS) or the X (Windows) in the corner of the Preview window to close it.

Sharing your designs

At any point in the design process you may want to share your saved documents with others for collaboration to gather feedback, pass design specifications like font size and color to developers, and more. You can share the entire project, or a subset of artboards, with reviewers by providing them a web link they can use to view your prototype, test it, present it, or look at design specs in a web browser.

● **Note:** You'll learn about sharing an entire project or a subset of artboards in Lesson 10.

Next, you'll take a quick look at how you can share your design and what that means. In Lesson 10, "Sharing Your Designs," you'll learn about sharing your prototypes and design specs with others.

1 Click Share in the upper-left corner of the application window to enter Share mode.

2 In the Properties panel on the right, click the View Setting to show a menu.

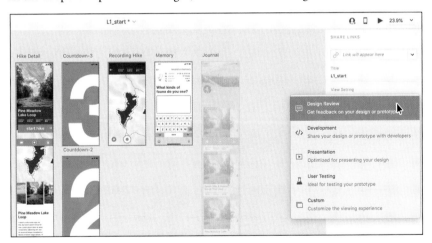

You can share your document for a variety of purposes, including for a design review, development, a presentation, user testing, and more. If you make changes later, you can always update what you share or create a new version from the current design.

3 Press the Esc key or click away from the View Setting menu to hide it.

Switching between documents

When working in Adobe XD, you can have multiple documents open at one time. To switch between open documents, you'll first open another file to have another document open to work with.

- Choose File > Open or Open From Your Computer (macOS) or, on Windows, click the menu icon (≡) and choose Open or Open From Your Computer. Navigate to a second file and open it in Adobe XD.

  The document opens in a separate application window.

- To switch to another open document, on macOS either choose Window > [name of file] or press Command+~, or, on Windows, press Alt+Tab to switch between the open documents.

Finding resources for using Adobe XD

For complete and up-to-date information about using Adobe XD, choose Help > Learn & Support (macOS) or, with a document open on Windows, click the menu icon (≡) and choose Help > Learn & Support from within Adobe XD. The helpx.adobe.com/support/xd.html page will open in a web browser. From that web page you can explore the library of tutorials, projects, and articles to learn more about Adobe XD.

● **Note:** The web page you see will most likely look different, and that's okay.

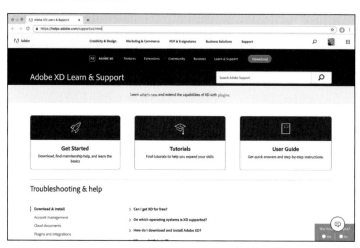

- Choose File > Close (macOS), or click the X in the upper-right corner of the open window (Windows), to close the L1_start.xd file. If you're asked whether you want to save your changes, click Don't Save.

Review questions

1 Briefly, what is Adobe XD?

2 What is meant by a low-fidelity (low-fi) wireframe?

3 What are two ways to change the view of a document?

4 What is a prototype used for?

5 What are the two methods for previewing a prototype?

6 What purpose does sharing serve?

Review answers

1 Adobe XD is a complete end-to-end solution for designing user experiences for websites, mobile apps, and presentations. You can design, prototype, preview, and share in the same tool.

2 A low-fidelity wireframe is a way to determine the functional elements of a page or screen without diving into design specifics like colors and fonts. It is a quick method of exploring the basic structure of content in an app or website using rough representations of graphics and layout.

3 To change the zoom level of a document, you can choose commands from the View menu (macOS) or the Zoom menu (macOS and Windows). You can also use the Zoom tool (Q) in the toolbar and click in or drag over a document to enlarge or reduce the view. In addition, you can use keyboard shortcuts to magnify or reduce the display of artboards.

4 Interactive prototypes allow us to test our designs and to gather feedback on the feasibility and usability of our designs.

5 Currently, the two main methods for previewing (testing) a prototype are by using Desktop Preview with Adobe XD or by using the Adobe XD app on your iOS or Android device.

6 Sharing a document is useful for collaboration, testing a prototype, gathering feedback on your design, sharing design specs, and more.

2 SETTING UP A PROJECT

Lesson overview

In this lesson, you'll learn how to do the following:

- Create and save a new document.
- Understand cloud documents.
- Create and edit artboards.
- Add grids to artboards.
- Work with multiple artboards.
- Manage artboards with the Layers panel.

 This lesson will take about 45 minutes to complete. To get the lesson files used in this chapter, download them from the web page for this book at www.adobepress.com/XDCIB2020. For more information, see "Accessing the lesson files and Web Edition" in the Getting Started section at the beginning of this book.

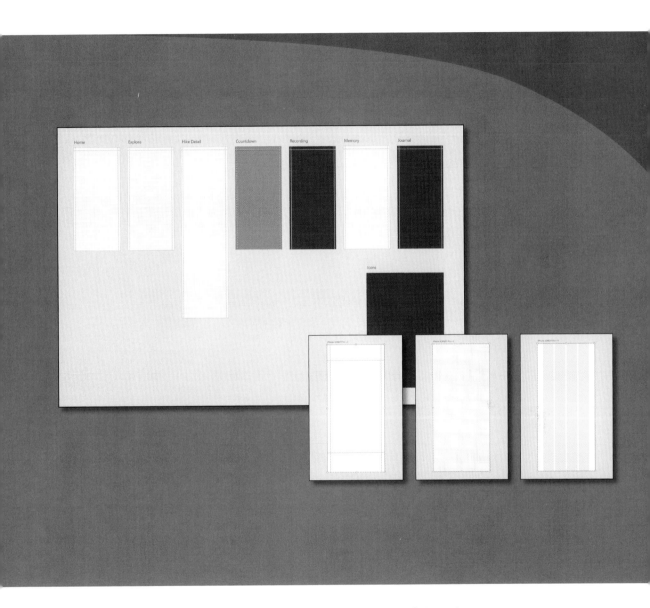

In this lesson, you'll start a new app design project and create and manage the artboards that will become the screens in your project.

Starting the lesson

In this lesson, you'll create your first project in Adobe XD and begin to set up design screens for a hiking app you will design, prototype, and share. To start, you'll open a final lesson file to get an idea of what you'll create in this lesson.

● **Note:** If you have not already downloaded the project files for this lesson to your computer from your Account page, make sure to do so now. See the "Getting Started" section at the beginning of the book.

1   Start Adobe XD, if it's not already open.

2   On macOS, choose File > Open From Your Computer. On Windows, click the menu icon (☰) in the upper-left corner of the application window and choose Open From Your Computer. Open the file named L2_end.xd, which is in the Lessons > Lesson02 folder that you copied onto your hard disk.

● **Note:** For either macOS or Windows, if the Home screen is showing with no files open, click Your Computer in the Home screen. Open the file named L2_end.xd, which is in the Lessons > Lesson02 folder that you copied onto your hard disk.

● **Note:** The screen shots for this lesson were taken on Windows. On macOS, you'll see the menus above the application window.

3   Choose View > Zoom To Fit All (macOS), or choose Zoom To Fit All from the Zoom menu (Windows) in the upper right.

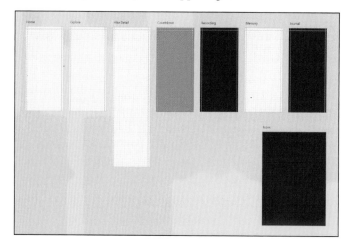

This file shows you what you will create by the end of the lesson.

4   You can either leave the file open for reference or close it. To close it, choose File > Close (macOS) or, on Windows, click the X in the upper-right corner of the open window to close the file.

Creating and saving a new document

You'll now begin your app design by creating a new document. In Adobe XD, you can have a number of project files open at one time and easily move between them.

1   If the Home screen isn't showing (if you have the L2_end.xd file open), choose File > New (macOS) or, on Windows, click the menu icon (☰) and choose New.

    With Adobe XD, you can start your document using a range of screen sizes. In the Home screen that opens, you'll find a row of icons representing the generic device sizes used in app design, web design, and more. From left to right, the icons represent phones, tablets, general web pages, and custom screen sizes. Within Adobe XD, screens are represented by artboards. Know that no matter what screen size you start with, you can always edit that size in your document later.

2   In the Home screen, click the iPhone X/XS/11 Pro name to reveal a menu of sizes. Click iPhone XR/XS Max/11 (414 x 896), and a new document opens with a single artboard showing.

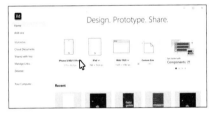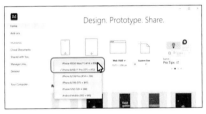

3   Choose View > Zoom To Fit All (macOS), or choose Zoom To Fit All from the Zoom menu (Windows) in the upper right.

    The file that opens is your working file and will include all of the screens (artboards), images, colors, and more that make up your project.

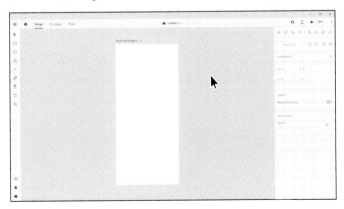

Tip: To show the Home screen, with a document open, you could also click the Home button (🏠) in the upper-left corner of the application window.

Note: You may see different screen sizes in the Home screen, and that's okay. The Home screen reflects the most widely used screen sizes and will change over time.

Tip: In the Home screen, you can click the Custom Size icon (not the W and H fields) to create a new document without any artboards.

Adobe XD and Retina (HiDPI)

By default, artboards in Adobe XD are considered 1x, or non-Retina (non-HiDPI) in size. If you want to design at 2x, or Retina sizing (HiDPI), you will need to create custom artboards that are twice the size (scale) of the default artboards.

For instance, by default the iPhone 6/7/8 artboard size in Adobe XD is 375 x 667. To design at Retina (HiDPI) size, you need to change the artboard dimensions to 750 x 1334.

Raster content you import will need to be of sufficient pixel density, which you'll learn about in Lesson 3, "Adding Images, Graphics, and Text." When you export content, which you'll do in Lesson 11, "Exporting and Integration," you can change the Designed At option to get the correct export sizes, whether you designed at 1x or 2x (Retina).

● **Note:** You will learn more about cloud documents in Lessons 9 and 10.

When you create a new document in Adobe XD, by default it is saved as a cloud document. If you look above the document at the title, you'll see a cloud icon (☁) and "Untitled-1" (or something similar, like "Untitled-2").

Cloud documents are stored and managed in Creative Cloud and are counted toward your Creative Cloud storage quota. If you work on a cloud document offline, changes will be saved to your local device and synced back to the cloud when you reconnect. Cloud documents and local XD documents are both fully compatible with XD.

Adobe XD's cloud-native document type has a number of unique benefits that a locally saved XD file does not, including the following:

- **Autosave:** When you save your document to Creative Cloud, the autosave feature ensures that your document is updated and you don't lose your work.

- **Faster sharing:** You can share XD documents right from within XD and use co-editing to simultaneously edit XD documents with others.

- **Access all of your work:** You can use the Cloud Document Organizer to quickly find all your documents, and the documents shared with you, right from within XD. You can see any cloud documents you save by visiting assets.adobe.com/cloud-documents.

- **Access documents across devices:** You can save your documents as cloud documents and access them across devices, including mobile preview using the XD mobile app.

- **See previous design versions:** Manage document revisions.

While working through the lessons, you will work on a document saved to your hard drive (local) rather than in the cloud.

4   Choose File > Save As (macOS), or on Windows click the menu icon (☰) in the upper-left corner of the application window and choose Save As, to reveal a menu of options.

In the menu of options that appears, you can change the name of the document and click Save to save the document to Creative Cloud as a cloud document. If you want to save the document locally, you can click Your Computer and navigate to a location on your computer.

▶ **Tip:** Another way to save a file is to click the filename above the document, revealing the menu of options.

5   Change the name to **Travel_Design**. Click Your Computer, then click the folder icon beneath the option to open an operating system dialog box.

Windows

macOS

6   In the dialog box that opens, navigate to the Lessons folder on your computer, and click Choose (macOS) or Select Folder (Windows). Click Save.

The XD document is now saved locally. In Lesson 9, "Previewing a Prototype," and Lesson 10, "Sharing Your Designs" you'll learn about saving as cloud documents in Adobe XD, which will allow you to share cloud documents.

Working with cloud documents 🎥

To learn about how to save and work with cloud documents in Adobe XD, check out the video "Working with Cloud Documents," which is part of the Web Edition of this book. For more information, see the "Web Edition" section of "Getting Started" at the beginning of the book.

Creating and editing artboards

When you first set up a document in Adobe XD, you typically start with a single artboard at a size you choose. You can then add as many artboards as you need of similar or different sizes and orientations. Each artboard represents a screen in your app design, web design, presentation, and so on. For example, to create a web design, you might create different artboards for the mobile, tablet, and desktop versions of that web page. Alternatively, if you're creating an app, you may want to create a single file with a separate artboard for each screen in your app.

Artboards in XD lay the groundwork for your design and are a feature you will spend a fair amount of time working with. In this part of the lesson, you'll use different methods to create and edit artboards in the hiking app you're designing.

Creating artboards with the Artboard tool

In this section, you'll learn about the different ways to create artboards with the Artboard tool ( ). Later, you'll use faster ways to create artboards, including duplicating existing artboards.

1   Select the Select tool ( ) and double-click the artboard name (iPhone XR/XS Max/11 – 1). Change the name to **Home** and press Return or Enter to accept the name.

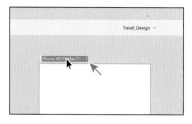 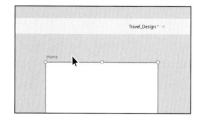

Naming artboards helps you keep track of your screens when you're editing your design content, for targeting specific artboards for interactivity during prototyping, and more.

2   Click in an empty area away from the artboard to deselect it.

▶ **Tip:** To access the Artboard tool, you can press the A key.

3   Select the Artboard tool ( ) in the toolbar on the left.

Notice the preset screen sizes, grouped by device platform—Apple, Google, and so on—that appear in the Property Inspector on the right side of the workspace.

4   Click the iPhone XR/XS Max/11 size in the Property Inspector to add a new artboard to the document at that size.

Note: With content selected in the document and the Artboard tool selected, you will see content properties as well as the default artboard sizes listed in the Property Inspector.

Because of the ever-changing nature of technology, the preset screen sizes you see may be different, and that's okay. By default, the new artboard is added to the right of the currently selected artboard. If there are other artboards to the right of the selected artboard, the new artboard is added to the far right of the other artboards.

5 Choose View > Zoom Out (macOS), or press Command and – (macOS) or Ctrl and – (Windows) once, to zoom out.

6 Double-click the artboard name (iPhone XR/XS Max/11 – 1) above the new artboard and change it to **Explore**. Press Return or Enter to accept the name change.

Note: Be careful if you double-click an artboard name with the Artboard tool selected. If you miss, you may wind up creating an artboard instead.

Tip: To delete an artboard, simply click its name to select it, and then press Delete or Backspace. Deleting an artboard also deletes any content associated with that artboard.

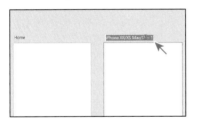
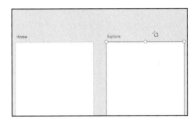

To select an artboard with the Artboard tool selected, you need to click the artboard name. With the Select tool selected, there are other methods for selecting artboards, which you will learn about later.

7 With the Artboard tool selected, click to the left of the artboard named Home to add another.

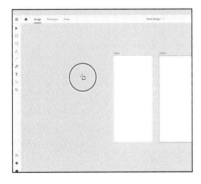
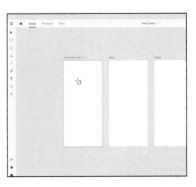

8 Double-click the name of the new artboard and change it to **Countdown**. Press Return or Enter to accept the name change.

9 With the Artboard tool still selected, press Command and – (macOS) or Ctrl and – (Windows) a few times to zoom out.

10 Click in the Explore artboard to add another artboard to the right.

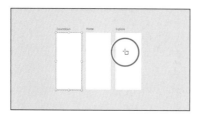 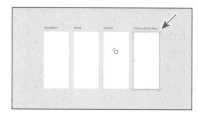

In this step, you can see that if there are other artboards to the right of the selected artboard (Countdown), the new artboard is added to the far right of the other artboards.

11 Change the new artboard name to **Hike Detail**. Press Return or Enter to accept the name. This artboard will eventually contain detailed information about a hike.

There are many ways to add artboards, including drawing a custom-size artboard, which is what you'll do next.

Note: You may need to scroll up in the Property Inspector to see the Width and Height values.

12 Move the pointer to the right of the Hike Detail artboard, in line with its top edge. An aqua guide appears, telling you when the pointer is aligned with the top edge. Drag down and to the right to draw an artboard. As you drag, you'll see the Width and Height values changing in the Property Inspector. Release the mouse button when the artboard roughly matches the size you see in the second part of the figure.

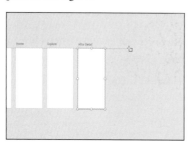 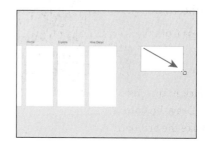

Tip: As you draw an artboard, you can press the Option (macOS) or Alt (Windows) key to draw from the center, or press the Shift key to constrain the proportions. When you are finished drawing, make sure to release the mouse button and then the key(s).

You can draw an artboard of almost any size or orientation, and artboards you create can also overlap.

13 Change the name of the new artboard to **Icons**. Press Return or Enter to accept the name.

You can work a lot of different ways, including creating the artboards you need at the start of the project or duplicating artboards with existing content and resizing the design content and artboards to match different screen sizes.

14 Choose File > Save (macOS), or on Windows click the menu icon (≡) in the upper-left corner of the application window and choose Save.

Editing artboards

While creating your design, you will most likely need to change the position of artboards, resize them, and more. Next, you'll see how to reposition, resize, and duplicate artboards as well as set a few other properties for them.

1   With the new Icons artboard still selected, in the Property Inspector on the right side of the workspace you can now see options specific to that selected artboard. Change Width to **700** and Height to **1000** in the Property Inspector. Press Return or Enter after the last value entered.

2   Make sure that the Portrait option (▯) is selected. It should be, since the dimensions you enter will change the orientation of the selected artboard.

> ▶ **Tip:** You can select the Lock Aspect icon (🔒) before resizing so that width and height change together proportionally.

You can change properties such as width and height for a single artboard or multiple selected artboards at one time. Changing the size or orientation of an artboard does not affect the artwork on that artboard.

3   Press Command+0 (macOS) or Ctrl+0 (Windows) to see all of the artboards and center them in the document window.

4   Select the Select tool (▶) in the toolbar. Click in the Hike Detail artboard to select it. Drag the bottom-middle point down to make the artboard taller.

You can resize any of the existing artboards using the Select tool or the Artboard tool. You will notice that a dashed line and widget appear on the artboard when the height of the artboard is taller than the original size. This indicates the original height of the artboard and the start of scrollable content, which you'll learn about in Lesson 5, "Organizing Content."

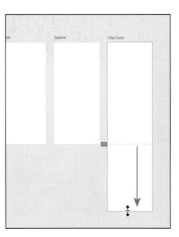

5 With the Select tool still selected, drag the Icons artboard below the row of smaller artboards. Don't worry about its exact position right now.

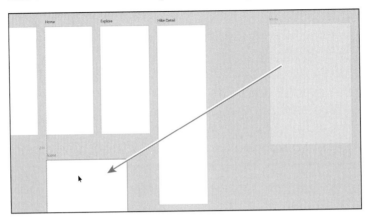

With the Select tool, you can select an artboard by clicking its name, by clicking in the artboard area if the artboard is empty, or by dragging across the artboard. You can arrange your artboards in a configuration that makes sense for your project and process.

Next, you'll arrange the artboards in an order that makes sense for the flow of screens in the app, and make copies to create new artboards. This can be done with either the Artboard tool or the Select tool selected.

6 Drag the Countdown artboard to the right. Drag until purple spacing guides show a value of 70 and you see aqua horizontal guides (indicating it is aligned with the others).

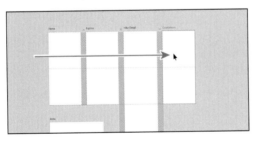

The purple spacing between the objects (artboards, in this case) appears when the space between them is the same.

7 Option-drag (macOS) or Alt-drag (Windows) from within the Countdown artboard to the right. Drag until the purple spacing guides show a value of 70 and you see aqua horizontal guides (indicating it is aligned with the others). Release the mouse button and then the key.

Note: If the Artboard tool is selected, in order to drag-duplicate an artboard, you need to drag it by the artboard name, not from within the artboard.

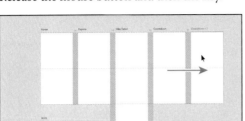

8 Change the name of the new artboard to **Recording**. Press Return or Enter to accept the name.

Option/Alt-dragging an artboard is a great way to make a copy of an artboard and all of its content, placing it where you want. In Adobe XD, you'll find that there are a lot of ways to create artboards. If you just want to add artboard copies in the same row, you can use a keyboard command to duplicate them.

Tip: You can also copy and paste artboards, even between documents.

9 With the Recording artboard still selected, press Command+D (macOS) or Ctrl+D (Windows) to create a duplicate that is placed to the right.

10 Change the name of the new artboard (Recording - 1) to **Memory**. Press Return or Enter to accept the name.

Note: If you zoom out far enough, the artboard names may appear truncated.

11 With the artboard named Memory selected, press Command+D (macOS) or Ctrl+D (Windows) to create a duplicate to the right. Leave the name as is for now.

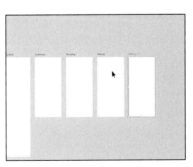

12 Choose File > Save (macOS), or on Windows click the menu icon (≡) in the upper-left corner of the application window and choose Save.

Changing artboard appearance

You can change several properties for each artboard in your document, including the background color, size, grids, and more. Changing the background color could be useful for showing white icons on a dark background or previewing a screen designed with a dark background, for instance. Next, you'll change the appearance of an existing artboard.

1   Press Command+0 (macOS) or Ctrl+0 (Windows) to fit all artboards in the Document window.

2   With the Select tool (▶) selected, click in the Countdown artboard to select it.

3   In the Property Inspector on the right, deselect the Fill option.

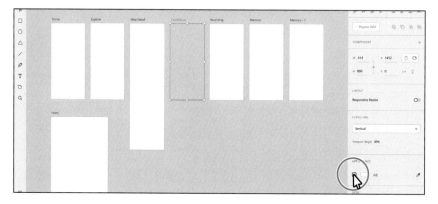

You can turn off the default fill of an artboard, but notice that the artboard outline is still visible.

▶ **Tip:** You can select multiple artboards and change the background color for all at once.

4   Select the Fill option in the Property Inspector to turn the default white fill back on.

5   Click the Fill color box, to the right of that same option, to show the color picker. Drag the circle in the vertical color slider to an orange color (first part of the following figure). Drag the Saturation/Brightness slider toward the upper-right corner to select an orange color (second part of the following figure).

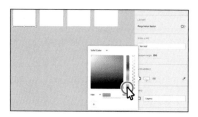 

Adobe XD offers a lot of ways to edit color, including visually.

6   Press the Esc key or click somewhere to hide the color picker.

Working with multiple artboards

You can change properties like background color and size for multiple artboards at one time. This can greatly speed up your design process. Next, you'll apply a background color to multiple artboards.

1 With the Select tool (▶) selected, click in the Recording artboard to select it. To also select the Memory – 1 artboard, Shift-click in the Memory – 1 artboard.

   You need to apply a background color to the Recording and Memory – 1 artboards so those app screens have a blue background. Next, you'll apply a color you were given as HSB (Hue, Saturation, and Brightness) values.

2 Click the Fill color box in the Property Inspector to show the color picker. Choose HSB from the color menu in the lower left corner of the color picker, and change the values to H=**205**, S=**88**, B=**35**. Press Return or Enter after typing the last value.

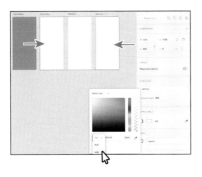 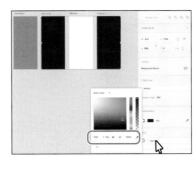

● **Note:** Even though the Memory artboard appears to be selected on your screen, it isn't.

3 Press the Esc key to hide the color picker.

4 Choose File > Save (macOS), or on Windows click the menu icon (≡) in the upper-left corner of the application window and choose Save.

Aligning artboards

You can easily select and align or distribute the spacing between artboards to keep them more visually organized. As you drag artboards, alignment guides and spacing guides make it relatively easy to align them, but you can also align and distribute artboards using the alignment methods at the top of the Property Inspector. Next, you'll align the Icons artboard to the Memory – 1 artboard so the Icon artboard is closer to that group of artboards.

1 Click in the Icons artboard and Shift-click the Memory – 1 artboard.

2 Click the Align Right option (⮐) at the top of the Property Inspector to align the right edge of the Icons artboard to the right edge of the Memory – 1 artboard.

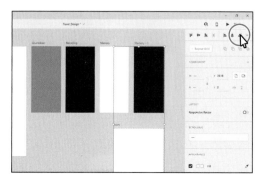

The Align options are pinned at the top of the Property Inspector, which means they are always showing. They are also contextual, which means they are dimmed when they're not available. You'll learn all about aligning content and artboards in Lesson 5.

3 Click in the gray pasteboard area to deselect the artboards.

4 Choose File > Save (macOS), or on Windows click the menu icon (≡) in the upper-left corner of the application window and choose Save.

● **Note:** You'll learn all about responsive resize in Lesson 7, "Using Effects, Repeat Grids, and Responsive Layout."

Artboards and responsive layouts

When designing for a multi-device landscape today, it's important to consider the wide variety of screen sizes available across mobile, tablet, and desktop resolutions. Since not all designers use similar devices, designers need to consider how content works across multiple screen sizes.

To solve this user problem, Adobe XD has developed a feature, called responsive resize, that allows you to resize objects while maintaining spatial relationships at different sizes to best adapt to multiple screen sizes.

—From XD Help

Adding grids and guides to artboards

In Adobe XD, there is a universal pixel grid that you can snap content to. In addition, there are several ways to position and lay out objects with precision: square grids, layout grids, and artboard guides.

Note: Adobe XD uses a virtual pixel for most of its measurements and font sizes, which is the same unit of measurement as a CSS pixel, the basic unit of measurement in iOS. The virtual pixel is roughly equal to one physical pixel on a 72 dpi monitor (and is equal to one point). You cannot change the unit of measurement in Adobe XD.

Square grids provide horizontal and vertical guides that you can align content to. When you draw or transform content, objects snap to the grid automatically when the edges of the object are within the grid's snap-to zone. Square grids can be useful for aligning objects and also for giving an idea of measurement when designing, and they are most often used when designing apps.

Layout grids can be used to define columns on each artboard. A layout grid helps you define the underlying structure of your design and how each component in it responds to different breakpoints for responsive designs (web design). In Lesson 7, you'll learn about responsive resize, which allows you to resize artboards while maintaining spatial relationships at different sizes to best adapt to multiple screen sizes.

Artboard guides will be discussed later in this section.

Working with square grids

In this section, you'll explore turning on a square grid for artboards and changing the appearance of grids. Square grids provide horizontal and vertical guides that you can align content so they can be useful for determining the measurements of objects.

1   With the Select tool (▶) selected, click in the Home artboard to select it. Press Command+3 (macOS) or Ctrl+3 (Windows) to zoom in to that artboard.

Note: The default grid you see may look different. That's okay, since you'll change the grid type shortly.

Tip: You can also choose View > Show Square Grid (macOS) or press Command+' (macOS) or Ctrl+' (Windows) to toggle the square grid on and off for the selected artboard(s).

2 Choose Square from the Grid menu in the Property Inspector. Make sure that the option is selected to turn the default square grid on for all artboards.

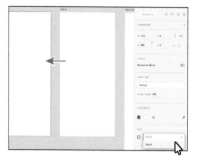 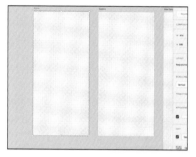

When you enable a square grid for one artboard, square grids are added globally to all artboards in the document. You can customize the appearance of the grid, like color and grid size, on different artboards.

3 In the Property Inspector, click the color box to the left of Square Size to open the color picker, and change the appearance of the grid. Drag the Alpha slider (on the far right in the color picker) down to make the grid less visible. You can adjust the color to whatever makes sense to you.

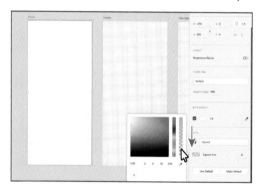

Notice that the grid on the Home artboard is the only one affected by the subtle color change. If you want to change the appearance of the square grid on more than one artboard, you would select those artboards first.

Layout grids and square grids overlay the design content of the artboard. Later, when you add content to these artboards, making the layout grid more transparent can make it easier to focus on the content rather than the grid. You can also toggle the visibility of a grid, which is what you will do at times in later lessons.

4 Select the Square Size value, and change it to **20**. Press Return or Enter to accept the value.

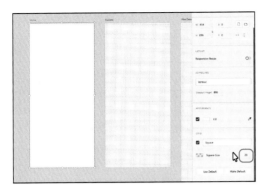

Once again, the selected artboard (Home) is the only one affected by the change. You'll notice that the smaller the grid size number, the denser the grid is, and the larger the grid size number, the looser the grid is. An 8 pt grid system is relatively standard—or at least a grid system whose lines are divisible by 8.

5 Change the Square Size value back to **8**.

Units in Adobe XD

Adobe XD is unit-less and focuses on the relationships between elements.
So, for example, if you design an iPhone 6/7/8 artboard at 375x667 units, and it uses type with a 10 unit font size, that relationship remains the same, no matter what physical size your design is scaled to.

—From XD Help

6 Click the Make Default button to ensure that these square grid settings are the default for square grids you apply going forward. You may need to scroll down in the Property Inspector to see it.

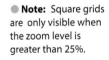
Note: Square grids are only visible when the zoom level is greater than 25%.

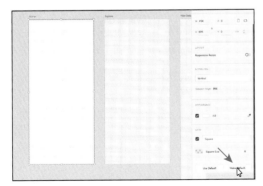

Now you'll select a series of artboards and apply the new default square grid appearance to them all at once.

7 Press Command+0 (macOS) or Ctrl+0 (Windows) to fit all artboards in the document window.

▶ **Tip:** When dragging to select multiple artboards, only one of them needs to be fully encompassed within the selection area.

8 Move the pointer off the upper-left corner of the Explore artboard. Drag down and across the artboard. Keep dragging until the blue marquee box surrounds the entire artboard. When the artboard is highlighted (selected), continue dragging across all of the artboards in the same row, and release the mouse button to select them all. See the figure. Make sure not to select the Icons artboard.

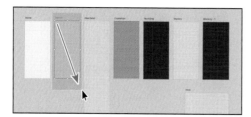 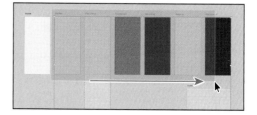

With a series of artboards selected, you could also change other values that appear in the Property Inspector, like Fill or Width and Height. Selecting a series of artboards and applying properties like Width and Height can be a great way to ensure uniformity.

9 Click the Use Default button in the Property Inspector to apply the default square grid appearance to the selected artboards. You may need to scroll down in the Property Inspector to see the button.

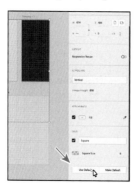 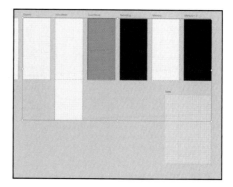

The square grid on each of the selected artboards should now match the default square grid you set on the Home artboard.

10 Choose File > Save (macOS), or on Windows click the menu icon (≡) in the upper-left corner of the application window and choose Save.

Applying a layout grid

Now you'll apply a layout grid to artboards in a new web design document you create. In Lesson 7, you'll learn about responsive resize which allows you to resize artboards while maintaining spatial relationships at different sizes to best adapt to multiple screen sizes.

1 To create a new document, choose File > New (macOS) or, on Windows, click the menu icon (≡) and choose New.

2 In the Home screen, click the Web 1920 name to reveal a menu of sizes. Choose Web 1920 (1920 x 1080), and a new document opens with a single web design sized artboard showing.

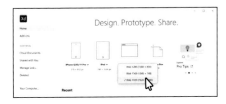

3 Choose View > Zoom To Fit All (macOS), or choose Zoom To Fit All from the Zoom menu (Windows) in the upper right.

4 Choose File > Save As (macOS), or on Windows click the menu icon (≡) in the upper-left corner of the application window and choose Save As, to reveal a menu of options.

5 Change the name to **Travel_Design_web**. Click Your Computer, then click the folder icon beneath the option to open an operating system dialog box.

6 In the dialog box that opens, navigate to the Lessons folder on your computer, and click Choose (macOS) or Select Folder (Windows).

7 Click Save.

8 Choose Layout from the grid menu in the Grid section of the Property Inspector, if it isn't already, and make sure that the option is selected to turn the default layout grid on for the selected artboard.

▶ **Tip:** You can also choose View > Show Layout Grid (macOS) or press Shift+Command+' (macOS) or Shift+Ctrl+' (Windows) to toggle the Layout grid on and off for the selected artboard(s).

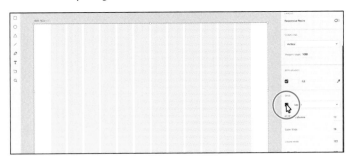

The number and size of the columns displayed in the artboard depends on the size of the artboard. For example, a phone-sized artboard has fewer and narrower columns than does the default layout grid for a desktop artboard. If you resize an artboard, the column widths in the layout grid change to fit the new artboard size. You can change grid properties depending on your design needs. You'll do that next.

● **Note:** You may need to adjust the Gutter Width and Column Width values to achieve those margin values.

9 Scroll down in the Property Inspector, if you need to and click the Different Margin For Each Side (▣) button, and ensure that the values for the margins are 0, 32, 0, and 32, as shown in the figure. After entering the last value, press Return or Enter. You may need to scroll in the Property Inspector to see the values.

● **Note:** Lots of designers will create a grid based on their design. You can do a quick drawing of your layout on paper to get an idea for the number of columns. Many popular frameworks also use a grid system of 12 columns, which usually divides the page area (artboard, in this case) easily into 12 even sections.

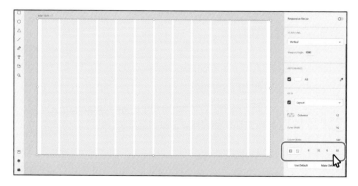

Gutter Width and Column Width are automatically calculated based on the size of the artboard, the number of columns, and the margins set. The Gutter Width is the distance between the columns, and the Column Width is the width of each column. You can change either the Gutter Width or the Column Width values at this point, depending on your design needs. Values you see in the Grid section of the Property Inspector are values automatically calculated by XD. Leave the columns set to 12.

There are two options for setting margins: Linked Left/Right Margins (▫) (default) or Different Margin For Each Side (▣). If you need to set different margins on any of the sides of the artboard, you can select Different Margin For Each Side and change the value(s).

10 Choose File > Save (macOS), or click the menu icon (☰) in the upper-left corner of the application window and choose Save (Windows).

11 To close the Travel_Design_web document, choose File > Close (macOS) or click the X in the upper-right corner (Windows).

You should be back in the Travel_Design.xd document.

Creating artboard guides

You can also add custom guides to each artboard or a series of artboards to help you position and lay out objects with precision. In this section, you'll add a few guides to dictate where content will go in later sections.

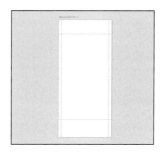

1   Press Command+0 (macOS) or Ctrl+0 (Windows) to fit all artboards in the document window.

2   With the Select tool (▶) selected, click in the Home artboard to select it. Press Command+3 (macOS) or Ctrl+3 (Windows) to zoom in to that artboard.

● **Note:** You don't need to select an artboard in order to add guides to it.

3   To create a guide that you can use to position status bar content that contains the wireless signal icon, time, and more, at the top of each artboard, move the pointer just off the top edge of the artboard, below the "Home" name. When you see a double-arrow (⬍), press and drag down into the artboard area. As you drag, you'll see a Y position, indicating the distance between the guide and top edge of the artboard. When you see a Y value of approximately 26, release the mouse button to create a horizontal guide.

● **Note:** If there are other guides on the artboard, the distance between the guides is displayed off the left edge (for horizontal guides) or top edge (for vertical guides) of the artboard.

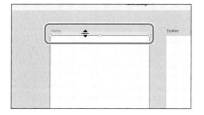
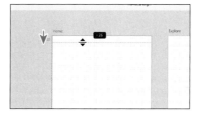

With the guide created, now you'll create two vertical guides so that content you add to the artboards will have a visible margin between the content and the left and right edges of the artboard.

4   Move the pointer just off the left edge of the artboard. When you see a double-arrow (◀▶), press and drag to the right, into the artboard area. When you see an X position (the distance from the left edge of the artboard and the new guide) of 16, release the mouse button to create a vertical guide.

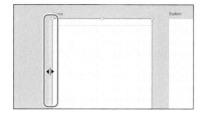
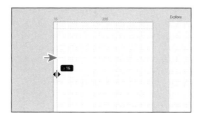

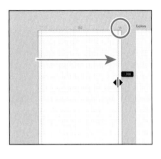

Tip: To delete a guide, drag the guide off of the artboard. To delete all the guides on an artboard, select the artboard and choose View > Guides > Clear Guides (macOS) or right-click an artboard and choose Guides > Clear Guides (Windows).

Tip: Press the Shift key when dragging guides to snap them to 10 pixel increments.

5 Move the pointer just off the left edge of the artboard. When you see a double-arrow (◀▶), press and drag to the right, into the artboard area. When you see a distance of approximately 16 above the top edge of the artboard (circled in the figure), indicating the distance between the new guide and the *right* edge of the artboard, release the mouse button to create a vertical guide.

Now you'll copy those three guides to all of the artboards.

6 Press Command+0 (macOS) or Ctrl+0 (Windows) to see all the design content in the document.

7 Choose View > Guides > Copy Guides (macOS) or, on Windows, right-click in the Home artboard (the artboard with the guides on it) and choose Guides > Copy Guides to copy all three guides on the selected artboard.

8 To paste the guides, move the pointer off the upper-left corner of the Explore artboard. Drag down and across the artboard. Keep dragging until the blue marquee box surrounds the entire artboard. When the artboard is highlighted (selected), continue dragging across all of the artboards in the same row, and release the mouse button to select them all. Make sure not to select the Icons artboard.

9 Press Cmd+V (macOS) or Ctrl+V (Windows) to paste the guides on all of the selected artboards.

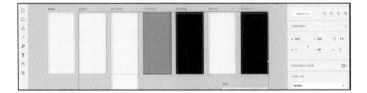

Duplicating an artboard also duplicates the guides created on that artboard.

Tip: To lock all of the guides in your document you can press Cmd+Shift+; (macOS) or Ctrl+Shift+; (Windows).

10 To lock the guides, so you can't accidentally move them, choose View > Guides > Lock All Guides (macOS) or right-click the artboard and choose Guides > Lock All Guides (Windows).

While the guides are locked, you can create guides and snap objects to guides, but you cannot change their position on the canvas.

Managing artboards with the Layers panel

In Lesson 1, "An Introduction to Adobe XD," you were introduced to the Layers panel and saw how you could use it to navigate artboards in your documents. In this section, you'll see how you can also create and manage your artboards from the Layers panel. As you proceed through the lessons, you'll use what you learn here.

1   With the Select tool (▶) selected, click in the gray pasteboard area to deselect.

    It's important that nothing be selected for the next step.

2   Click the Layers panel button (◆) in the lower-left corner of the application window to open the Layers panel.

    In the Layers panel, with nothing selected, you'll see a list of all the artboards in the document. Notice that the artboards are listed in the order in which they were created, with the last artboard you created at the top of the list.

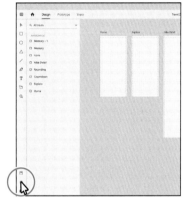

▶ **Tip:** You can also press Command+Y (macOS) or Ctrl+Y (Windows) to toggle the visibility of the Layers panel.

3   Click Home in the Layers panel list.

    When you select an artboard in the list, the artboard is selected in the document, as you saw in Lesson 1. Selecting artboards using the Layers panel can sometimes be easier.

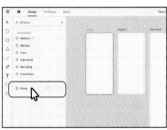

4   Drag the Home artboard up in the Layers panel list to the top. When you see a line appear above the first item in the list (mine is "Memory – 1"), release the mouse button.

    I tend to drag the artboards in an order that matches the path the user takes from one screen to another in the document. In

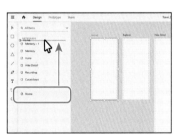

other words, in an app you may have a login screen. After the user enters their login information, the next screen they may see in the app is *their* home screen. The home screen artboard would follow the login screen artboard in the flow (usually from left to right). This can also make the artboards easier to find later. You can organize them however you want.

5 Drag the artboards into the order in the Layers panel you see in the figure. It follows the general flow of the screens.

6 Double-click the Memory – 1 artboard name in the Layers panel to select the name. Change the name to **Journal** and press Return or Enter.

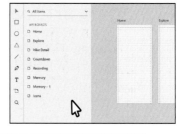

7 Right-click the Journal artboard name in the Layers panel and choose Copy.

In the context menu that appears when you right-click, you will see a series of commands, such as Copy, Delete, Duplicate, and more. These commands can be applied to selected artboards. Performing these kinds of operations in the Layers panel can sometimes be faster, especially when dealing with a lot of artboards at once.

8 Right-click the Icons artboard name in the Layers panel and choose Paste Appearance to paste the blue fill.

The guides on the Journal artboard are not part of the appearance, so they aren't copied to the Icons artboard, but the square grid was. If your zoom level is 25% or less, you may not see the grid.

9 Click in the gray pasteboard area in the document to deselect all content.

10 Choose File > Save (macOS), or click the menu icon (≡) in the upper-left corner of the application window and choose Save (Windows).

11 If you plan on jumping to the next lesson, you can leave the Travel_Design.xd file open. Otherwise, for each open document, choose File > Close (macOS) or click the X in the upper-right corner (Windows).

Review questions

1 What does an artboard represent in Adobe XD?

2 By default, when you resize an artboard to be taller, a dashed line appears on the artboard. What does that dashed line indicate?

3 Which tool must be selected to see the preset artboard sizes that come with Adobe XD with a document open?

4 What purpose does an artboard grid serve?

5 What are at least two things you can do with artboards in the Layers panel?

Review answers

1 In Adobe XD, artboards represent a screen (app) or page (website) in your design. Each Adobe XD file can contain many artboards of similar or differing sizes and orientations.

2 The dashed line that appears on an artboard after making the artboard taller indicates the original height of the artboard and the start of scrollable content. It's useful for determining what's initially visible on the device.

3 To see the preset artboard sizes that come with Adobe XD when a document is open, you must have the Artboard tool ( ) selected.

4 In Adobe XD, each artboard can contain either a layout grid or a square grid that provides guides for aligning content. Grids can be useful for aligning objects and can also help you get a quick idea of measurement when designing.

5 In the Layers panel, you can change artboard names, reorder the artboards, copy an artboard, delete an artboard (and its contents), select and zoom in to an artboard, and much more.

3 ADDING IMAGES, GRAPHICS, AND TEXT

Lesson overview

In this lesson, you'll learn how to do the following:

- Import images.

- Transform images.

- Bring in content from Adobe Photoshop.

- Bring in content from Adobe Illustrator.

- Mask content.

- Add and format text.

 This lesson will take about 45 minutes to complete. To get the lesson files used in this chapter, download them from the web page for this book at www.adobepress.com/XDCIB2020. For more information, see "Accessing the lesson files and Web Edition" in the Getting Started section at the beginning of this book.

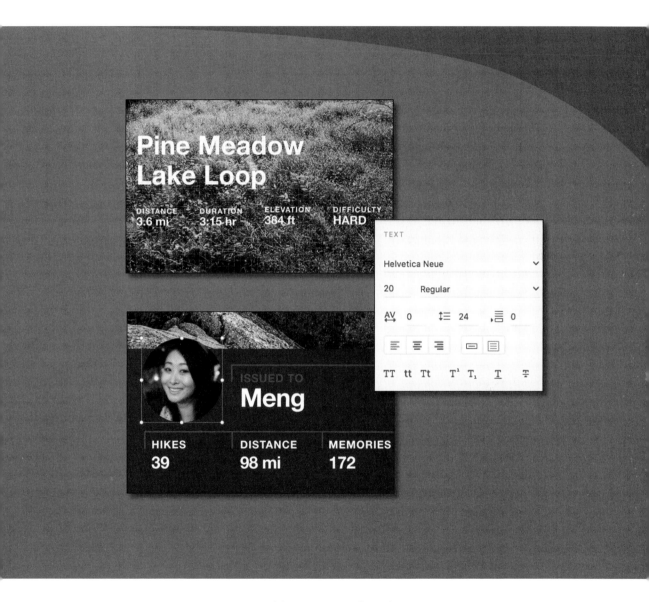

In Adobe XD, images and text play an important part in any design. This lesson focuses on importing and transforming images, as well as adding and formatting text.

Starting the lesson

In this lesson, you'll bring raster images and vector graphics into, and add text to, your app design. To start, you'll open a final lesson file to get an idea for what you will create in this lesson.

● **Note:** If you have not already downloaded the project files for this lesson to your computer from your Account page, make sure to do so now. See the "Getting Started" section at the beginning of the book.

● **Note:** The figures in the lesson were taken on macOS, so on Windows the XD interface will be a little different.

1 Start Adobe XD, if it's not already open.

2 On macOS, choose File > Open From Your Computer. On Windows, click the menu icon (≡) in the upper-left corner of the application window and choose Open From Your Computer. Open the file named L3_end.xd, which is in the Lessons > Lesson03 folder that you copied onto your hard disk.

● **Note:** For either macOS or Windows, if the Home screen is showing with no files open, click Your Computer in the Home screen. Open the file named L3_end.xd, which is in the Lessons > Lesson03 folder that you copied onto your hard disk.

3 If the Assets panel opens on the left and you see a Missing Fonts message, close the panel by clicking Assets panel icon (⊟) in the lower left.

4 Press Command+0 (macOS) or Ctrl+0 (Windows) to see all of the content.

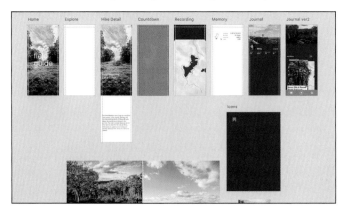

This file shows you what you will create by the end of the lesson.

5 You can either leave the file open for reference or close it. To close it, choose File > Close (macOS) or, on Windows, click the X in the upper-right corner of the open window to close the file.

Assets and Adobe XD

In the previous lesson, you set up your document and worked with artboards. In this lesson, you'll learn about the different types of image assets you can import into Adobe XD; the different methods for bringing them in from programs like Illustrator, Photoshop, and Sketch; and how to work with them to fit your design.

Adobe XD supports PSD, AI, PNG, GIF, SVG, JPEG, and TIFF images. In Adobe XD, images (both raster and vector) that you import are embedded in the XD file, since there is no default image-linking workflow, as you would find in Adobe InDesign.

▶ **Tip:** In Lesson 6, "Working with Assets and CC Libraries," we discuss CC Libraries, which do allow for an image-linking workflow.

Importing an image

In Adobe XD, there are several methods for adding assets to your projects. In this section, you'll bring a few assets into your design using the Import command.

1   Choose File > Open From Your Computer (macOS) or click the menu icon (☰) in the upper-left corner of the application window and choose Open From Your Computer (Windows). Open the Travel_Design.xd document in the Lessons folder (or where you saved it).

2   Press Command+0 (macOS) or Ctrl+0 (Windows) to see all of the content.

3   To temporarily disable the square grids on the artboards, choose View > Hide Square Grid (macOS) or right-click in the gray pasteboard and choose Hide Square Grid (Windows).

4   With the Select tool (▶) selected, click in the Home artboard.

5   Choose File > Import (macOS) or click the menu icon (☰) in the upper-left corner of the application window and choose Import (Windows). Navigate to the Lessons > Lesson03 > images folder. Click to select the image named home_1.jpg. Click Import.

● **Note:** If you are starting from scratch using the jumpstart method described in the section "Getting Started," open L3_start.xd from the Lessons > Lesson03 folder.

● **Note:** To learn more about image sizing and Adobe XD, see the sidebar "Sizing raster images for Adobe XD."

JPEG images you import into Adobe XD are placed at half size. That means a JPEG that is 400 pixels x 400 pixels will be placed at 200 pixels x 200 pixels. The image is placed in the center of the selected artboard and is larger than the artboard. Any image content that is outside the bounds of the artboard is hidden. With the image selected, XD shows the masked content as semi-transparent to give you a preview of what is hidden.

Tip: You can also scale an image non-proportionally if needed. Before dragging to resize, with the image selected, you can turn off the Lock Aspect option (🔒) in the Property Inspector on the right.

6 With the Select tool (▶) selected, drag the image until the bottom edge snaps to the bottom edge of the artboard, and ensure that it's still centered on the artboard (a vertical aqua guide will appear when it's centered).

7 Drag the top-middle handle of the image down until the image is as tall as the artboard.

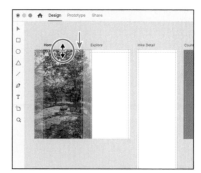

The proportions of raster images are maintained when resizing by dragging.

8 Click away from the image, in a blank area of the document window, to deselect it. You should now see that the image content that is outside the bounds of the artboard is hidden.

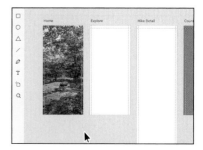

Sizing raster images for Adobe XD

If you're designing using the default artboard sizes (1x), you need to pay attention to the sizing of any raster images (JPEG, GIF, PNG) that you import into your design. The sizing is especially important if you will later need to export production-ready assets for a website or app.

It's best to edit your raster images in a program like Photoshop to be the maximum size you need before you import them into XD. In the case of an image for a website, if your image spans the entire width of a 1920 x 1080 artboard, you'll want to ensure that your image is 3840 pixels across (twice the width of the intended use in XD). Be careful about simply importing overly large images each time you need an image, since large file sizes can slow down load time.

If you're designing for iOS and designing at 1x, you'll want to make sure that any raster images you import are scaled at 3x (three times the size they are in your Adobe XD design); for Android make sure they are 400% (or 4x).

Importing multiple assets

In Adobe XD, you can import multiple assets using a variety of methods. In this section, you'll import an SVG file and a PNG using the Import command.

1   Choose File > Import (macOS) or click the menu icon (☰) in the upper-left corner of the application window and choose Import (Windows). Navigate to the Lessons > Lesson03 > images folder. Click to select the image named journal_header.png and Command-click (macOS) or Ctrl-click (Windows) the image named red_map.svg. Click Import.

● **Note:** In the images folder, you'll see an Illustrator document named red_map.ai. You can import native Illustrator documents (.ai) into Adobe XD as well.

● **Note:** If an image seems to disappear, it's because it was placed on one of the artboards, and most of it may be hidden. You can drag the image away from the artboard.

The assets are placed next to each other, in the center of the document window. Any imported assets that touch an artboard are placed on that artboard. If a placed image doesn't overlap the first artboard, it will be placed on the next artboard to the right, and so on. Images that don't overlap an artboard will be placed on the empty pasteboard.

2   Drag one of the assets down to drag them both away from the artboards.

3   With the Select tool selected, click in a blank area away from the selected assets to deselect them. Click the red map artwork to select it.

4 Right-click the selected map artwork and choose Cut. Right-click in the Countdown artboard and choose Paste.

  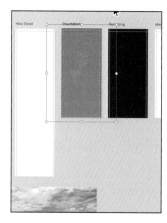

5 Drag the other image you placed, journal_header.png, from its center, onto the Journal artboard. Make sure the person is approximately centered on the artboard and the pointer is within the bounds of the Journal artboard and release the mouse button.

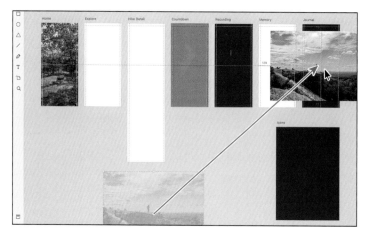

The image is placed on the Journal artboard and is cropped by the bounds of the artboard.

Importing assets via drag and drop

Another method for bringing assets into Adobe XD is to drag and drop from the Finder (macOS) or File Explorer (Windows). Aside from adding assets to your design, this is also a great way to insert images into existing frames (as you'll see in a later section, "Masking with an image fill") or as a more precise placement option.

1 With the Select tool (▶) selected, click in a blank area away from the artboards to deselect all.

2 Go to the Finder (macOS) or File Explorer (Windows), open the Lessons > Lesson03 > images folder, and leave the folder open with XD showing in the background.

3 With XD and the folder showing, click the image named scene_1.png. Shift-click the image named scene_2.png to select both images. Release the key and drag either of the selected images into XD, just below the Home artboard.

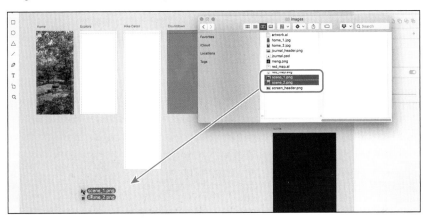

● **Note:** If an image seems to disappear, it's because it was placed on one of the artboards, and most of it may be hidden. You can drag the image away from the artboard.

The images are placed next to each other on the pasteboard as a row of images. If you were to release the mouse button over an artboard, any images that touch the artboard would be placed on that artboard. Images that don't overlap an artboard will be placed on the empty pasteboard.

4 Click in Adobe XD to make it the focus again, if necessary.

Replacing an image

If you need to replace an image in your design, you can do so by dragging an image from your desktop onto an existing image to replace it. Next, you'll replace a copy of an image in your design.

1   Go to the Finder (macOS) or Windows Explorer (Windows), open the Lessons > Lesson03 > images folder, and leave the folder open with XD showing in the background.

2   With XD and the folder showing, click the image named home_2.jpg. Drag the image on top of the home_1.jpg image on the Home artboard. When it shows a blue highlight, release the mouse button to replace the image.

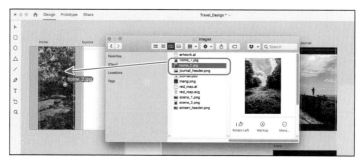

The image will resize to fit the shape but keep its proportions, and will most likely be masked by the shape (parts of the new image may be hidden). This may mean that the new image is scaled if the image you are replacing is larger or smaller than the image you are dragging in.

3   With the image on the Home artboard selected, press Command+C (macOS) or Ctrl+C (Windows) to copy it.

4   With the Select tool selected, click in the Hike Detail artboard to make it the active artboard. Press Command+V (macOS) or Ctrl+V (Windows) to paste it.

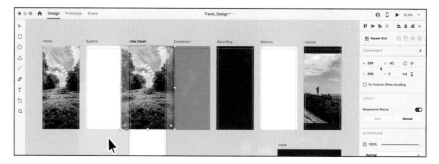

Tip: If you copy and paste using keyboard commands or menu items (macOS) and you want to paste on a particular artboard, click in a blank area of an artboard or select it to make it the active artboard before pasting.

Content copied from one artboard to another is pasted in the same position, relative to the upper-left corner.

Transforming images

Images you import into Adobe XD can be transformed in a variety of ways—from scaling and rounding corners to rotating and positioning. In this section, you'll apply a few transformations to the images you've imported so far.

1   Click the image on the Journal artboard. Press Command+3 (macOS) or Ctrl+3 (Windows) to zoom in to the selection.

2   Press Command and – (macOS) or Ctrl and – (Windows) a few times to zoom out.

3   Drag the image to reposition it. Notice that as you drag, if an edge of the image comes close to an artboard edge or guide, it snaps. As you drag, press the Command (macOS) or Ctrl (Windows) key to temporarily turn off snapping. Position the image as you see in the second part of the following figure. Release the mouse button and then the key.

4   Drag the lower-left bounding point of the box around the image up and to the right to make it smaller. Make sure it's still a little wider than the artboard.

5   With the image still selected, in the Property Inspector, change the X value to **0** and press Return or Enter. Leave the Y value (vertical position) as is. Leave the image selected.

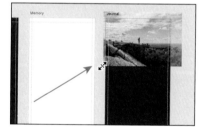

Note: If the image doesn't scale in proportion, make sure the Lock Aspect (🔒) option is selected in the Property Inspector and try scaling it again. You can also press the Shift key while scaling to constrain the proportions.

The X (horizontal) value and Y (vertical) value each start at zero (0) in the upper-left corner of each artboard. Content such as the image is positioned from its upper-left corner relative to the upper-left corner of the artboard. Positioning content using the X and Y values can help you work more precisely.

Resizing an image in its frame

Images you bring into XD are contained within a frame. When you transform an image frame, the image is transformed as well. You can also select the image within the frame and transform it separately. Next, you'll resize an image within its frame. This can be an easy way to hide parts of an image you don't want showing.

1   With the image at the top of the Journal artboard still selected, zoom in to the selected image by pressing Command+3 (macOS) or Ctrl+3 (Windows) or by using any other method you've learned up to this point.

2   To zoom out a little, press Command and – (macOS) or Ctrl and – (Windows).

3   Double-click the image to reveal bounding points around it.

The points you see around the perimeter of the image are used to resize the image within the frame. Currently you can't edit the individual anchor points for the shape of the image frame.

Later in this lesson, you'll learn about masking an image with a shape. In that case, you will be able to edit the frame or the image within the frame.

4   Drag the bottom-middle point of the image down to make it larger within the frame.

The bottom part of the image will be hidden, or *cropped*, when you drag beyond the edge of the frame it's in.

5   Press the Esc key to stop resizing the image and show the bounding box of the image again.

6   Drag the lower-right point of the bounding box toward the center of the image to make it a bit smaller. Make sure it still covers the width of the artboard.

7   Press Command+0 (macOS) or Ctrl+0 (Windows) to see everything.

8   Choose File > Save (macOS) or click the menu icon (≡) in the upper-left corner of the application window and choose Save (Windows).

Bringing in content from Photoshop

There are a lot of ways to bring content from Photoshop into XD: copy and paste, export from Photoshop and import into XD, import a Photoshop file (.psd) (which places the PSD content into the XD file), open a Photoshop file (.psd) directly in XD (which opens the PSD as a separate XD file), or place the content in a Creative Cloud Library and drag it into your design from the Creative Cloud Library panel in XD. In this section, you'll use a few different methods to bring content from Photoshop into your design in Adobe XD.

Note: If you don't have the latest version of Adobe Photoshop installed on your machine, in Adobe XD you can choose File > Import (macOS) or, on Windows, click the menu icon (≡) in the upper-left corner of the application window and choose Import. Navigate to the Lessons > Lesson03 > images folder and import the screen_header.png image file.

Copying and pasting from Photoshop to XD

To start, you'll open a Photoshop document in Photoshop and copy content that you will then paste into your Adobe XD project.

1   Open the latest version of Adobe Photoshop.

2   Choose File > Open. Click On Your Computer in the dialog box that appears. Navigate to the Lessons > Lesson03 > images folder, select the file named journal.psd, and click Open. If the New Library From Document dialog box appears, click Cancel.

   The Photoshop file contains a design with multiple artboards that contains layers of imagery, text, vector content, and more. Next, you'll copy image content and paste it into Adobe XD as a flattened raster image.

3   Choose View > Fit On Screen.

   The image at the top of the Journal artboard (the artboard on the left) needs to be copied into your XD project, without the time and other status bar information currently on top of it. You can make a selection, select specific layers, and copy what you need or simply copy a selected area and paste a flattened raster image of that content.

4   Make sure the Layers panel is open. You can choose Window > Layers to see it.

   In Photoshop, the Layers panel lists artboards along with layers. They're marked by disclosure triangles, as groups are, but they lack the folder icons that groups display.

5   In the Layers panel, click the disclosure triangle next to the Journal artboard name (it should be at the top of the list) to reveal the contents of the artboard. Scroll down in the Layers panel, if necessary, to see the layer named "Journal header image." Click to select it, if it isn't already.

6   Command-click (macOS) or Ctrl-click (Windows) the layer thumbnail to the left of the layer name in the panel to make a selection from the layer content.

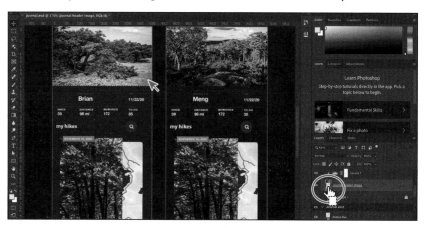

7   Choose Edit > Copy to copy the image within the selection marquee.

8   Close Photoshop without saving, if asked. Back in Adobe XD, in the Travel_Design document, press Command+0 (macOS) or Ctrl+0 (Windows) to see all of the artboards, if you don't already.

9   With the Select tool selected, click in the gray pasteboard away from the artboards to deselect all.

● **Note:** Content you paste from Photoshop is a single flattened image in Adobe XD.

10 With nothing selected, press Command+V (macOS) or Ctrl+V (Windows) to paste the content into the center of the document window.

11 Drag the image below the Icons artboard.

12 Choose File > Save (macOS) or click the menu icon (≡) in the upper-left corner of the application window and choose Save (Windows).

Opening a Photoshop file in Adobe XD

You can open Photoshop (.psd) files in Adobe XD, and they will be converted into XD files. When a Photoshop file is opened in XD, Photoshop elements and effects that can be mapped to XD's functionality are available. The rest of the elements either are rasterized or don't appear in the XD file.

Next, in Adobe XD you'll open a design started in Photoshop.

1   In Adobe XD, choose File > Open From Your Computer (macOS) or click the menu icon (≡) in the upper-left corner of the application window and choose Open From Your Computer (Windows). Open the journal.psd document in the Lessons > Lesson03 > images folder.

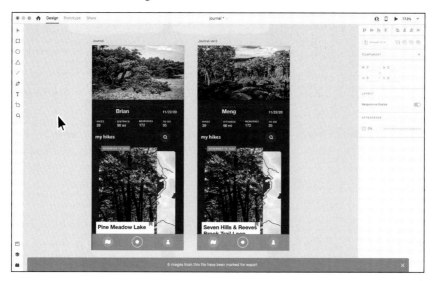

The Photoshop document is now an XD document called journal that is open in Adobe XD. You may see a blue bar at the bottom of the document window. You can click the X on the end to close it. By default, images in a PSD you open are marked for export. You'll learn more about that in Lesson 11.

2   Press Command+0 (macOS) or Ctrl+0 (Windows) to see all of the content.

Most of the content on the two artboards is still editable in XD, but there are a few exceptions. For a listing of the supported features when you open Photoshop files in Adobe XD, see helpx.adobe.com/xd/kb/open-photoshop-files-in-xd.html.

3   With the Select tool (▶) selected, click the text "Brian" in the Journal artboard.

4 Open the Layers panel by clicking the Layers panel button (≋) in the lower-left corner of the application window, if it isn't already open. In the Layers panel, you'll see a folder icon (🗀) to the left of the selected content named "Hike info," which indicates a group of content. Click the folder icon to reveal everything in it. All of the text is still editable.

5 Click the white status bar content at the top of the Journal artboard on the left.

The status bar content has been rasterized and is now a single image. You can tell because of the image icon (▣) in the Layers panel to the left of the name. Next, you'll copy one of the artboards into your project.

6 Click in a blank area, away from the artboards, to deselect all. Then click the Journal ver2 artboard name above the artboard on the right. Press Command+C (macOS) or Ctrl+C (Windows) to copy the artboard and all of its content.

7 Choose File > Close (macOS) or click the X in the upper-right corner (Windows) to close the Journal document without saving it.

8 Back in the Travel_Design.xd document, press Command+V (macOS) or Ctrl+V (Windows) to paste the artboard and content to the right of the Journal artboard.

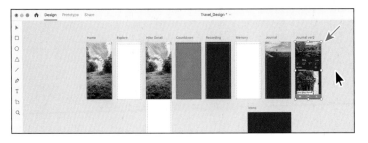

9   With the artboard still selected, zoom in by pressing Command+3 (macOS) or Ctrl+3 (Windows) or by using any other method you've learned up to this point.

10 Drag the group with the "Meng" text to the Journal artboard and drop it below the image.

11 To center the content on the Journal artboard, click the Align Center (Horizontally) button (⬍) at the top of the Property Inspector. The group is aligned to the horizontal center of the artboard.

Editing an image in Photoshop

As you learned earlier, images you place in XD are embedded. But after placing JPEG, PNG, GIF, or BMP images in XD, you can update them in real-time in Photoshop. You need Photoshop installed for this to work. Next you'll edit the image at the top of the Journal ver 2 artboard.

1   Move the pointer over the image at the top of the Journal ver 2 artboard and right-click. Choose Edit In Photoshop from the context menu that appears.

The image opens as a new file in Photoshop with the same name as the image layer name in XD. If Photoshop is not installed, this option is dimmed.

2 With the image open in Photoshop, choose Layer > New Adjustment Layer > Black & White. Click OK to create the new adjustment layer.

3 In the Properties panel (Window > Properties), click Auto to apply the auto settings.

4 Choose File > Save. Quit Photoshop and return to XD.

The image is automatically sent to XD as a flattened bitmap image. If Photoshop were kept open when you returned to XD, you could go back to Photoshop and undo, revert, or make further changes to the image in Photoshop. The layers you create are preserved.

Note: You can only open Sketch files created using Sketch version 43 or newer. If you have an older file, save the file using the latest version of Sketch, and then open the file in XD.

Tip: You can drag images directly from all modern web browsers onto your artboards. You can also drag the images into an object on an artboard; when you do so, the image size is automatically adjusted to fit the object.

Bringing in assets from Sketch

You can directly open Sketch (.sketch) files in XD and convert them to XD files. After you open Sketch files, you can edit them in XD, wire interactions, and share them.

You can also move Sketch content into XD and continue working on your design systems. Sketch symbols and elements are converted to XD components, and you can also use them as linked assets.

To learn more, visit helpx.adobe.com/xd/help/working-with-external-assets.html#sketch.

Bringing in content from Adobe Illustrator

There are several ways to bring content from Illustrator into Adobe XD: open the Illustrator file directly in Adobe XD, copy and paste from Illustrator to XD, export assets from Illustrator, add the Illustrator artwork to a Creative Cloud library, and import into XD. In this section, you'll open an Illustrator document (.ai) in XD.

1 In Adobe XD, choose File > Open From Your Computer (macOS), or click the menu icon (≡) in the upper-left corner of the application window and choose Open From Your Computer (Windows). In the Lessons > Lesson03 > images folder on your hard disk, select the artwork.ai file, and click Open.

   Note: For a list of supported and non-supported features when opening Illustrator files in XD, visit helpx.adobe.com/xd/kb/open-illustrator-files-in-xd.html.

   The Illustrator file contains artwork that you will incorporate into your design in Adobe XD. There were two artboards in the Illustrator document that remain in the document opened in XD, and the vector graphics and text are still editable. You can now copy and paste or drag and drop this content into your other projects.

2 Press Command+0 (macOS) or Ctrl+0 (Windows) to see all of the content.

   The content on the left artboard contains a banner icon and other content, and the artboard on the right contains a topographical map illustration. You'll copy the content and paste it into your Travel_Design.xd document.

3 Press Command+A (macOS) or Ctrl+A (Windows) to select all of the content.

4 Right-click directly on the content and choose Copy to copy it.

5 Choose File > Close (macOS), or click the menu icon (≡) in the upper-left corner of the application window and choose Close (Windows). Don't save the file. XD converted it to a new XD file that you don't need to keep.

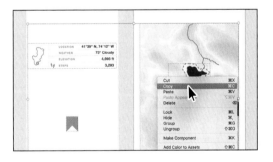

6 In the Travel_Design.xd document, press Command+0 (macOS) or Ctrl+0 (Windows) to see all of the content.

7 Click in the gray pasteboard to deselect. Press Command+V (macOS) or Ctrl+V (Windows) to paste the content. Drag the selected artwork away from the artboards so it doesn't touch any of them.

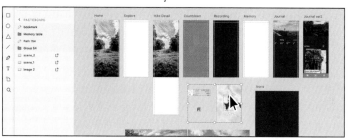

● **Note:** If some of the artwork disappears even when it's not touching an artboard, you may want to restart XD and reopen the files and try again.

8 Click away from the artwork to deselect it. Drag across the topography illustration (the map) to select it. To keep it together, group it by pressing Command+G (macOS) or Ctrl+G (Windows).

9 Drag the group onto the center of the Recording artboard.

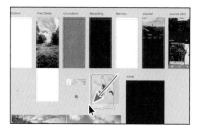 

10 Drag the artwork you pasted with the Location, Weather, Elevation, and Steps text (not the orange-red banner icon) onto the top of the Memory artboard.

11 Drag the remaining orange-red banner icon onto the Icons artboard.

12 Press Command+S (macOS) or Ctrl+S (Windows) to save the file.

Exporting artwork from Illustrator for Adobe XD ◼◄

To learn about how to easily export artwork from Illustrator to be used in Adobe XD, check out the video "Exporting Artwork from Illustrator for Adobe XD," which is a part of the Web Edition of this book. For more information, see the "Web Edition" section of "Getting Started" at the beginning of the book.

Masking content

You can easily hide portions of images or shapes (paths) using two different methods of masking in Adobe XD: mask with shape or image fill. Masks are nondestructive, which means that nothing that is hidden by the mask is deleted. In either case, you can adjust the mask, if required, to highlight another portion of the masked content.

Masking with a shape or path

The first method for masking you will learn is masking with a shape. This method of masking (hiding) portions of artwork or images is similar to masking in a program like Illustrator. The mask is either a closed path (shape) or an open path (like a path in the shape of an "s," for instance). To mask content, the masking object is on top of the object to be masked. Next, you'll mask a portion of artwork.

1 Click in the gray pasteboard area to deselect all.

2 Open the Layers panel, if it isn't already open, by clicking the Layers panel button (◆) in the lower-left corner of the application window. In the Layers panel, double-click the artboard icon (□) to the left of the Recording artboard to select it and zoom in to it.

3 Click to select the topography illustration (the map) on the Recording artboard.

4 Select the Rectangle tool (□) in the toolbar on the left. Starting below the top edge of the map artwork on the left edge of the artboard, drag down and to the right corner of the artboard.

▶ **Tip:** Pressing the R key will select the Rectangle tool.

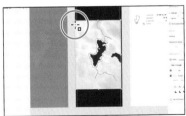
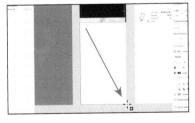

5 Press the V key to select the Select tool. With the shape still selected, in the Layers panel, Shift-click the Group 120 object name (or whatever you see) to select the map artwork behind the shape as well.

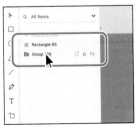

You selected the rectangle you just created and the map group so the rectangle can be used to mask the group. Also, the numbers you see in the names of objects in the Layers panel ("Rectangle 65," for example) may be different, and that's okay.

6 Choose Object > Mask With Shape (macOS) or right-click and choose Mask With Shape from the menu that appears (Windows).

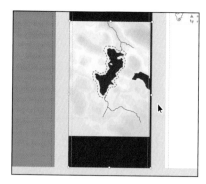

7 With the Layers panel open and the content still selected on the artboard, click the Mask Group 1 thumbnail in the Layers panel list to reveal the content, if necessary.

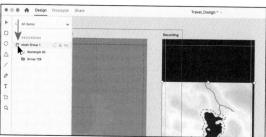

The mask shape and the object that is masked (the map group) are now part of a group.

Editing a mask

When you mask content, you may later want to crop it in a different way, revealing more or less of that content. When you mask with a shape, as you did in the previous section, you can easily edit both the mask and the object masked. Next, you'll change how the content from the previous section is masked.

● **Note:** If you select content within the map group, you can click in the pasteboard to deselect and double-click the map to try again to select the mask shape.

1 With the Select tool (▶) selected and the content still selected, double-click the map artwork to enter mask editing mode. The mask (rectangle) will be selected.

Double-clicking a masked object will temporarily show the mask and the masked object (the map artwork, in this instance) in the window. That way, you can edit either the mask or the object that is masked.

2 In the Layers panel, click the "Group 129" (or whatever you see) to select the map object. On the artboard, Shift-drag the lower-right handle of the map artwork down a little to make it larger than the artboard.

3 Move the pointer just off a corner of the artwork, and when you see rotate arrows, drag clockwise to rotate it a little. See the second part of the figure.

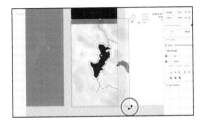 

4 Drag the selected artwork into the center of the artboard. Make sure that it fills the mask shape and covers the lower corners of the artboard. You may need to make it larger.

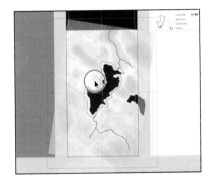

You could transform the masked content in different ways, or you could select the shape that is the mask (the rectangle, in this case) and reposition or resize it. You can also copy and paste other content into the mask.

5 In the Layers panel, click the rectangle object (the mask you drew).

6 In the Property Inspector on the right, click the Different Radius For Each Corner button (⬚). To round the top two corners of the rectangle, change the first two values to **30**, pressing Return or Enter after typing in the second value. Leave the last two values at 0.

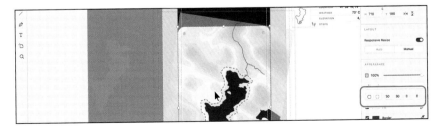

● **Note:** Any appearance property changes you make to the rectangle shape that is the mask, like fill or border, will not show when you exit the editing mode.

▶ **Tip:** In Path Edit mode, you can add, delete, and move anchor points as well as convert them between smooth and corner (and back) by double-clicking.

If you wanted to edit the mask shape further, you could double-click the edge of the mask and enter Path Editing mode to edit the anchor points.

Tip: To remove a mask, you could select the mask group and choose Object > Ungroup Mask (macOS) or, on Windows, right-click the group and choose Ungroup Mask. You can also press Shift+Command+G (macOS) or Shift+Ctrl+G (Windows).

7 Press the Esc key to exit the mask editing mode. The map artwork is once again masked.

● **Note:** Masked content is cropped like you see on the artboard when the asset is exported. You'll learn about exporting in Lesson 11.

8 Click in a blank area away from the artboards to deselect the masked content.

9 Choose File > Save (macOS) or click the menu icon (≡) in the upper-left corner of the application window and choose Save (Windows).

Masking with an image fill

Another method for masking is to drag and drop an image into an existing shape or path. The image becomes the fill of the shape. This method of masking is great when creating boxes as placeholders for content to come later, for instance. Next, you'll import a new image for a profile picture and mask it with a shape.

1 Double-click the artboard icon (□) to the left of the artboard name "Journal" in the Layers panel to fit the artboard in the document window.

2 To show the square grids on the artboards, choose View > Show Square Grid (macOS) or right-click in the gray pasteboard and choose Show Square Grid (Windows).

Tip: If the circle doesn't have a width and height of exactly 144, you could set the Lock Aspect option (🔒) in the Property Inspector and change either Width or Height to 144 to change both together.

3 Select the Ellipse tool (○) in the toolbar. Shift-drag on the Journal artboard to create a circle. Release the mouse button and then the key when you see a width and height of approximately 144 in the Property Inspector.

As you drag, you'll notice that the Width and Height values change by 8 because the circle is snapping to the square grid.

4 Go to the Finder (macOS) or File Explorer (Windows), open the Lessons > Lesson03 > images folder, and leave the folder open. With the folder showing and XD in the background, find the image named meng.png in the folder, and drag the image on top of the circle you drew in the Journal artboard. When the circle is highlighted in blue, release the mouse button to drop the image into the frame.

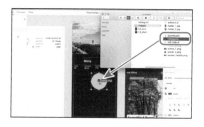

By dragging an image onto a shape, the image becomes the fill of the shape.

Editing an image fill mask

Dropping an image into a shape so that it becomes the fill of the shape means the image is always centered in the shape. Next, you'll explore the editing capabilities of this type of mask.

1   With the Select tool (▶) selected, double-click the image to enter Path Edit mode. The image will be selected.

2   Drag a corner of the image to make it larger. Then, drag within the image so that more of her face is in the circle.

● **Note:** Unlike with the Mask With Shape command you used in the previous section, you cannot edit the anchor points of the shape in this type of mask.

3   Press the Esc key to stop editing the image within the circle.

4   Deselect the Border option in the Property Inspector to turn it off.

● **Note:** The Width and Height values may change by different values in the Property Inspector, depending on the zoom level of the document. If you are zoomed out far enough, the width and height will change by 8.

5   With the masked image still selected, Shift-drag a corner of the bounding box to make the image smaller. When Width and Height are 80 in the Property Inspector, release the mouse button and then the key.

▶ **Tip:** If the circle doesn't have a width and height of exactly 80, that's okay. You could set the Lock Aspect option (🔒) in the Property Inspector and change either Width or Height to 80 to change both together.

The image remains centered in the shape. If the shape is resized, the image is resized proportionally to fill the shape. Unlike with images you place, the Lock Aspect option (🔒) is not selected for masked content by default. That's why you held the Shift key down when resizing it.

6 Drag the image into position, as you see in the figure.

7 Choose File > Save (macOS) or click the menu icon (≡) in the upper-left corner of the application window and choose Save (Windows).

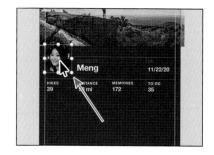

Working with text

When adding text to your design in Adobe XD, you have two main methods to choose from: adding it at a point or in an area. *Text at a point* is a horizontal line of text that begins where you click and expands as you enter characters. Each line of text is independent—the line expands or shrinks as you edit it but doesn't wrap to the next line unless you add a paragraph return or a soft return (Shift+Return [macOS] or Shift+Return [Windows]). Entering text this way is useful for adding a headline or a few words to your artwork.

Text in an area uses the boundaries of an object to control the flow of characters. When text reaches a boundary, it automatically wraps to fit inside the defined area. Entering text in this way is useful when you want to create one or more paragraphs. In this section, you'll explore the different ways to create text and change the formatting of text.

Adding text at a point

With some design content on the Home artboard in place, next you'll focus on adding text to it. Since this new text will be a single line, creating text at a point is the best option, as you'll soon see.

1 Press Command+0 (macOS) or Ctrl+0 (Windows) to see all of the content.

2 Click in a blank area away from the artboards to deselect everything. In the Layers panel, double-click the artboard icon (▢) to the left of the Home artboard to zoom in to it and select the artboard.

3 To temporarily turn off the square grids, in the Property Inspector, deselect the Square grid option.

4 Select the Text tool (**T**) in the toolbar. Click to the left of the Home artboard and type **field**. If you see an auto-correct menu below the text that shows the text "Field," click the X to the right to keep the lowercase "field."

The auto-correct functionality is a part of Spelling and Grammar, which is turned on by default in Adobe XD. To learn more, see the sidebar "Spelling and grammar in XD."

5 Press Return or Enter, and type **guide** to create text at a point. Once again, to keep the text lowercase, you may need to click the X to the right of the auto-correct menu that appears beneath the text.

Note: The figures in the lesson were taken on macOS, so you will see Helvetica Neue being used. The default font for Adobe XD on Windows is Segoe UI.

If you continue to type, the text will continue to the right until you either press Return/Enter for a paragraph return or press Shift+Return (macOS) or Shift+Enter (Windows) for a soft return.

6 Press Esc to select the text object.

A single point appears at the bottom of the bounding box around the text. This is one way to tell that this is text at a point.

7 Drag the point at the bottom of the text object down and up to see the font size change. Stop dragging when you see a font size of approximately 100 in the Property Inspector.

Tip: If you move the pointer just off the single anchor point on text at a point, the pointer will change (↖). You can then rotate the text.

8 With the text object still selected, click the Fill color box in the Property Inspector. Change the color to white in the Color Picker that appears.

9 Select the Select tool (▶) and drag the text into the center of the Home artboard.

10 Choose File > Save (macOS) or click the menu icon (≡) in the upper-left corner of the application window and choose Save (Windows).

Creating a text area

To create text in an area, you drag with the Text tool (T). Doing that creates an area to type text into. After you draw the text area, the cursor appears, and you can type. Next, you'll create a text area for body copy that you'll add to your design.

1 Press the spacebar to access the Hand tool (✋), and drag in the document window to see the Hike Detail artboard to the right of the Home artboard. You can also drag on a trackpad with two fingers to pan in the document window.

2 Select the Text tool (T) in the toolbar, and over the bottom half of the image, drag from the left artboard guide to the right artboard guide to create a text area between them. Type **Pine Meadow Lake Loop** (without a period).

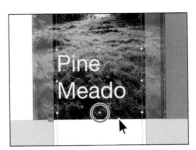

You may notice that your text doesn't fit within the text area (but you see it all) since the formatting is the same as the last text and is rather large. Also, the text is wrapping within the bounds of the text object.

3 Select the Select tool (▶) and notice the very small dot in the bottom-middle point of the box around the text. That dot indicates that there is *overset* text, or text that doesn't fit.

To make all of the text visible, you could drag the bottom-middle point down until it all shows. Since the text is so large, in this case, you will simply change the font size.

4 Double-click the text to select it. You should now see all of the highlighted text.

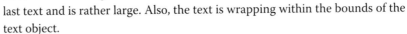
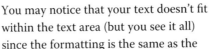
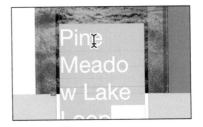

5 Select the Font Size value in the Property Inspector and type **36**. Press Return or Enter to accept the change. Make sure the text color is white.

6 Press the Esc key to select the text object again and not the text within.

Importing text

Next, you'll add more text to the design from a text file. This can be a great method for adding text to your designs from an external source.

1 Press Command+0 (macOS) or Ctrl+0 (Windows) to see all of the content.

2 Choose File > Import (macOS) or click the menu icon (≡) in the upper-left corner of the application window and choose Import (Windows). Navigate to the Lessons > Lesson03 folder and select the file named Hiking.txt. Click Import to place the text in its own type object on the same artboard.

3 With the Select tool (▶) selected, drag the text you just placed down toward the bottom of the artboard.

You may need to zoom in a little to see the bottom part of the artboard.

4 Press Command+3 (macOS) or Ctrl+3 (Windows) to zoom in to the text.

5 Drag the text area so the left edge is snapped to the guide on the left (see the following figure).

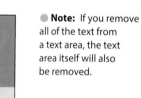

● **Note:** If you remove all of the text from a text area, the text area itself will also be removed.

6 Drag the middle-right point of the text area to the right to make it wider. Stop dragging when it snaps to the guide near the right edge of the artboard.

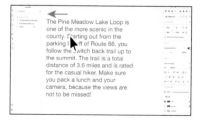
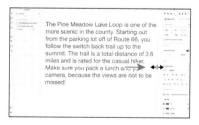

7 Press Command+0 (macOS) or Ctrl+0 (Windows) to see all of the content.

8 Click in a blank area of the document window away from content to deselect.

Styling text

In Adobe XD, the text-formatting options are found in the Property Inspector and include formatting such as type (point or area text), font size, text alignment, and more. In this section, you'll get a feel for formatting text in Adobe XD by applying formatting to text.

1   Double-click the artboard icon (⬚) to the left of the artboard name "Home" in the Layers panel to fit the Home artboard in the document window.

2   With the Select tool (▶) selected, click to select the text "field guide."

● **Note:** The figures in this lesson were taken on macOS, so you will see Helvetica Neue being used.

3   Make sure that Helvetica Neue (macOS) or Segoe UI (Windows) is selected for the font in the Property Inspector. Click the arrow next to "Regular" to reveal the Font Weight menu, and choose Bold.

● **Note:** The Font menu in Adobe XD shows all of your system fonts and any active Adobe fonts.

For both text at a point and area text, you can change the formatting for all of the text by simply selecting the type object with the Select tool. If you want to apply different formatting to different text within text at a point or a text area, you can select text with the Text tool.

4   To adjust the space between the lines of text, change Line Spacing (‡≡) to **96** in the Property Inspector. Press Return or Enter.

Line spacing is the space between lines of text and is similar to leading in programs like Adobe Illustrator.

▶ **Tip:** To change values in fields, you can select the value and press the up arrow or down arrow key. If you press Shift+up arrow or down arrow key, the value changes by 10.

5   Press the spacebar to access the Hand tool (✋), and drag in the document window to see the "Pine Meadow Lake Loop" text on the Hike Detail artboard. You can also drag on a trackpad with two fingers to pan in the document window.

6   With the Select tool (▶) selected, click the text "Pine Meadow Lake Loop." Make sure Font Size is **36** and Font Weight is Bold in the Property Inspector. Change Line Spacing to **40**. Press Return or Enter after the last value entered.

7 Drag the right-middle point of the text area to the left so the text wraps like it does in the figure.

8 Drag the bottom-middle bounding point up to just below the text (first part of the following figure).

This is meant to make the frames as small as they can be so that it will be easier to select a lot of content in a small area.

9 Drag the text to snap to the guide near the left side of the artboard, if it isn't already (second part of the following figure).

10 With the Select tool (▶) selected, click in the gray pasteboard to deselect.

11 Select the Text tool (T), and below the Pine Meadow Lake Loop text, click the guide on the left side of the artboard, to add text. Type **Distance**, press Return or Enter, and type **3.6 mi**.

12 Press Command+A (macOS) or Ctrl+A (Windows) to select all of the text in that type object. In the Property Inspector, change the font size to **10** and the line spacing to **16**.

13 Double-click the text Distance to select it. Change the character spacing (the spacing between each character) to **100** and press Return or Enter. Click the Uppercase button (**TT**) to make the text uppercase.

I zoomed in to the text to more easily see it.

14 Drag across the 3.6 mi text to select it. Change the font size to **16**. Press Return or Enter. Press the Esc key to select the text area.

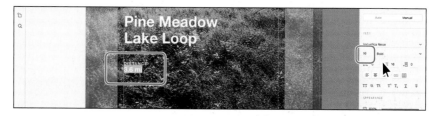

Fixing missing fonts

When you open an XD file that uses Adobe Fonts, they are automatically activated when you open your XD document. If non-Adobe fonts are used in the XD document that you don't have installed on your computer, the Assets panel will open, indicating that the fonts are missing.

You can replace missing fonts by right-clicking the name of the font in the Assets panel list and choosing Highlight On Canvas to see where they are used, and choosing Replace Font to choose a different font to be used wherever the missing font appears.

Duplicating text

One way to reuse text formatting is to copy a text object that has the formatting you want and change the text. You can also click in text with formatting you want and then create a new text object and use the formatting from the original text. In this final section, you'll copy text and change it.

1   With the Select tool (▶) selected, drag the DISTANCE text object so its left edge aligns with the guide near the left edge of the artboard. See the first part of the following figure for the position. Also note the vertical position.

2   Option-drag (macOS) or Alt-drag (Windows) the DISTANCE text object straight to the right. When horizontal alignment guides appear, indicating the copy is aligned with the original, release the mouse button and then the key.

3   Select the Text tool and double-click in the *copied* DISTANCE text to select it, and type **duration** to replace the text. The text should be uppercase because it inherits the formatting from the original DISTANCE text. Double-click in the *copied* 3.6 mi text to select it, and type **3:15 hr** to replace the text.

● **Note:** If you see an auto-correct menu below the text, click the X to the right to keep the text uppercase.

4   Press Esc to select the text object. Select the Select tool (▶), and Option-drag (macOS) or Alt-drag (Windows) the DURATION text object straight to the right. This time, you may see a gap value and a pink bar appear between all three text objects when the gap is the same value. Release the mouse button and then the key.

You may not see the gap values because the text is snapping to the square grid. If, when dragging, you don't see the gap values, you can either zoom in further or turn off the square grid for the artboard and try dragging again. To turn off the square grid for the artboard, press Command+' (macOS) or Ctrl+' (Windows). After dragging, you can then turn the grid back on by pressing the same keyboard shortcut.

5 Change the text to **elevation 384 ft** (see the figure).

6 Repeat the last two steps to create another copy. Change the text to **difficulty HARD** (see the figure).

7 Press Command+0 (macOS) or Ctrl+0 (Windows) to see all of the artboards.

8 Click in a blank area of the document window away from content to deselect.

9 Choose File > Save (macOS) or click the menu icon (≡) in the upper-left corner of the application window and choose Save (Windows).

● **Note:** If you started with the L3_start.xd jumpstart file, then keep that file open.

10 If you plan on jumping to the next lesson, you can leave the Travel_Design.xd file open. Otherwise, choose File > Close (macOS) or click the X in the upper-right corner (Windows) for each open document.

Spelling and grammar in XD

In Adobe XD, by default, spelling check and grammar check are enabled. You can access Spelling and Grammar by choosing it from the Edit menu (macOS) or by clicking the menu icon (≡) in the upper-left corner of the application window (Windows).

With Spelling and Grammar enabled, and the cursor in text or text selected, misspelled words are underlined in red. You can right-click the word and choose from alternatives, among other options.

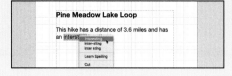

Review questions

1 What are at least three asset types you can import into Adobe XD?

2 Briefly, how do you temporarily disable snapping when dragging an image?

3 How do you replace an image?

4 What are the two methods for masking?

5 What are at least two methods for bringing Photoshop content into Adobe XD?

6 What is the difference between text at a point and area text?

Review answers

1 Types of asset files you can import into Adobe XD are .txt, PSD, AI, Sketch, SVG, GIF, JPEG, PNG, and TIFF.

2 When dragging an image, you can press the Command (macOS) or Ctrl (Windows) key to temporarily disable snapping.

3 You can drag an image from your desktop onto an existing image to replace it.

4 In Adobe XD, you can easily hide portions of images or shapes (paths) using two different methods: mask with shape or image fill. Masks are nondestructive, which means that nothing that is hidden by the mask is deleted.

5 There are several ways to bring content from Photoshop into Adobe XD: copy and paste, export from Photoshop and import into XD, import a Photoshop file (.PSD) (which places the .PSD content into the XD file), open a Photoshop file (.PSD) directly in XD (which opens the .PSD as a separate XD file), or place the content in a Creative Cloud Library and drag it into your design from the CC Libraries panel in XD.

6 Text at a point begins where you click and expands as you enter characters. Each line of text is independent—the line expands or shrinks as you edit it but doesn't wrap to the next line unless you add a paragraph return or a soft return. Text in an area uses the boundaries of an object to control the flow of characters. When text reaches a boundary, it automatically wraps to fit inside the defined area.

4 CREATING AND EDITING GRAPHICS

Lesson overview

In this lesson, you'll learn how to do the following:

- Create and edit shapes.
- Change the fill and border of content.
- Combine shapes using Boolean operations.
- Draw with the Pen tool.
- Edit paths and shapes.
- Work with UI kits.

 This lesson will take about 60 minutes to complete. To get the lesson files used in this chapter, download them from the web page for this book at www.adobepress.com/XDCIB2020. For more information, see "Accessing the lesson files and Web Edition" in the Getting Started section at the beginning of this book.

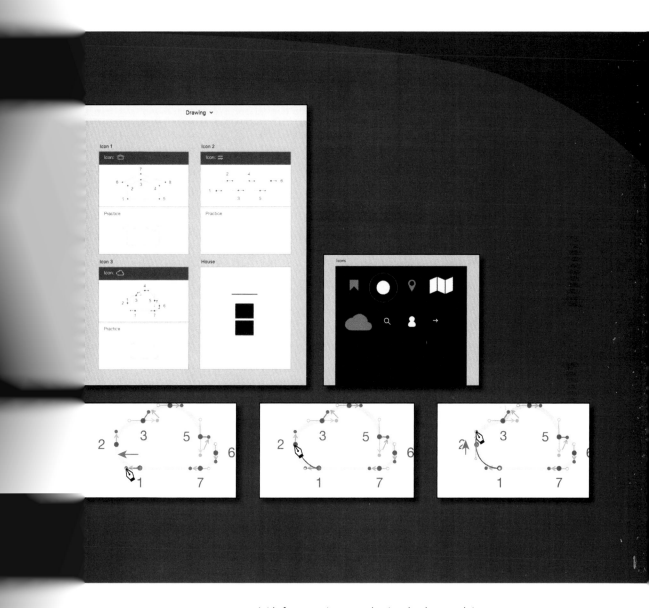

Aside from creating artwork using the shape tools in Adobe XD, you can also create artwork using the Pen tool. With these tools, you can precisely draw straight lines, curves, and more complex shapes.

Starting the lesson

In this lesson, you'll create vector shapes in the form of buttons, icons, and other graphic elements. To start, you'll open a final lesson file to get an idea of what you will create in this lesson.

● **Note:** If you have not already downloaded the project files for this lesson to your computer from your Account page, make sure to do so now. See the "Getting Started" section at the beginning of the book.

1 Start Adobe XD, if it's not already open.

2 On macOS, choose File > Open From Your Computer. On Windows, click the menu icon (≡) in the upper-left corner of the application window and choose Open From Your Computer. Open the file named L4_end.xd, which is in the Lessons > Lesson04 folder that you copied onto your hard disk.

● **Note:** For either macOS or Windows, if the Home screen is showing with no files open, click Your Computer in the Home screen. Open the file named L4_end.xd, which is in the Lessons > Lesson04 folder that you copied onto your hard disk.

3 If the Assets panel opens on the left and you see a Missing Fonts message, close the Assets panel by clicking Assets panel icon (▢) in the lower left.

4 Choose View > Zoom To Fit All (macOS) or Zoom To Fit All from the Zoom menu (Windows) in the upper right and leave the file open for reference.

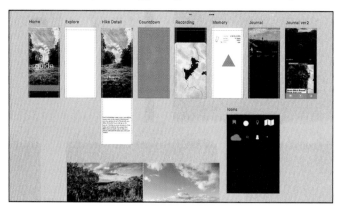

This file shows you what you will create by the end of the lesson.

5 Leave the file open for reference, or choose File > Close (macOS) or click the X in the upper-right corner of the open window (Windows) to close the file.

Graphics and Adobe XD

In Adobe XD, you'll create and work with *vector graphics* (sometimes called vector shapes or vector elements). Vector graphics are made up of lines and curves defined by mathematical objects called *vectors* and can be created in Adobe XD or a program like Adobe Illustrator.

In Lesson 3, "Adding Images, Graphics, and Text" you learned about the different types of images you can import into Adobe XD and how to work with them, including bringing in vector artwork from Illustrator. Using a variety of methods and tools in Adobe XD, you can freely move or modify shapes or paths you import or create. These can be in the form of icons, buttons, and other design elements.

Creating and editing shapes

Creating vector artwork in Adobe XD is easy thanks to the array of drawing tools available. If you're coming from other Adobe applications, you'll find the drawing tools in Adobe XD to be streamlined and efficient, with a few differences. For more complex vector content, you can use Illustrator and easily bring the vector artwork into XD.

1 Choose File > Open From Your Computer (macOS), or click the menu icon (☰) in the upper-left corner of the application window and choose Open From Your Computer (Windows). Open the Travel_Design.xd document in the Lessons folder (or where you saved it).

● **Note:** If you are starting from scratch using the jumpstart method described in the section "Getting Started," open L4_start.xd from the Lessons > Lesson04 folder.

2 Press Command+0 (macOS) or Ctrl+0 (Windows) to see all of the content.

3 Click the artboard name "Home" in the document window to select that artboard. Press Command+3 (macOS) or Ctrl+3 (Windows) to zoom in.

4 Select the Select tool (▶) and click away from the artboards to deselect all.

Creating rectangles

In this section, using the Rectangle tool, you'll create a rectangle that will be used as a button on the home screen.

▶ **Tip:** When drawing shapes, you can hold down Option (macOS) or Alt (Windows) to draw from the center, or press Shift to constrain the proportions of the shape. In the case of the Rectangle tool, pressing the Shift key constrains the shape to a square as you draw.

▶ **Tip:** You can also press the R key to select the Rectangle tool.

1 Select the Rectangle tool (☐) in the toolbar. Near the bottom of the Home artboard, move the pointer over the left edge of the artboard until that edge of the artboard turns aqua. This change in color indicates that the shape will snap or align to the edge of the artboard. Drag down and to the right to draw a rectangle, stopping on the right edge of the artboard. When alignment guides appear on the right, release the mouse button. Don't worry about the height for now.

Alignment guides are always on and can be very helpful for aligning, snapping, and spacing content you create or transform.

2 With the rectangle selected, drag the top-middle point of the shape up or down until you see a Height value of approximately 80 in the Property Inspector.

Drag to resize the rectangle   The result in the Property Inspector

Similar to editing artboards, as you draw or edit shapes the Width and Height values in the Property Inspector change to reflect the current sizing of the selected content.

Creating ellipses

Another drawing tool you can use is the Ellipse tool. In this section, you'll create several circles that will be used as a button in the app footer.

1 Press Command+Shift+A (macOS) or Ctrl+Shift+A (Windows) to deselect all so that you will be able to see all of the artboards in the Layers panel.

2 Click the Layers panel button (▲) in the lower-left corner (or press Command+Y [macOS] or Ctrl+Y [Windows]) to open the Layers panel, if it isn't already open. Double-click the artboard icon (▯) to the left of the artboard name "Icons" in the Layers panel to fit the artboard in the document window.

As you make your way through the lessons, you'll see that there are a lot of ways to navigate between artboards. The Layers panel is a method that you learned about in Lesson 1, "An Introduction to Adobe XD."

3 Choose Square from the Grid menu in the Property Inspector to turn it on. Click the Use Default button to apply the default square grid you set up previously.

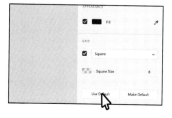
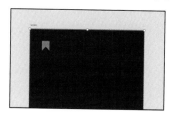

Note: If you started with the L4_start.xd file, the default grid you see may not be the same. Ensure that Square Size is 8, and click the Square Size color to ensure that the Alpha value in the color picker is 20%.

Tip: You can press Command+' (macOS) or Ctrl+' (Windows) to show or hide the square grid for a selected artboard or artboards.

Next you'll create a record button that will be used on the Recording artboard.

4 Select the Ellipse tool (○) in the toolbar (or press the E key to select the Ellipse tool). Hold down the Shift key and drag to create a circle on the artboard. As you drag, pay attention to Width and Height in the Property Inspector. When you see a width of 152 and height of 152, release the mouse button and then the key.

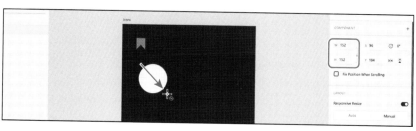

You may notice that as you drag, the Width and Height values are changing by multiples of 8. That's due to the square grid setting of 8.

5   Right-click the circle and choose Copy. Then right-click and choose Paste to paste a copy directly on top of the original.

6   To make the new circle half its size, drag a corner toward the center. As you drag, hold down Option+Shift (macOS) or Alt+Shift (Windows) to resize it from the center and maintain its proportions. Release the mouse button and then the keys.

Creating polygons

The last type of shape you'll explore is the polygon. Using the Polygon tool, you'll create a triangle shape that will be used on the Memory artboard.

1   Press Command+Shift+A (macOS) or Ctrl+Shift+A (Windows) to deselect all so that you can see all of the artboards in the Layers panel.

2   In the Layers panel, double-click the artboard icon (⬚) to the left of the artboard name "Memory" to fit the artboard in the document window.

3   To turn off the square grid, deselect the Square option in the Grid section of the Properties panel. This allows you to draw without snapping to the square grid.

4   Select the Polygon tool (△) in the toolbar.

5   Move the pointer in an empty area of the artboard. By default, the Polygon tool creates a triangle (a three-sided shape), but you'll edit the shape as you draw it. Drag down and to the right to begin drawing a polygon, but *don't release the mouse button yet*. Press the up arrow key twice to increase the number of sides on the polygon to five, and don't release the mouse button yet. Hold down the Shift key to straighten and constrain the shape. Release the mouse button and then the key. Leave the shape selected.

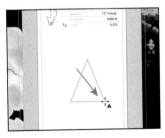 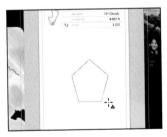 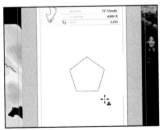

In the Properties panel, you will now see a Corner Count option (⬠), the Corner Radius option (⌒), and the Star Ratio (✩). The corner count is used to change the number of sides on the shape after you've created it, and the star ratio is used to turn the polygon into a star shape.

6 Change the Corner Count option to **3** and press Return or Enter. Leave the triangle selected.

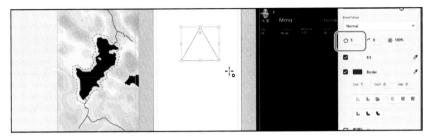

Creating stars

To create a star shape using the Polygon tool, start by drawing a polygon on the artboard. Then, click the Star Ratio handle in the upper right corner of the polygon, and drag in towards the radius. You can also adjust the star ratio by clicking the Star Ratio field in the Property Inspector. The ratio can be a value between 1 and 100. Use the Corner Count field to define the number of sides you want to have for the polygon. You can draw a star polygon from a regular triangle and go up to a hundred-sided polygon.

Hold down Shift key while dragging the Star Ratio handle to change it in increments of 10%. Alternatively, place the cursor on the Star Ratio field, and press the up and down arrow keys to control the ratio size.

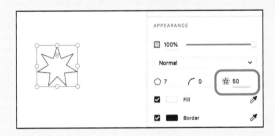

—From XD Help

Changing fill and border

Now that you have a few shapes in your design, you'll start to change appearance properties for them. You'll start by sampling color with the Eyedropper.

1. Press Command+0 (macOS) or Ctrl+0 (Windows) to see all of the content.

2. Select the Select tool (▶) in the toolbar. Shift-click the rectangle you drew toward the bottom of the Home artboard to select it and the triangle.

▶ **Tip:** You can also click the Eyedropper to the right of the Fill box in the Property Inspector (circled in the figure) to be able to sample a color for the fill.

3. Press the I key to select the fill Eyedropper so you can sample a color and apply it to the fill of selected content. Move the pointer over the orange-red color in the Countdown artboard and click to sample the color.

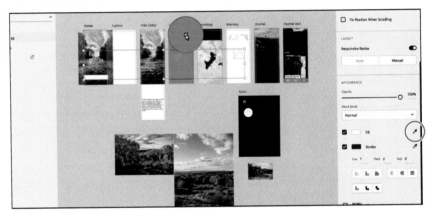

4. To save the orange-red color, click the Fill color in the Property Inspector and click the plus (+) at the bottom of the Color Picker. Press the Esc key to hide the panel.

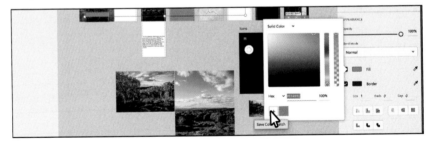

5. Deselect the Border option to turn the border off for the selected shapes.

6. Click the larger circle you drew on the Icons artboard to select it. Press Command+3 (macOS) or Ctrl+3 (Windows) to zoom in to it.

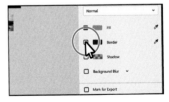

7   Deselect the Fill option in the Property Inspector to remove the fill.

8   Click the Border color to show the Color Picker. Change the border color to white by dragging in the Saturation/Brightness field.

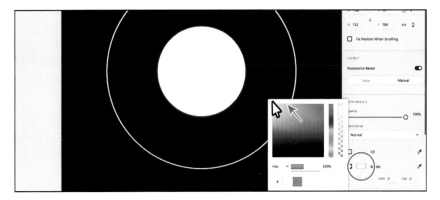

9   Click the plus (+) at the bottom of the color picker to save the white color.

Fill and border colors you create can be saved in this way. The colors you save using this method appear in the color picker for this document only. You can't give names to these saved colors.

▶ **Tip:** To delete a color swatch, drag the swatch away from the color picker window.

10 Click to select the smaller circle and deselect the Border option to turn it off.

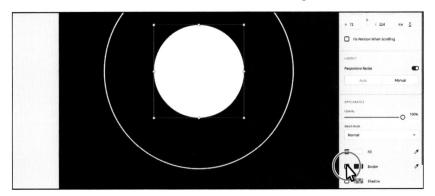

11 Drag across both circles to select them, and choose Object > Group (macOS) or right-click and choose Group to keep them together as a group.

12 Press Command+S (macOS) or Ctrl+S (Windows) to save the file.

Working with border options

Now, you'll create a simple magnifying glass search icon from a circle and path. You'll explore border alignment and changing the line cap to get the final look.

1 Press Command and – (macOS) or Ctrl and – (Windows) a few times to zoom out.

2 Press the spacebar and drag to the left to see more of the Icons artboard to the right of the circles. You can also drag on a trackpad with two fingers to pan in the document window.

3 Select the Ellipse tool (○) in the toolbar. Shift-drag to create a circle on the artboard. As you drag, pay attention to Width and Height in the Property Inspector. When you see an approximate width of 20 and height of 20, release the mouse button and then the key.

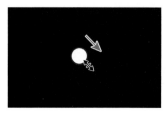 

4 Deselect the Fill option in the Property Inspector to remove the fill.

5 Click the Border color to show the Color Picker. Click the white color you saved previously to apply it to the border. Press the Esc key to hide the panel.

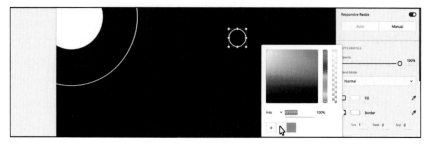

6 Change Border Size to **4** and press Return or Enter.

7 Click the Outer Stroke button (⌐) to align the border to the outside of the shape.

By default, borders are aligned to the inside of paths in Adobe XD. Next you'll draw the handle of the search icon.

8 Press Command+Shift+A (macOS) or Ctrl+Shift+A (Windows) to deselect.

9 Select the Line tool (╱) in the toolbar on the left and Shift-drag to make a small angled line, as you see in the figure. This will be the handle of the magnifying glass.

10 Change the border color to white, change the border size to **4**, and press Return or Enter. Click the Round Cap button (∈) to round the ends of the line.

● **Note:** You may want to reposition the handle before you group the objects in the next step.

11 Select the Select tool and drag across both objects and press Command+G (macOS) or Ctrl+G (Windows) to group them.

Rounding corners

When it comes to rectangles, you can easily round all of the corners of a rectangle at once or each individually. In this next section, you'll create a rounded-corner rectangle that will become part of an icon.

1 With the Select tool (▶) selected, zoom out by pressing Command and – (macOS) or Ctrl and – (Windows).

To zoom in or out you can also pinch using a trackpad or Option-scroll/Alt-scroll using a mouse.

2 Select the Rectangle tool (▢) in the toolbar and Shift-drag to create a square next to the search icon you just created. Release the mouse button and then the key when it shows an approximate width of 30 and height of 30 in the Property Inspector.

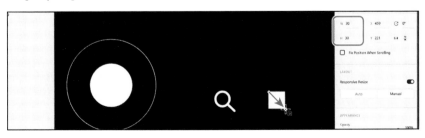

3 Deselect the Border option in the Property Inspector to remove the border.

For the next step, you may need to zoom in to see the corner radius widgets.

▶ **Tip:** You can drag any of the corner widgets on the shape away from the center of the shape to remove the corner radius.

4 Drag any one of the corner radius widgets () toward the center of the shape to round all of the corners at once. Drag as far as you can to make a circle.

Next, you'll round corners independently on a shape.

5 To duplicate the circle, press Command+D (macOS) or Ctrl+D (Windows). A copy is placed on top of the original.

6 Press the letter V to select the Select tool and drag the new circle straight down, away from the original, making sure they still overlap a little.

7 Option-drag (macOS) or Alt-drag (Windows) the middle point on the right side of the shape to the right to make the shape wider from both sides at the same time.

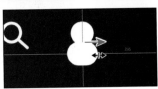

8 Change the Corner Radius value in the Property Inspector to **0** to remove the rounded corners from the copy.

9 Option-drag (macOS) or Alt-drag (Windows) the upper-left corner radius widget () toward the center of the shape. Drag until you see a Top Left Corner Radius value of approximately 30 in the Property Inspector.

Dragging with the Option/Alt key held down allows you to change one of the corner radii. When you change a single corner radius by dragging with the Option/Alt key, the Different Radius For Each Corner option ( ) becomes selected in the Property Inspector, allowing you to change each corner radius independently. If you find that you can't change the radius value to 30—maybe you can only change it to 26, for instance—it may be that the rectangle is smaller than it is in the figure. That's okay.

10 Change the Corner Radius values in the Property Inspector to **50, 50, 30**, and **30** (or similar values) and press Return or Enter to accept the values. Leave the shape selected.

▶ Tip: If you want to ensure that all of the radius values are the same again, you can click the Same Radius For All Corners button ( ).

● Note: By default, when you transform a shape, the corner radius values do not scale (change).

11 With the Select tool selected, drag across both objects and press Command+G (macOS) or Ctrl+G (Windows) to group them.

Editing shapes

If you've ever edited shapes in other Adobe programs, like Illustrator, you're likely used to switching tools to accomplish shape editing tasks. In Adobe XD, shape editing is easily accomplished with a single tool, the Select tool. In this section, you'll create and edit shapes for a map icon.

1 Choose View > Show Square Grid (macOS), or right-click the Icons artboard and choose Show Square Grid (Windows).

2 Select the Rectangle tool ( ) in the toolbar and, starting on the square grid, drag to create a rectangle that is wider than it is tall. Make sure to snap the right edge of the rectangle to the square grid. See the figure. The rectangle in the figure has a height of 40 and a width of 72.

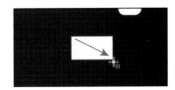

In this case, the square grid can be a useful way to create shapes because it ensures whole-number values for width and height. Every shape you create has a bounding box around it when selected. This is used for transforming the shape in different ways.

3 Select the Select tool (▶) and double-click the selected rectangle.

Double-clicking an object enters Path Edit mode, which allows you to edit the anchor points of the object. At this point, you could select existing anchor points and edit or delete them and add new anchor points, but you can't move or transform the entire shape.

4 Drag across the top two anchor points to select them both. You could have also pressed the Shift key and clicked both anchor points to select them.

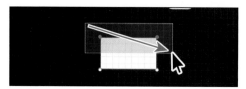

5 Drag one of the anchor points to the left, keeping it in line with the original position of the anchor points. Snap the anchor point you are dragging to the square grid.

6 Press the Esc key to exit Path Edit mode. The bounding box is now showing again, and the anchor points are hidden.

7 With the shape still selected, move the pointer just off one of the corners. When the pointer changes (↗), Shift-drag clockwise to rotate the shape. When you see 90 in the Rotation field of the Property Inspector, release the mouse button and then the Shift key.

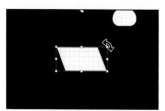
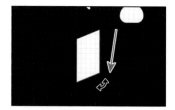

8   With the Select tool (▶) and the shape still selected, press Command+D (macOS) or Ctrl+D (Windows) to paste a copy right on top of the original.

Next, you'll flip the shape copy.

9   Click the Flip Horizontally button (▷◁) in the Property Inspector to flip the shape.

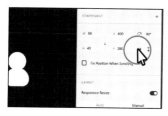 

10 Drag the shape you just flipped to the right. When there is a gap of 3 pixels between the shapes, stop dragging and release the mouse button. Aqua alignment guides appear, indicating it is still aligned horizontally with the original shape.

11 Option-drag (macOS) or Alt-drag (Windows) the shape on the left to the right to make a copy. When it looks like the figure, release the mouse button and then the key.

● **Note:** If you find that the shape is snapping to the square grid and the Gap value you see is 8, try zooming in further. By zooming in, the shape will snap to the pixel grid and the square grid.

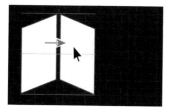 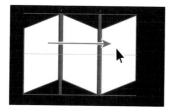

12 Drag across all three shapes and press Command+G (macOS) or Ctrl+G (Windows) to group them together and make a map icon.

13 Deselect the Border option in the Property Inspector to remove the border.

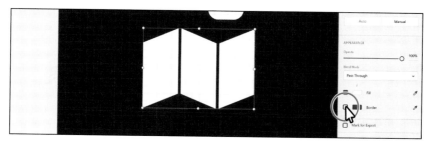

Combining shapes

Like many other drawing applications, Adobe XD offers several Boolean operations for combining shapes in different ways. There are four Boolean operations you can choose from: Add, Subtract, Intersect, and Exclude Overlap. Using Boolean operations can be very useful for creating more complex artwork from simpler shapes. To me, the best part of combining shapes using Boolean operations in Adobe XD is the ability to edit each individual shape, even after multiple shapes have been combined. Next, you'll combine shapes to create a map pin icon.

1 Zoom out a bit by pressing Command and – (macOS) or Ctrl and – (Windows) a few times.

2 Select the Ellipse tool (○) in the toolbar. In a blank area of the artboard, Shift-drag to create a circle. Don't worry about the size for now. Just make it large enough to work with. Release the mouse button and then the key.

3 With the Select tool (▶) and the shape still selected, press Command+D (macOS) or Ctrl+D (Windows) to paste a copy right on top of the original.

4 Option+Shift-drag (macOS) or Alt+Shift-drag (Windows) a corner to make the circle smaller.

● **Note:** You may need to deselect the smaller circle first, before attempting to select the larger circle.

5 Click the larger circle to select it. Double-click the shape to enter Path Edit mode and see the anchor points. See the first part of the following figure.

6 Click the anchor point on the bottom of the circle to select it. You should see little direction handles appear on either side of the point. These control the curve of the path on either side of the anchor point.

 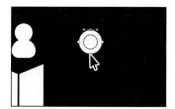

For the next step, if you don't see the aqua alignment guide, you may need to zoom in.

7 Drag the bottom anchor point down to reshape the circle. As you drag, a vertical aqua alignment guide should appear when the point is aligned with the anchor point at the top of the shape. Drag down until it looks good to you.

8 Double-click the same point to convert it to a corner point (not a curve).

▶ **Tip:** You can double-click the same point again to convert it back to a corner point.

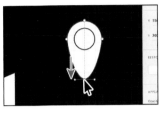 

In Adobe XD, you can easily edit existing shapes without having to switch tools from the Select tool. Later in this lesson, in the section "Drawing with the Pen tool," you'll learn about creating and editing paths with the Pen tool and the Select tool.

9 Press the Esc key to exit Path Edit mode. You should see the bounding box around the shape, not the anchor points on the shape. Drag across both shapes to select them.

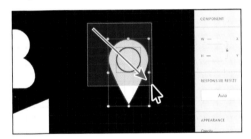

10 Click the Subtract button (⬚) in the Property Inspector to subtract the smaller circle from the shape under it.

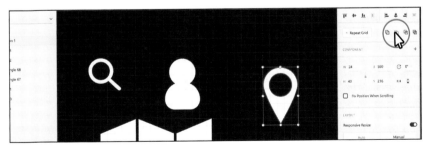

Look in the Property Inspector and notice that the Subtract option is on. The Boolean operations, such as Subtract, can be toggled off later, returning the shapes to two separate shapes.

11 Deselect the Border option in the Property Inspector to remove the border.

Tip: In Lesson 6, "Working with Assets and CC Libraries," you'll learn about saving colors and working smarter.

12 Click the Fill color box in the Property Inspector to show the Color Picker. Select the orange-red color you saved, at the bottom of the panel, to apply it.

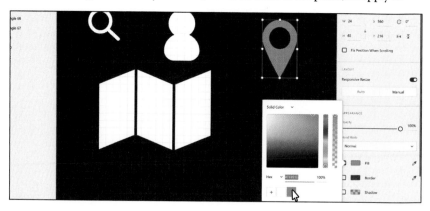

13 Press the Esc key to hide the color picker.

Editing combined shapes

No matter which of the operations you use for combining shapes, you can always edit the underlying shapes you started with. Next, you'll edit shapes from the map pin icon you just created.

1 Double-click the newly combined pin icon to enter editing mode for the selected shapes.

2 Click in the smaller circle in the center to select it, if it's not already selected.

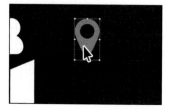 

Notice the blue outline around the entire pin icon. When you double-click combined shapes, the outline appears, indicating the combined shapes that you are editing. You can see the outline in the following figure.

3 Zoom in to the pin icon.

4 Option+Shift-drag (macOS) or Alt+Shift-drag (Windows) a corner to make the circle even smaller. Release the mouse button and then the keys.

5 Press the Esc key to stop editing the individual shapes, and select the entire combined pin icon.

6   Choose Object > Path > Convert To Path (macOS) or, on Windows, right-click and choose Path > Convert To Path.

The Convert To Path command is useful if you want to make the path combination permanent (you can no longer edit the individual paths) and also to be able to edit the anchor points of the combined path.

7   Press Command+S (macOS) or Ctrl+S (Windows) to save the file.

Creating dashed lines

In addition to changing the color and size of a border for content, you can also apply a dash. With a path or shape selected, in the Property Inspector you can assign specific quantities to the Dash and Gap values. The Dash value is the length of each dash segment on the line, and the Gap value is the distance between those dash segments.

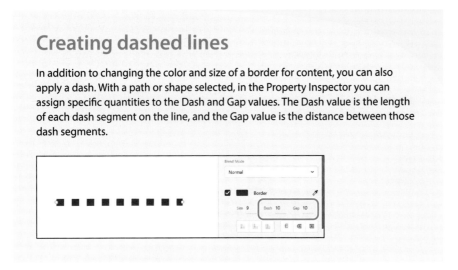

Aligning content to the pixel grid

When you're creating vector content in Adobe XD or bringing in vector content from other sources, it's important that the images you export later look sharp. To create pixel-accurate designs, you can align artwork to the pixel grid using the Align To Pixel Grid option. The *pixel grid* is an invisible grid of 72 squares per inch. Align To Pixel Grid is an object-level property that enables an object to have its vertical and horizontal paths aligned to the pixel grid. Next you'll draw an arrow icon and align it to the pixel grid.

1   Choose View > Hide Square Grid (macOS) or, on Windows, right-click the artboard and choose Hide Square Grid.

With the square grid off, content you create will no longer be aligned to the grid.

2   Press the spacebar and drag to the left to see more of the Icons artboard to the right of the other icons. You can also drag on a trackpad with two fingers to pan in the document window.

● **Note:** If you find that this zoom command won't work, you can pinch-zoom on a trackpad or select the Zoom tool to zoom in.

3   Select the Line tool (⁄) in the toolbar and Shift-drag to make a horizontal line, as you see in the figure. Release the mouse button and then the key.

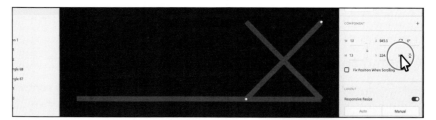

4   Press Command+3 (macOS) or Ctrl+3 (Windows) to zoom in to the line.

5   To deselect the line, press the Esc key.

Now you'll draw the arrowhead.

6   With the Line tool selected, starting on the right end of the path you drew, Shift-drag up and to the left to make a line that is angled at 45 degrees.

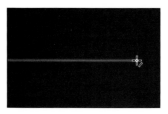

7   Press Command+D (macOS) or Ctrl+D (Windows) to duplicate the line in place. Click the Flip Horizontally button (▷|◁) in the Property Inspector.

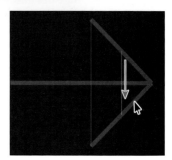

8   Select the Select tool and drag the flipped line straight down. Aqua alignment guides will appear to help you align it.

9   Drag across all of the paths and then right-click them and choose Group.

10 In the Property Inspector, change the border color to white, change the border size to **4**, and press Return or Enter. Click the Round Cap button (∈) to round the ends of the line.

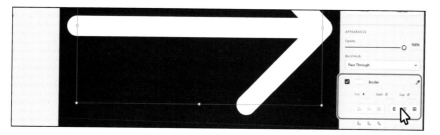

11 Shift-drag a corner to make it smaller. Drag until you see a width of around 24 in the Property Inspector. Release the mouse button and then the key.

Looking in the Property Inspector, you may see that the Width and Height values are not whole numbers. Next, you'll align the artwork in the group to the pixel grid, and those values will become whole numbers.

12 Choose Object > Align To Pixel Grid (macOS) or right-click the selected artwork and choose Align to Pixel Grid.

● **Note:** To see the change to the Height and Width values in the Property Inspector, you may want to click away from the arrow artwork, then click to select it again.

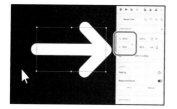

Not pixel-grid aligned

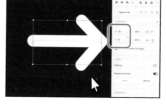

After aligning to the pixel grid

You probably noticed the subtle shift in the shapes as the paths were aligned to the pixel grid. To give you an idea of what just happened, take a look at the following figure. On the left is artwork that I didn't align to the pixel grid before I exported it as a PNG; on the right is artwork that is aligned to the pixel grid.

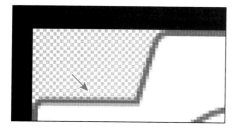

Not aligned before exporting as PNG

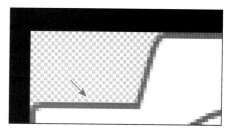

Aligned before exporting as PNG

You can clearly see the difference on the horizontal and vertical paths.

13 Press Command+0 (macOS) or Ctrl+0 (Windows) to see all of the artboards.

14 Click in a blank area of the gray pasteboard to deselect all.

15 Press Command+S (macOS) or Ctrl+S (Windows) to save the file.

Drawing with the Pen tool

Another way to create artwork is to use the Pen tool in Adobe XD. With the Pen tool, you can create freeform and more precise artwork, and edit existing shapes. In this section, you'll explore the Pen tool by drawing artwork using straight and curved lines, and then you'll learn how to edit shapes with both the Pen and Select tools. First, you'll open an existing file and begin drawing some icons using the Pen tool.

1   Choose File > Open From Your Computer (macOS), or click the menu icon ($\equiv$) in the upper-left corner of the application window and choose Open From Your Computer (Windows). Locate the file named Drawing.xd, which is in the Lessons > Lesson04 folder that you copied onto your hard disk. Select the file and click Open.

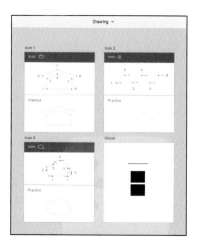

This document has three icons you'll create. You'll use templates provided for tracing paths, and then you can practice on your own.

2   In the Layers panel, double-click the artboard icon ($\square$) to the left of the artboard name "Icon 1" to fit the artboard in the document window.

Drawing straight lines

You may have some experience with the Pen tool in an application like Illustrator or Photoshop. The Pen tool in Adobe XD is similar, but in XD creating paths with the Pen tool may seem easier and more intuitive. To start drawing with the Pen tool in Adobe XD, you'll create an icon in the shape of a house.

▶ **Tip:** You can press the P key to select the Pen tool.

1   Select the Pen tool ($\mathscr{O}$) in the toolbar. Move the pointer over point 1 and click to create an anchor point; then release the mouse button. Make sure you have released the mouse button and move the pointer away from the point you just created, and you'll see a line connecting the first point and the pointer, no matter where you move the pointer. That line gives you a preview of the next line segment you will draw.

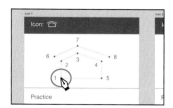
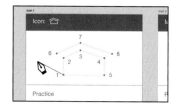

Later, as you create curved paths, it will make drawing them easier because you can preview what the path will look like.

2 Move the pointer over point 2, above point 1. When the pointer is vertically aligned with the first point, the preview line will turn aqua to show that it's aligned. Click point 2 to create another anchor point.

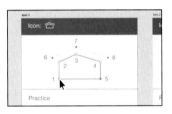

● **Note:** If the path looks curved, you have accidentally dragged with the Pen tool. Press Command+Z (macOS) or Ctrl+Z (Windows) to undo, and then click again without dragging.

You just created a path. A simple path is composed of two anchor points and a line segment connecting those anchor points. You use the anchor points to control the direction, length, and curve of the line segment.

3 Continue clicking points 3, 4, and 5 to create a house shape, releasing the mouse button every time you click to create another anchor point.

The aqua snap guides are very useful for aligning anchor points you create to existing anchor points. Notice that only the last anchor point is filled (not hollow like the rest of the anchor points), indicating that it is selected.

4 Click the first anchor point you created to close the path and stop drawing.

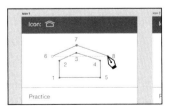

After closing a path, the Select tool (▶) is automatically selected. Next, you'll create a path that will be the roof of the house. This will be an open path, not closed.

▶ **Tip:** Instead of relying on alignment guides to align points as you create them, you can also press the Shift key and click to create an anchor point. The Shift key constrains the angle of the segment to a multiple of 45 degrees.

5 Select the Pen tool and move the pointer over point 6. Move the pointer around and you most likely will see aqua snap guides. Press and hold Command (macOS) or Ctrl (Windows) and move the pointer around. You will no longer see the aqua alignment guides since dragging with the Command (macOS) or Ctrl (Windows) key down temporarily disables the alignment guides. With the key still held down, click point 6.

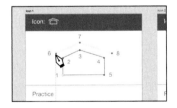

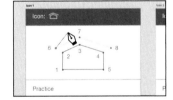

6 With the key held down, click to add a point at 7. Release the key and click point 8 to create a roof.

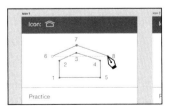

Releasing the Command (macOS) or Ctrl (Windows) key before adding point 8 allowed the alignment guides to work again.

7   Press the Esc key to stop drawing the path, which also automatically switches to the Select tool.

If you want to practice without the template, try tracing the same shape below the template in the area labeled Practice.

Drawing with a square artboard grid turned on

Drawing on an artboard with the grid turned on means that what you draw will snap to the grid lines. This can make creating icons or other vector objects easier and more precise. To avoid snapping to the grid, you can press the Command (macOS) or Ctrl (Windows) key while dragging the mouse and drawing an object.

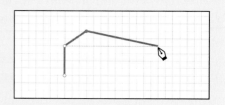

Drawing curves

Along with creating straight paths with the Pen tool, you can also draw curves. As you draw, you create a line called a *path*. A path is made up of one or more straight or curved segments. The beginning and end of each segment are marked by anchor points, which work like pins holding a wire in place.

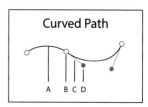

Curved Path

A. Line segment
B. Anchor point
C. Direction line
D. Direction point

A path can be closed (for example, a circle) or open, with distinct endpoints (for example, a wavy line). You change the shape of a path by dragging its anchor points or the direction points at the end of direction lines (together, direction points and direction lines are called *direction handles*) that appear at anchor points.

Creating curves with the Pen tool can be tricky, but with some practice you'll soon be on your way. Next, you'll create a curved path. To do this, you'll drag away from a point you create.

▶ **Tip:** You can press the spacebar to access the Hand tool and then drag in the document window to move to a blank area of the artboard.

1   Press Command+Shift+A (macOS) or Ctrl+Shift+A (Windows) to deselect all.

2   Double-click the artboard icon (⬚) to the left of the artboard name "Icon 2" in the Layers panel to fit the artboard in the document window.

3 Select the Pen tool (✐) in the toolbar. Move the pointer over the gray point labeled 1. Press and drag to the right, to the blue dot, to create a direction line.

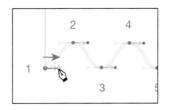

The angle and length of direction lines determine the shape and size of the curve. As you drag away from a point, there are typically two direction handles (except for on a starting point), one before the point and one after it. Direction lines move together by default and only show when you're editing paths.

4 Move the pointer over point 2; then press and drag to the right. *After you begin dragging,* press the Shift key to constrain the movement to a multiple of 15 degrees. When you reach the blue dot, release the mouse button and then the key to create direction lines.

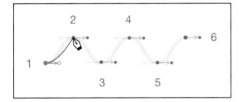 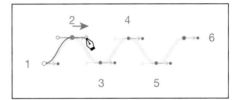

Next, you'll create a corner point with no direction lines, and then go back and change it to a smooth point.

5 Move the pointer over point 3. Click and release without dragging to create a corner point with no direction lines.

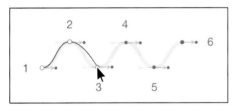

6 Move the pointer over point 4, and press and drag to the right. After you start dragging, press the Shift key. When you reach the blue dot, release the mouse button and then the key to create a direction line.

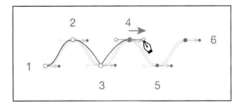

7   Move the pointer over the anchor point at 3. When the point turns blue and the pointer changes (➤), double-click to convert the point to a smooth point with direction handles you can edit.

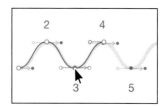

While drawing with the Pen tool in Adobe XD, you can always edit the path you are currently drawing without switching tools.

8   Move the mouse pointer over point 5 and drag to the right. As you drag, press the Shift key. When you reach the blue dot, release the mouse button and then the key to create a direction line.

9   Move the mouse pointer over point 6 and drag to the right. As you drag, press the Shift key. When you reach the blue dot, release the mouse button and then the key to create a direction line.

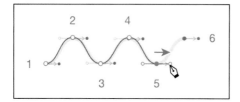 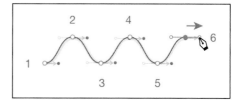

10 Press the Esc key to stop drawing and automatically switch to the Select tool.

11 Change Border Size to **3** in the Property Inspector. Press Return or Enter.

12 With the Select tool selected, click in a blank area of the gray pasteboard to deselect the last path.

If you want to practice without the template, try tracing the same shape below the template in the area labeled Practice.

Changing path direction

The last icon you will create is a cloud. The path will contain an anchor point whose direction lines are "split." This means that a curve can be followed by a straight path, for instance.

1   Double-click the artboard icon (▯) to the left of the artboard named Icon 3 in the Layers panel to fit the artboard in the document window. To zoom in a bit further, press Command and + (macOS) or Ctrl and + (Windows).

2   Select the Pen tool (✐) in the toolbar. Press and drag from point 1 to the left, to the blue dot, to create a direction line. Release the mouse button.

3 Move the mouse pointer over point 2 and drag up to the blue dot to create a direction line.

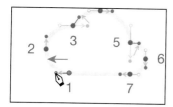 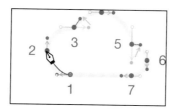 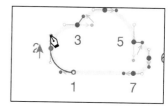

Now you need the next part of the path to switch directions at the anchor point and create another curve. You will *split* the direction lines to convert a smooth point to a corner point. This involves a keyboard modifier.

4 Move the pointer over point 3 and drag to the gold dot to create a direction line. Release the mouse button.

5 Press the Option (macOS) or Alt (Windows) key and drag the end of the direction line to the blue dot. Release the mouse button and then the key.

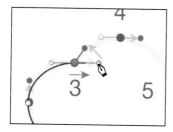 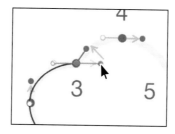 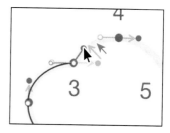

The direction lines are now split, which means you can move them independently of each other. The trailing direction line controls the curve of the path *leading up to* the anchor point, and the leading direction line controls the curve of the path *after* the anchor point.

▶ **Tip:** To make the handles move together again, you can double-click the corner anchor point twice.

6 Move the mouse pointer over point 4 and drag to the right, to the blue dot, to continue drawing the path.

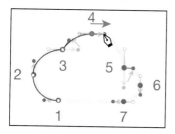

When it comes to smooth points (curved), you'll find that you spend a lot of time focusing on the path segment that is created when you place a new anchor point. Remember, by default there are two direction lines for a point. The previous direction line controls the shape of the previous segment.

7 Move the pointer over point 5 and drag to the gold dot to create a direction line. When the path between points 4 and 5 looks good, release the mouse button.

8 Press the Option (macOS) or Alt (Windows) key and drag the end of the direction line to the blue dot. Release the mouse button and then the key.

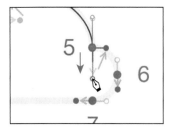 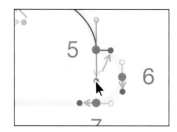 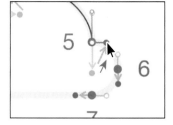

9 Move the mouse pointer over point 6 and drag down, to the blue dot, to continue drawing the path.

10 Move the mouse pointer over point 7 and drag to the left, to the blue dot, to continue drawing the path.

11 Move the mouse pointer over point 1 and click to close the cloud path.

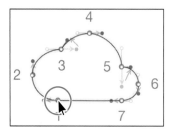

If you want to practice without the template, try tracing the same shape below the template in the area labeled Practice.

12 Deselect the Border option in the Property Inspector.

13 Click the Fill color, and in the color picker change the Hex value to an orange-red (**#FF491E**). You may need to make sure that Hex is chosen from the menu in the lower left corner of the color picker first.

▶ **Tip:** When editing the Hex value, you can enter Hex values using shorthand. You can type any Hex value to have it repeated for all six values. For instance, typing a single character, such as "f," and pressing Return or Enter repeats that character for all values (#ffffff). Typing two characters, such as "ab," repeats in order (#ababab). Typing three characters, such as "123," repeats each character in order (#112233).

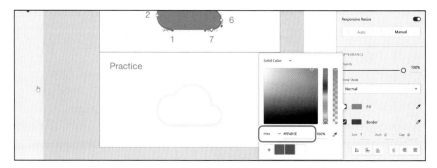

Editing artwork with the Pen tool

In Adobe XD, you can edit shapes and paths as you are drawing vector artwork or after the artwork is created. In the next few exercises, you'll focus on editing shapes using Path Edit mode.

1   Press Command+Shift+A (macOS) or Ctrl+Shift+A (Windows) to deselect all.

2   Double-click the artboard icon (⬚) to the left of the House artboard in the Layers panel to fit the artboard in the document window.

3   With the Select tool (▶) selected, double-click the top rectangle shape to enter Path Edit mode.

4   Move the pointer over the top border of the path, as you see in the first part of the following figure. When the Pen tool icon (✎) appears, click to create a new anchor point and release the mouse button.

When in Path Editing mode, you don't have to switch tools from the Select tool to add, delete, and edit points.

5   Drag the anchor point up.

6   Double-click the line above the house shape to enter Path Editing mode. Move the pointer over the path, and when you see the Pen tool icon, click to add a new anchor point. See the first part of the following figure.

7   Drag that same anchor point up a bit. See the second part of the following figure.

8   Press the Esc key to exit Path Edit mode.

At this point, the anchor points aren't visible, and you cannot edit them; only the bounding box of the shape is visible.

9   Drag the path down, above the house icon. See the last part of the following figure.

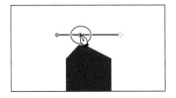
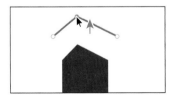

To finish the house artwork, you'll edit the rectangle below the path to look like a curving sidewalk.

10 Double-click the rectangle below the house shape to enter Path Editing mode.

● **Note:** The figure also shows the anchor points closer to the house icon above.

11 Drag the top two anchor points on the selected shapes closer together.

12 Move the pointer over the lower-left anchor point and double-click to convert it to a smooth point. The path at that anchor should now be a curve.

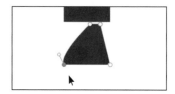

13 Click the end of the direction handle pointing down. Press Delete or Backspace to remove it. The path on that side of the anchor point is now straight.

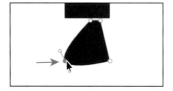 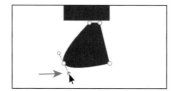 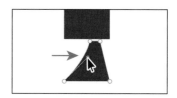

14 Drag the remaining direction handle up and to the right to curve the path.

15 Repeat steps 12–14 on the anchor point in the lower-right corner of the same shape.

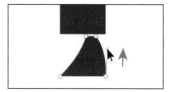

Copying the cloud icon

Next, you'll copy the cloud icon you created to the Travel_Design.xd document.

1 Press Command+0 (macOS) or Ctrl+0 (Windows) to zoom out.

2 With the Select tool selected, right-click the cloud icon and choose Copy.

● **Note:** If you started with the L4_start.xd jumpstart file, then return to that file.

3 To close and save the Drawing document, choose File > Close (macOS) or click the X in the upper-right corner (Windows).

You should be back in the Travel_Design.xd document.

4 Right-click the Icons artboard and choose Paste to paste the cloud icon.

5 Drag the icons around on the artboard so they are more evenly spaced. That will make it a little easier to select them later. You may want to zoom in to the artboard.

6 Press Command+0 (macOS) or Ctrl+0 (Windows) to see everything, if necessary.

Working with UI Kits

In Adobe XD you have access to a series of UI (user interface) kits for Apple iOS, Microsoft Windows, Google Material (Android), and wireframes. UI kits and wireframes can save time when you're designing for different device interfaces and platforms. They are XD files that include common design elements such as icons, keyboard layouts, navigation bars, inputs, buttons, and more. You can use a UI kit as a starting point or copy and paste elements into your own design. These resources can help you create a design that matches a specific design language (like iOS).

Downloading the UI kit

In this section, you'll download and unzip a UI kit from the developer.apple.com website. You'll then open an XD file from the downloaded files and copy a few elements into your design.

● **Note:** If you are on Windows or cannot access the Adobe XD file on the Apple website, you can open the UI_kit_content.xd document in XD, located in the Lessons > Lesson04 folder. You can then press Command+A (macOS) or Ctrl+A (Windows) to select all of the content in the document, copy it, and paste it into the Travel_Design.xd file that is still open.

1   Choose File > Get UI Kits > Apple iOS (macOS) or, on Windows, click the menu icon (≡) in the upper-left corner of the application window and choose Get UI Kits > Apple iOS.

   The UI kits listed in the menu you see are links to the websites that they can be downloaded from. By choosing Apple iOS, the developer.apple.com website is opened in your default browser to a page (developer.apple.com/design/resources/) where you can download a UI kit specifically for Adobe XD.

2   On the web page that opens in your default browser, click Download For Adobe XD. A DMG file is downloaded to your computer.

3   Find the DMG file that was downloaded and double-click it. After you accept an agreement, you can view the contents in a window. Double-click the iOS 13 Adobe XD folder to view its contents.

4   Save the UI Elements + Design Templates + Guides *folder* to the Lessons folder on your hard drive so you can easily find the contents.

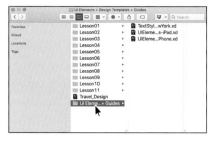

● **Note:** If you've already closed the window, you can open developer.apple.com/ fonts/ in your browser.

5   On macOS, in the same window that you double-clicked the iOS 13 Adobe XD folder, double-click the file "Download San Francisco.webloc" to go to a web page in your browser. On that page, click the button to download the SF Pro fonts.

● **Note:** If you are on Windows or you don't install the San Francisco fonts, you may still proceed. You will most likely continue to see a missing fonts warning every time you open a file that uses the content from these UI kits.

6   After the DMG for the fonts is downloaded, locate it and double-click it to view the contents. Follow the installation instructions to install the fonts.

Opening and copying from the UI Kit

With the UI kit downloaded and the San Francisco Pro fonts installed (macOS only), now you'll open one of the downloaded files and copy content into your Travel_Design.xd document.

● **Note:** Once again, if you are on Windows or cannot access the Adobe XD file on the Apple website, you can open the UI_kit_content.xd document in XD, located in the Lessons > Lesson04 folder. Press Command+A (macOS) or Ctrl+A (Windows) to select all of the content in the document, copy it, and paste it into the Travel_Design.xd file that is still open.

1   Back in Adobe XD, on macOS, choose File > Open From Your Computer (macOS). Navigate to the Lessons > UI Elements + Design Templates + Guides folder. Open the UIElements+DesignTemplates+Guides-iPhone.xd file in that folder.

On Windows, click the menu icon (≡) in the upper-left corner of the application window and choose Open From Your Computer (Windows). Open the UI_kit_content.xd document in XD, located in the Lessons > Lesson04 folder. Press Command+A (macOS) or Ctrl+A (Windows) to select all of the content in the document, copy it, and paste it into the Memory artboard of the Travel_Design.xd file that is still open.

2   Press Command+0 (macOS) or Ctrl+0 (Windows) to see all of the content.

The content in the UI kit is very well organized, and content is grouped together to make selections easier. You will find, however, that it can be challenging to select individual objects since there are a lot of groups nested within groups.

3   With the UIElements+DesignTemp-
    lates+Guides-iPhone.xd document
    open (macOS), in the Layers panel
    (Command+Y [macOS]), type
    status bars into the search field (🔍) at
    the top of the Layers panel to filter the
    list of content that appears in the panel
    (circled in the figure). Click the name
    "Status Bars" (with the folder icon to
    the left) to select that content in the document.

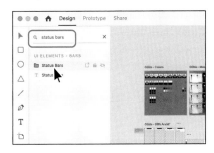

4   Press Command+3 (macOS) or Ctrl+3 (Windows) to zoom in to the status bars.

5   Click the X to the right of the search
    field (🔍) (circled in the figure) at the
    top of the Layers panel to clear the
    filtering. You should now see all of the
    content for the UI ELEMENTS - BARS
    artboard listed in the Layers panel.

6   Click the folder icon (📁) (circled in the following figure) to the left of the
    Status Bars object in the Layers panel to see the contents of the group.

    You need to select and copy a dark version of the status bar and a light version.

7   Click the "Status Bar" name to the
    right of each folder icon until you see
    the top, black text status bar selected
    (see the figure).

8   Click the folder icon for the selected
    Status Bar to show the content (circled
    in the following figure).

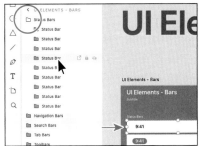

9   Click the name "Status Bar" to the left
    of the remaining folder icons until you
    see the top, white text status bar selected (see the figure).

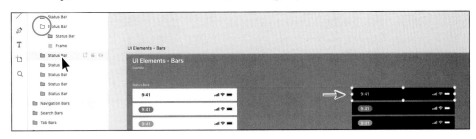

10 Click the folder icon for the selected status bar to show the content.

11 Press the Command key (macOS) or Ctrl key (Windows), and in the Layers panel, click the black status bar and then click the white status bar to select both (see the figure for which to select). Right-click either of them and choose Copy to copy them.

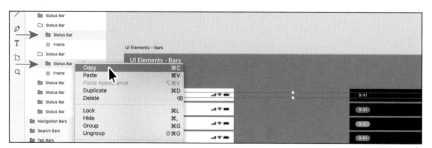

● **Note:** If you started with the L4_start.xd jumpstart file, then return to that file.

12 Choose File > Close (macOS) to close the file and return to the Travel_Design.xd document.

13 Back in the Travel_Design.xd document, press Command+V (macOS) or Ctrl+V (Windows) to paste the status bars in the center of the document window. Drag the pasted content above the Memory artboard for now.

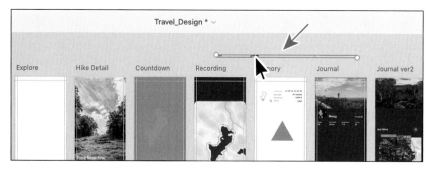

When you drag the pasted content, you may wind up deselecting it instead. In Adobe XD, you cannot just drag from within the bounds of the group; you need to drag from the content in the group. You may want to zoom in to make it easier to drag.

14 Press Command+S (macOS) or Ctrl+S (Windows) to save the file. If you plan on jumping to the next lesson, you can leave the Travel_Design.xd file open. Otherwise, for each open document, choose File > Close (macOS) or click the X in the upper-right corner (Windows).

Review questions

1 What is Path Edit mode?

2 How do you combine several shapes into one?

3 How do you draw straight vertical, horizontal, or diagonal lines using the Pen tool (✐)?

4 How do you draw a curved path using the Pen tool?

5 How do you convert a smooth point on a curve to a corner point?

6 What is a UI kit?

Review answers

1 Path Edit mode is when shape anchor points are visible but moving the mouse does not draw anything. In Path Edit mode, you can edit or delete existing anchor points or add new anchor points.

2 To combine several shapes into one, you can select the shapes and then apply one of the combine options in the Property Inspector to create new shapes out of the overlapping objects.

3 To draw a straight line, click with the Pen tool (✐) and then move the pointer and click again. The first click sets the starting anchor point, and the second click sets the ending anchor point of the line. To constrain the straight line vertically, horizontally, or along a 45 degree diagonal, press the Shift key as you click to create the second anchor point with the Pen tool.

4 To draw a curved path with the Pen tool, click to create the starting anchor point and release the mouse button. Move the mouse pointer to another part of the artboard, drag to set the direction of the curve, and then release the mouse button to end the curve.

5 To convert a smooth point on a curve to a corner point (or vice versa), double-click the shape or path with the Select tool (▶) to enter Path Edit mode. With the anchor points showing on the selected artwork, double-click an anchor point to convert it to the opposite. If it's currently smooth, it will become a corner point and vice versa.

6 A UI kit is a file or set of files that contains resources, such as user-interface elements (buttons, icons, and more), that are specific to an operating system. It can help you design apps (or websites) that match a design language like iOS.

5 ORGANIZING CONTENT

Lesson overview

In this lesson, you'll learn how to do the following:

- Arrange content.
- Work with the Layers panel.
- Create and edit groups.
- Align content and artboards.
- Position objects precisely.

 This lesson will take about 45 minutes to complete. To get the lesson files used in this chapter, download them from the web page for this book at www.adobepress.com/XDCIB2020. For more information, see "Accessing the lesson files and Web Edition" in the Getting Started section at the beginning of this book.

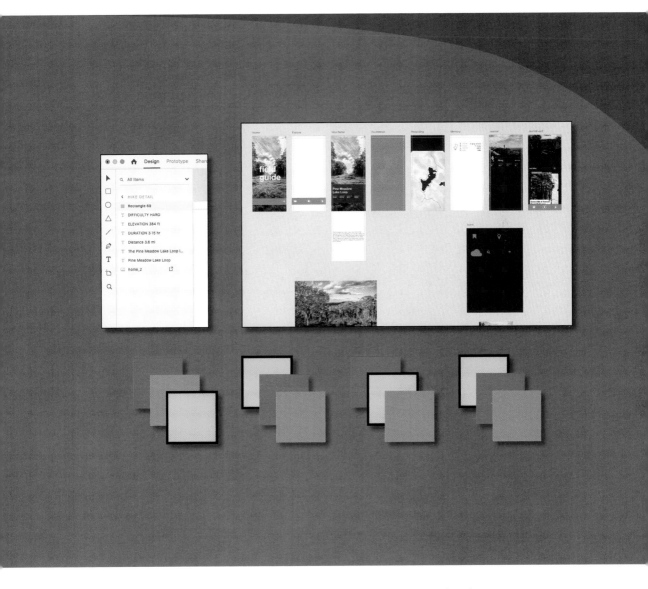

Using the Layers panel, you can organize artboards and control how content is exported, displayed, organized, selected, and edited. Within each artboard, you'll use arranging, grouping, positioning, and aligning to ensure that individual assets are organized and easy to access.

Starting the lesson

In this lesson, you'll learn ways to organize the design content in your app design. To start, you'll open a final lesson file to get an idea for what you will create in this lesson.

● **Note:** If you have not already downloaded the project files for this lesson to your computer from your Account page, make sure to do so now. See the "Getting Started" section at the beginning of the book.

● **Note:** The screen shots for this lesson were taken on macOS. On Windows, the menus can be accessed by clicking the hamburger menu.

1 Start Adobe XD, if it's not already open.

2 On macOS, choose File > Open From Your Computer. On Windows, click the menu icon (≡) in the upper-left corner of the application window and choose Open From Your Computer. Open the file named L5_end.xd, which is in the Lessons > Lesson05 folder that you copied onto your hard disk.

● **Note:** For either macOS or Windows, if the Home screen is showing with no files open, click Your Computer in the Home screen. Open the file named L5_end.xd, which is in the Lessons > Lesson05 folder that you copied onto your hard disk.

3 If the Assets panel opens on the left and you see a Missing Fonts message, close the panel by clicking Assets panel icon (▢) in the lower left.

4 Press Command+0 (macOS) or Ctrl+0 (Windows) to see all of the content.

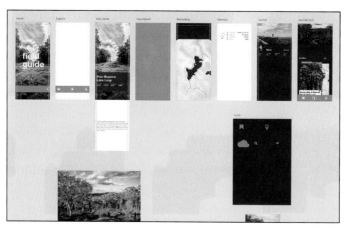

This file shows you what you will create by the end of the lesson.

5 Leave the file open for reference, or choose File > Close (macOS) or click the X in the upper-right corner of the open window (Windows) to close the file.

Arranging objects

As you add content to artboards, each new object goes on top of the previous object. This ordering of objects, called *stacking order*, determines how objects are displayed when they overlap. You can change the stacking order of objects in your artwork at any time, using either the Layers panel or arrange commands.

In the first part of the following figure, the red square was created first, the blue second, and the orange object last. An arrange command has been applied to the *orange* object for each example from left to right. Arrange commands (Send To Back, for instance) are found in the Object menu (macOS) or by right-clicking the object to be arranged (macOS or Windows).

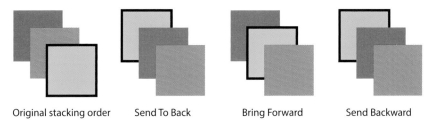

Original stacking order   Send To Back   Bring Forward   Send Backward

The Send To Back command sends selected content behind all other artwork. The Bring To Front command brings the selected content on top of all other artwork. The Bring Forward and Send Backward commands bring the object forward one object and backward one object, respectively. Next, you'll work with the arrange commands to change the stacking order of content.

1 Choose File > Open From Your Computer (macOS) or click the menu icon (≡) in the upper-left corner of the application window and choose Open From Your Computer (Windows). Open the Travel_Design.xd document from the Lessons folder (or where you saved it).

2 Press Command+0 (macOS) or Ctrl+0 (Windows) to see all of the content.

3 Zoom in to the image at the top of the Hike Detail artboard using any zoom method, including Option/Ctrl-scroll wheel, Option-swipe (Magic Mouse), or pinch (trackpad).

4 Select the Rectangle tool (□), and in the lower half of the artboard, draw a rectangle that spans the full width of the artboard and covers the text. Make sure it has a height of approximately 220 in the Property Inspector.

● **Note:** If you are starting from scratch using the jumpstart method described in the section "Getting Started," open L5_start.xd from the Lessons > Lesson05 folder.

5 Click the Fill color in the Property Inspector and, in the color picker that
   appears, choose HSB from the color mode menu so you can enter values in
   Hue, Saturation, and Brightness. Change the color values to H=**180**, S=**54**, B=**33**
   and the A (Alpha or transparency) value to **90** to apply a green color to the
   rectangle. Press Return or Enter after the last value is entered.

6 Select the Select tool (▶) in the toolbar.

7 Choose Object > Arrange > Send Backward (macOS), or right-click the
   rectangle directly and choose Send Backward (macOS) or Arrange > Send
   Backward (Windows). Leave the rectangle selected.

The rectangle is sent behind the previously last object created *on that artboard*,
which is some of the text. In Adobe XD, each artboard has its own stacking order.
In the next section, you'll explore working with the Layers panel, which offers
another way to arrange and organize content. You'll also finish arranging the
green rectangle.

Working with the Layers panel

The Layers panel in Adobe XD is optimized for UX design. In Adobe XD, we don't create layers or sublayers—instead, objects (individual objects, groups, etc.) found on a specific artboard are listed in the Layers panel. When you select content on an artboard, only the objects that are associated with the artboard are shown, so your Layers panel stays clean and uncluttered. In addition to organizing content, the Layers panel lists the artboards found in your document when nothing is selected, and it offers an easy way to select, hide, and lock content, and much more.

Up to this point you've been navigating artboards using the Layers panel. In this section, you'll see how the Layers panel can be used for arranging, organization, naming, and selection.

Reordering artboards and layer content

At the beginning of this lesson, you explored stacking order and arranging content. In this section, you'll work with the Layers panel to change the ordering of content on artboards and the ordering of the artboards. Changing the ordering of artboards may be useful for organizing your designs, whereas changing the ordering of content within an artboard in the Layers panel has the same effect as using arrange commands. Next, you'll use the Layers panel to arrange the green rectangle so it's where it needs to be in your design.

1 With the Select tool (▶) selected and the green rectangle still selected, look in the Layers panel.

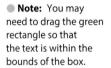

Note: Your rectangle may have a different name, and that's okay.

In the Layers panel, you will see all of the objects that are on the artboard, including the green rectangle, which is selected in the Layers panel. All of the text that is currently beneath the green rectangle needs to be on top so you can read it.

Note: You may need to drag the green rectangle so that the text is within the bounds of the box.

2 In the Layers panel, drag the selected rectangle (named Rectangle 69, or something similar) down below the bottom text object. When a line appears, release the mouse button.

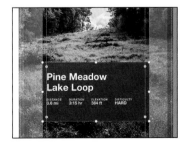

In the Layers panel, every object has an icon to the left of the name, indicating what type of object it is. For instance, the "T" means text, the image icon (🖼) means image, a pen icon (🖊) to the left of an object's name indicates that it's vector artwork, and so on.

3 In the document, click in the gray pasteboard to deselect the green rectangle.

Remember that with nothing selected, you see a listing of all artboards in the Layers panel.

▶ **Tip:** There are two ways to select multiple artboards in the Layers panel. If the artboards you want to select are next to each other in the Layers panel, hold Shift and click the first and last artboards in the list. To select artboards from various places in the list, hold Command (macOS) or Ctrl (Windows) while you click each one.

4 Drag the "Journal ver2" artboard down in the Layers panel list, below the "Journal" artboard. When a line appears, release the mouse button. Make sure the order of the artboards you see matches the figure.

If you look at the artboards in your design, nothing seems to have changed. As I mentioned in a previous lesson, that's because reordering artboards in the Layers panel affects how the artboards are stacked, if they overlap in the design, but not their position (X and Y coordinates). I tend to drag artboards into an order that makes sense to me. For instance, in a design where I include both the app design and the web design, I like to keep the artboards for the app together and the artboards for the web design together.

Selecting content using the Layers panel

There will be times when you have a lot of content in an area of your design and selection is more difficult. In that case, you can also make selections using the Layers panel. Next, you'll select the text on the Hike Detail artboard in the Layers panel to group all of it together.

1 In the Layers panel, double-click the artboard icon (🗋) to the left of the Hike Detail artboard name to center the artboard in the document window and show the content of the artboard in the Layers panel.

2 In the Layers panel, click the difficulty HARD text object and Shift-click the bottom-most Pine Meadow Lake Loop text object to select all of the text objects on the artboard.

With the text selected, you could change formatting options like font family, size, and color.

3   To deselect the paragraph of text toward the bottom of the artboard, Command-click (macOS) or Ctrl-click (Windows) the text object in the Layers panel whose name starts with "The Pine Meadow Lake Loop...."

Now you'll group the selected text.

4   Right-click one of the selected objects in the Layers panel and choose Group to create a group of the text.

Anytime you group content using the group command or bring in content that is grouped, the group icon () in the Layers panel, along with the object name, indicates that it's a group. In the section "Working with groups," later in this lesson, you'll learn more about working with groups.

5   Press the Esc key to deselect the group.

With nothing selected, you should see "Pasteboard" in the Layers panel along with all of the artboards in the document. When you have design content that's not on an artboard (it's on the gray pasteboard instead), "Pasteboard" appears in the Layers panel.

Note: You can also select content in your document that's not on an artboard (it's on the gray pasteboard) to show the pasteboard content in the Layers panel.

6   Double-click the name Pasteboard in the Layers panel to show the content.

All of the content that is in the gray pasteboard is now listed in the Layers panel. The ordering of the Pasteboard content in the Layers panel, by default, follows the order in which you added that content to the pasteboard. The topmost object in the Layers panel list is the last object added.

7   Press Command+0 (macOS) or Ctrl+0 (Windows) to see all of the content.

Note: Your image may be named something different, and that's okay. You can also select the image on the pasteboard to highlight the name of the image in the Layers panel.

8   Click the image named "scene_2" in the Layers panel to select that content. To cut the content, so you can paste it on another artboard, press Command+X (macOS) or Ctrl+X (Windows).

Selecting content this way is sometimes easier when there is a lot of content in your document.

9   Click the arrow to the left of the word PASTEBOARD at the top of the Layers panel to go back and show the listing of artboards again.

10 Right-click the Explore artboard name and choose Paste to paste the image onto the artboard. You'll resize and position the image in a later lesson.

11 Press the Esc key to deselect the image and show the artboards in the Layers panel again.

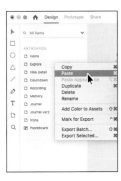 

12 Choose File > Save (macOS) or click the menu icon (≡) in the upper-left corner of the application window and choose Save (Windows).

Locking and hiding content

From time to time you may need to lock and hide content to make selecting easier, hide versions, and more. In this section, you'll see how to lock and hide content in the document and in the Layers panel.

1 With the Select tool (▶) selected, click the image in the background of the Home artboard.

You'll see the Home artboard content appear in the Layers panel and the home_2 image selected in the list of layers.

2 Press Command+L (macOS) or Ctrl+L (Windows) to lock the image.

A small lock icon appears in the upper-left corner of the image, and its bounding box is now gray. If you look in the Layers panel, a lock icon appears to the right of the object name, also indicating that the object is locked. When an object is locked, it cannot be moved, deleted, or edited. If you wanted to unlock the image, you could press Command+L (macOS) or Ctrl+L (Windows) or click the lock icon to the right of the object name in the Layers panel or in the upper-left corner of the image on the artboard.

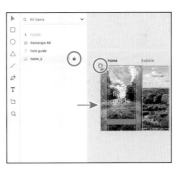

▶ **Tip:** You can also choose Object > Lock (macOS) or right-click the content and choose Lock (macOS and Windows) to lock the content. You can select a series of objects and lock them all at once using this method.

Next, you'll lock and hide content from the Layers panel.

3 Click in a blank area of the document window, away from artboards and content, to deselect everything.

4 Double-click the artboard icon (▢) to the left of the Explore artboard.

Tip: You can also press Command+; (macOS) or Ctrl+; (Windows), choose Object > Hide (macOS), or click the eye icon () in the Layers panel to the right of the object name to hide the content.

5   Right-click the image on the Explore artboard and choose Hide in the menu that appears.

When you right-click content, such as an image, you will see a lot of commands that you've already worked with, like the lock and arrange commands. As with locking, you can also hide content using a variety of methods. If you look in the Layers panel right now, you will see that the image object name is dimmed and the eye icon looks like this ().

6   Move the pointer over the eye icon (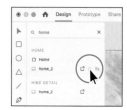) in the Layers panel and click several times to show and then temporarily hide the image. Make sure it's hidden. You will show it again in a later lesson.

Searching and filtering in the Layers panel

You can search the Layers panel to show only relevant layers and artboards containing the keyword, or you can filter layers shown in the panel by text, shapes, and image categories. In this section, you'll briefly explore filtering and understand why it might be useful.

1   Press the Esc key to see all of the artboards in the Layers panel.

2   At the top of the Layers panel, click in the search field and type **home**.

As you type, the list of objects and artboards is filtered.

3   Click the lock icon (🔒) in the Layers panel to unlock the image on the Home artboard.

4   To clear the Layers panel filtering, click the X to the right of the field at the top of the Layers panel.

In addition to searching and filtering the Layers panel list, you can filter what appears based on object type, such as text objects, images, and so on.

5 Click the arrow to the right of the search field and choose Text. All of the text objects in the document appear in the Layers panel, grouped according to the artboard they are on.

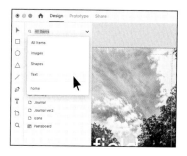

You may have noticed that what you typed ("home") appeared at the bottom of the menu. Recent search terms are temporarily saved in the filter menu for easy access. The recent search listing is reset when the file is closed.

6 Click the text object that starts with "The Pine Meadow Lake…." The text object with the paragraph of text is selected on the Hike Detail artboard.

7 Press Command+3 (macOS) or Ctrl+3 (Windows) to zoom in to the text.

8 Change the font size in the Property Inspector to **16** to make the text smaller.

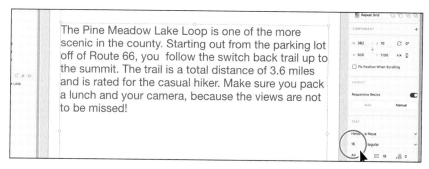

9 Click the arrow to the right of the search field and choose All Items to see all of the content on the Hike Detail artboard in the Layers panel.

10 Press the Esc key to deselect the text object and see the list of artboards in the Layers panel.

Working with groups

Objects in your design can be combined into a group so that those objects are treated as a single unit. You can then move or transform a group without affecting the attributes of the individual objects or positions relative to each other. Grouping content can also make selection of artwork easier later and help you keep your content organized in the Layers panel. Grouping in XD is similar to other Adobe applications, like Illustrator or InDesign, with a few differences.

Creating a group

In this first part, you'll explore a few ways to create a group of content.

1   Double-click the artboard icon (▢) to the left of the Hike Detail name in the Layers panel to fit the artboard in the document window.

2   With the Select tool (▶) selected, drag across the green rectangle and the Pine Meadow Lake Loop text group.

In the Layers panel (where you could have also selected the content), you will see three objects selected.

3   Shift-click the image in the background of the same artboard to deselect it.

> ● **Note:** Grouping content on different artboards is possible, but the grouped content will be moved to the topmost or leftmost artboard.

4   Press Command+G (macOS) or Ctrl+G (Windows) to group the selected content together.

5   Double-click the new group name in the Layers panel. Change the name to **Pine Meadow detail** and press Return or Enter.

You don't have to rename a group, but doing so can make it easier to find content in the Layers panel later. Also, when you export assets, the name of the content in the Layers panel will become the name of the asset.

> ▶ **Tip:** If the content for a group is collapsed in the Layers panel, the icon looks like this: ▥. If the content for a group is open in the Layers panel, the group icon looks like this: ▢.

6   Click the group icon (▥) to the left of the Pine Meadow detail name in the Layers panel to reveal the content of the group.

You'll see that the text objects are already grouped (you can tell because of the group icon [▥]). By grouping the text group and

136   LESSON 5   Organizing Content

the green rectangle, you created a nested group. Next, you'll add content to an existing group using the Layers panel.

7   Press the Esc key to deselect the group and show all of the artboards in the Layers panel.

8   Double-click the artboard icon (⬜) to the left of the Journal name in the Layers panel to fit the artboard in the window.

In the Layers panel, you should see a group named "Hike info" or something similar, the journal header image, and the image of Meng.

9   In the Layers panel, drag the meng image object onto the "Hike info" group name. When the "Hike info" group shows a highlight, release the mouse button to add the image of Meng to the group. Click the group icon (⬜) to collapse the Hike info group, if necessary.

10 Choose File > Save (macOS), or click the menu icon (≡) in the upper-left corner of the application window and choose Save (Windows).

Editing content within a group

There are several methods for editing content within a group. You can ungroup the grouped content, select the individual content by double-clicking the group, use a keyboard modifier to select content within a group, or select content within a group from the Layers panel. Double-clicking a group can save you a lot of time when making edits. Next, you'll make an edit to one of the grouped objects.

1   Press the Esc key twice to deselect the Meng image and then the group.

2   Click the image of Meng on the artboard once to select the group. Looking in the Layers panel, you can see that the group is selected. Then, double-click the image of Meng to select it within the group.

The image should be selected, with a blue border showing around the group that the image is in. The content for the entire group should be showing in the Layers panel.

3 Click away from the content, in the gray pasteboard, to deselect all.

4 Press Command (macOS) or Ctrl (Windows) and move the pointer over the content in the group on the artboard.

As you move across the different objects in the group, each will highlight. Whichever object is highlighted when you click will become selected.

5 With the key still held down, move the pointer over the 11/22/20 text. When you see a blue highlight around it, click to select the text object.

That text is now selected, and you could edit the properties in the Property Inspector. By Command-clicking or Ctrl-clicking, you are able to select any individual object in the group—even if it's a nested group. The blue border around the entire group means it is the parent object of the image.

6 Double-click the 11/22/20 text to select it. Change the text to **09/13/21**.

▶ **Tip:** Pressing the Esc key once more with the group selected would deselect all.

7 Press the Esc key to stop editing the text and select the text object; then press the Esc key again to select the entire group.

8 Choose File > Save (macOS), or click the menu icon (≡) in the upper-left corner of the application window and choose Save (Windows).

Aligning content

Adobe XD makes it easy to align and distribute multiple objects relative to each other and to the artboard. In this section, you'll explore the different ways to align and distribute objects.

Aligning objects to the artboard

Aligning objects to the artboard can be useful if, for instance, you need to center-align content. Next, you'll align some of the content to the center of an artboard.

1 Press Command+0 (macOS) or Ctrl+0 (Windows) to see all of the content in your document.

2 Click the Memory artboard name above the artboard in your design, and press Command+3 (macOS) or Ctrl+3 (Windows) to zoom in.

3 With the Select tool (▶) selected, click the map icon group in the top half of the artboard to select it. Click the Align Center (Horizontally) option (♣) at the top of the Property Inspector.

● **Note:** The name may not be showing if you are zoomed out far enough. Instead, it may show as three dots (...). If that's the case, either zoom or go to the Layers panel and double-click the artboard icon (▢). For this to work, first make sure that nothing is selected.

The group is horizontally aligned to the center of the artboard.

4 Click in a blank area away from the content to deselect.

5 Choose File > Save (macOS), or click the menu icon (≡) in the upper-left corner of the application window and choose Save (Windows).

Setting up objects for alignment

Aligning objects to each other can be useful if you need to align a series of profile images horizontally, for instance. In the next few sections, you'll align some icons on the Explore artboard to create a footer. But first, you'll set up the icons for alignment by getting them onto the correct artboard and finishing them.

1 Press Command+0 (macOS) or Ctrl+0 (Windows) to see all of the content in your document.

2 Right-click the orange-red rectangle on the Home artboard and choose Copy. Right-click in the Explore artboard to the right and choose Paste.

 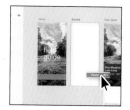 

Content you copy and paste from one artboard to another is pasted in the same relative position as the original artboard.

3 Press Command and + (macOS) or Ctrl and + (Windows) to zoom in a little. Make sure you can see the Explore and Icons artboards.

● **Note:** If your icons are larger or smaller than you see in the figure, that's okay. You'll resize them shortly.

4 Drag the map icon, the double-circle, and the person icon onto the orange-red rectangle on the Explore artboard.

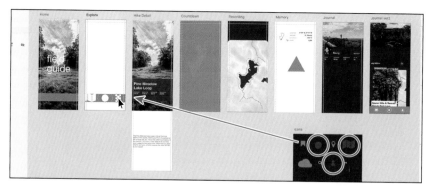

With the icons roughly in place, next you'll size them and add a circle behind the person and map icons. Then you'll align all of the icons to each other.

5 Zoom in to the icons at the bottom of the Explore artboard.

Now you'll resize the icons to better fit within the bounds of the orange-red rectangle.

6 Click the map icon. Shift-drag a corner until you see a height of approximately 20 in the Property Inspector. Release the mouse button and then the key.

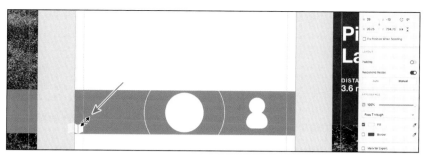

Note: If the height is snapping to larger increments, you can zoom in.

Tip: You can proportionally scale an object to a specific dimension using the Property Inspector, but the Lock Aspect option (🔒) needs to be on.

7 Resize the person icon by Shift-dragging so it also has an approximate height of 20. Select and then Shift-drag the double-circle icon so it has a height of approximately 48.

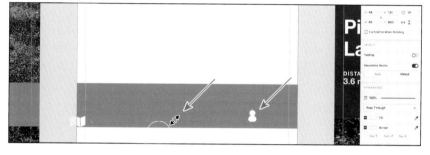

8 Select the Ellipse tool in the toolbar and draw a circle that has a width and height of approximately 48.

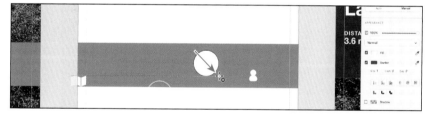

9 Deselect the Border option in the Property Inspector to turn off the border.

10 Click the Fill color box in the Property Inspector to open the color picker. Ensure that the fill color is white, and change Alpha (transparency) to **15**. Press Return or Enter, and then press Esc to hide the color picker.

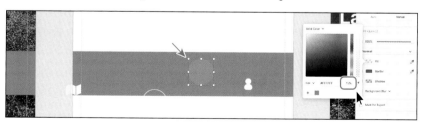

11 Select the Select tool (▶) and make sure the circle is still selected. To make a copy of the circle and paste it right on top of the original, press Command+D (macOS) or Ctrl+D (Windows).

12 Drag the copy away from the original so you can see both circles.

Next you'll align one of the circles with the person icon and the other circle with the map icon.

Aligning objects to each other

When you select more than one object and apply an alignment method, the selected objects align to each other, not to the artboard. Next, you'll align the content for each icon and then align the icons to each other.

1 With the Select tool (▶) selected, click the person icon. To arrange it on top of the circles you just created, choose Object > Arrange > Bring To Front (macOS), or right-click directly on the image and choose Bring To Front (macOS) or Arrange > Bring To Front (Windows).

2 Drag the person icon onto one of the circles you just created. Shift-click the circle to select both objects. Click the Align Middle (Vertically) button (◀▶) and the Align Center (Horizontally) button (↕) at the top of the Property Inspector.

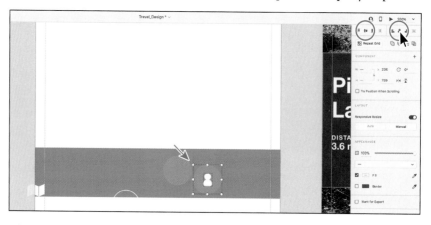

Alignment in Adobe XD is like it is in most Adobe applications, where aligning to top aligns all selected objects to the topmost object, aligning to bottom aligns all selected objects to the bottommost object, and so on.

3 To group the circle and person icon together, press Command+G (macOS) or Ctrl+G (Windows).

4 Click the map icon. To arrange it on top of the circles you just created, choose Object > Arrange > Bring To Front (macOS), or right-click directly on the image and choose Bring To Front (macOS) or Arrange > Bring To Front (Windows).

5   Drag the map icon onto the other circle you just created. Shift-click the circle to select both objects. Click the Align Middle (Vertically) button (⊞) and the Align Middle (Horizontally) button (⊞) at the top of the Property Inspector.

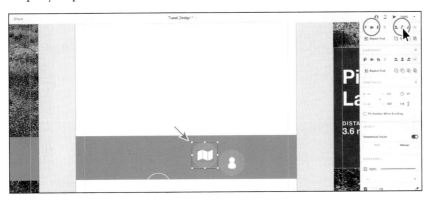

6   To group the selected content together, press Command+G (macOS) or Ctrl+G (Windows).

7   Drag each of the icons onto the orange-red rectangle as you see in the figure, if they aren't there already.

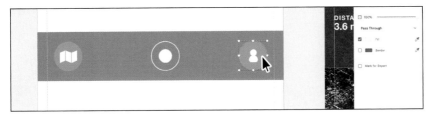

Distributing the icons

Distributing objects enables you to select multiple objects and distribute the spacing between the centers of those objects equally. Next, you'll position and then distribute the icons you were just working with.

1   Drag the map icon so that the left edge snaps to the guide near the left edge of the artboard.

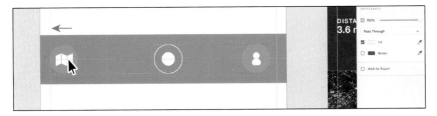

You may see horizontal alignment guides telling you the map group is aligning vertically to another icon to the right.

2 Drag across the icons and the orange-red rectangle to select them all. Click the Align Middle (Vertically) button (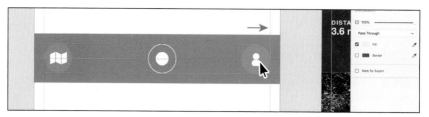) at the top of the Property Inspector. The icons should align to the orange-red rectangle.

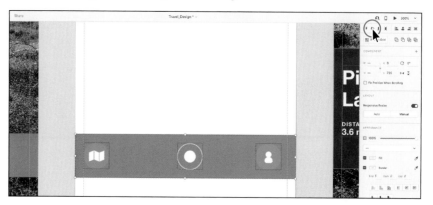

3 Click away from the selected artwork to deselect it all.

4 Drag the person icon so that its right edge aligns with the guide closest to the right edge of the artboard and you see the horizontal alignment guides, indicating it's aligned vertically with the other icons.

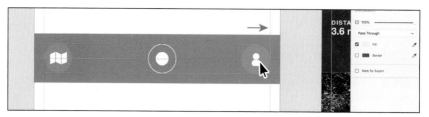

5 Drag across the icons and the orange-red rectangle to select them all. Shift-click the orange-red rectangle to deselect it, leaving the three icons selected.

6 Click the Distribute Horizontally button (‖) at the top of the Property Inspector.

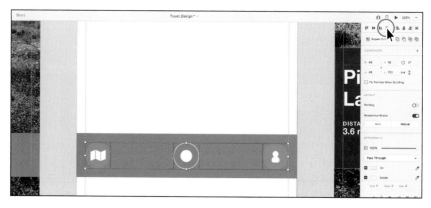

Distributing moves all the selected shapes so that the spacing between the centers of each is equal.

7 Drag across the orange-red rectangle and the icons to select them all. Press Command+G (macOS) or Ctrl+G (Windows) to group them together.

8 Press the Esc key to deselect the content.

9 Choose File > Save (macOS), or click the menu icon (☰) in the upper-left corner of the application window and choose Save (Windows).

Aligning and distributing artboards

As you work with your artboards, you may wind up dragging them around to better organize your designs. For instance, you may want to create a user flow in an app with a series of artboards.

In Adobe XD, you can easily align and distribute artboards just as you do objects. This can help you to visually organize your artboards. You can do this by selecting a series of artboards, and then clicking one of the alignment or distribution buttons at the top of the Property Inspector.

Positioning objects

Up to this point in the lessons, you've positioned objects without much precision. When precision is required, Adobe XD offers different methods, including working with guides for spacing and alignment, as well as changing position values in the Property Inspector.

Aligning with temporary guides

To start, you'll copy and paste an icon from the Icons artboard onto the Home button and use alignment guides to ensure that the content is aligned properly.

1 Double-click the artboard icon (▢) to the left of the Icons artboard to zoom in to it.

2 On the Icons artboard, right-click the small white arrow and choose Copy.

3 Press Command+0 (macOS) or Ctrl+0 (Windows) to see all of the artboards.

4 Click the orange-red rectangle on the Home artboard and press Command+3 (macOS) or Ctrl+3 (Windows) to zoom in to it.

5 Right-click the orange-red rectangle and choose Paste.

6 Drag the arrow so it's centered vertically in the rectangle and aligned with the guide on the right side. A horizontal magenta guide appears when the arrow is vertically center aligned in the rectangle (the tip of the arrow may extend past the guide on the right).

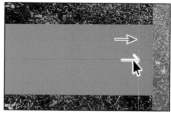

7 Shift-click the orange-red rectangle and press Command+G (macOS) or Ctrl+G (Windows) to group the two selected objects together.

8 Press the Esc key to deselect the group.

Positioning icons for the Memory artboard

Next you'll take a few more of the icons on the Icons artboard and add them to an artboard in the document so you can properly align them with existing content.

1 Double-click the artboard icon (☐) to the left of the Icons artboard to zoom in to it.

2 On the Icons artboard, click the orange-red cloud icon to select it; then Shift-click the orange-red pin icon to select it as well. Right-click one of them and choose Copy.

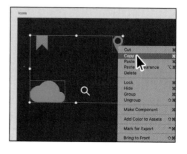

3 Press the spacebar to access the Hand tool, and drag in the window so you can see the Memory artboard. You can also drag on a trackpad with two fingers to pan in the document window.

4 Click in the Memory artboard and press Command+V (macOS) or Ctrl+V (Windows) to paste the icons. You may need to drag the icons so they are on the artboard.

5 Zoom in to the pasted icons, using any method, making sure you can still see the triangle you created in a previous lesson.

6 Click away from the icons; then click the cloud icon and Shift-click the triangle.

7 In the Property Inspector, make sure the Lock Aspect option (🔒) is selected. Change Height to **12**. Press Return or Enter.

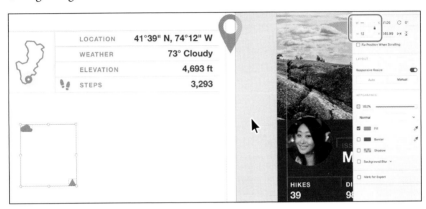

8 Click the map pin icon. In the Property Inspector, make sure the Lock Aspect option (🔒) is selected and then change Height to **18** in the Property Inspector. Press Return or Enter.

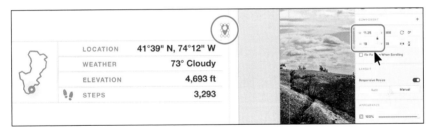

9 Drag the cloud icon to the left of the WEATHER text, the map pin icon to the left of the LOCATION text, and the triangle to the left of the ELEVATION text.

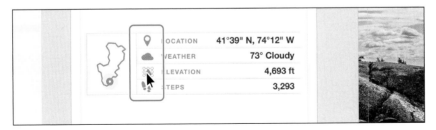

Notice that as you drag the icons into position, temporary alignment guides to help position the icons *relative to the text* are not showing. That's because the LOCATION and WEATHER text is part of a larger group.

Setting gap distances

When you drag to align content, temporary guides appear between objects when the distance between them is the same. This is referred to as the gap distance. This can be a quick visual way to ensure that content spacing is even without having to distribute content. In this section, you'll position a few icons using temporary guides.

1   Click the map pin icon. In the Layers panel, drag the selected Path object (the map pin icon) on top of the Memory table group and release the mouse button to add it to the group. Do the same for the cloud icon and the triangle in the Layers panel.

 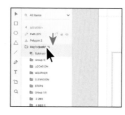 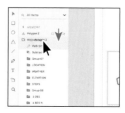

2   Zoom in closely to the map pin icon, triangle, and cloud icon.

3   Click the map pin, and pressing the Shift key, click both the cloud icon and triangle to select all three. Release the Shift key. Click the Align Center (Horizontally) button (✦) to align them to each other.

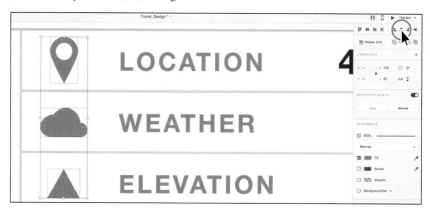

4 Drag the selected icons so they are vertically aligned with the shoe prints below them. A vertical aqua guide appears when they are aligned.

5 To deselect the icons, press Command+Shift+A (macOS) or Ctrl+Shift+A (Windows).

▶ **Tip:** Moving content with the arrow keys also displays alignment guides indicating when things are aligned.

6 Double-click the cloud icon and drag it up or down; you'll eventually see the magenta gap that indicates that the distance between the cloud icon and the gray line below it is the same as the distance between the triangle and the gray line above it.

If you don't see the gap distance, you may need to zoom in or out. The closer you zoom in, the more granular the movement you have when dragging.

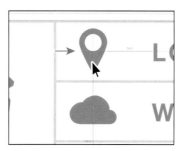

7 Zoom in to the map pin icon a little more, and drag the map pin icon so that it's aligned with the cloud icon and centered with the LOCATION text.

Once again, you may or may not see the alignment guides indicating alignment with the LOCATION text, depending on your zoom level.

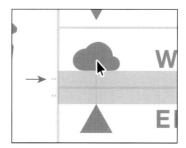

Viewing distances with temporary guides

Another great feature of temporary guides is the ability to view the distance between selected content and other objects or the edges of the artboard. This can be used to quickly ensure that several individual objects are the same distance from some other object, for instance.

1   Press Command and – (macOS) or Ctrl and – (Windows) a few times to zoom out so you can see more of the artwork around the icons.

Note: You may need to double-click the LOCATION text to select the text object.

2   Click the LOCATION text to select it. Press the Option key (macOS) or Alt key (Windows) and move the pointer to a blank area of the artboard.

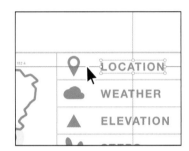

You will see four magenta lines extending from the edges of the text object, and values that represent the distance from the corresponding edge of the artboard. This is a quick way to see how far away from any edge of the artboard the selected object is.

3   While still pressing the Option key (macOS) or Alt key (Windows), move the pointer over content like the map pin icon.

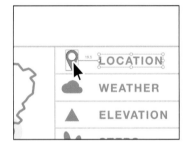

You can now see the distance between the LOCATION text and the object that the pointer is over.

4   Press Command+0 (macOS) or Ctrl+0 (Windows) to see all of the content in your document.

5   Click in a blank area of the gray pasteboard to deselect the content.

6   Choose File > Save (macOS), or click the menu icon (≡) in the upper-left corner of the application window and choose Save (Windows).

Note: If you started with the L5_start.xd jumpstart file, then keep that file open.

7   If you plan on jumping to the next lesson, you can leave the Travel_Design.xd file open. Otherwise, choose File > Close (macOS) or click the X in the upper-right corner (Windows) for each open document.

Review questions

1 What is stacking order?

2 On what layer in the Layers panel do you find content on the pasteboard?

3 What effect does reordering artboards have on your document?

4 How can you edit content within a group without ungrouping?

5 Describe how to show distance measurements between objects when not dragging content.

Review answers

1 Stacking order determines how objects display when they overlap. You can change the stacking order of objects in your artwork at any time, using either the Layers panel or arrange commands.

2 When you have design content that's not on an artboard (that is, it's on the gray pasteboard instead), "Pasteboard" appears in the Layers panel.

3 Reordering artboards in the Layers panel affects how the artboards are stacked in the design, not their position (X and Y coordinates). Changing the ordering of artboards may be useful for organizing your designs, whereas changing the ordering of content within an artboard in the Layers panel has the same effect as using arrange commands.

4 To edit content within a group without ungrouping, select content within the group by double-clicking the group, selecting the content from the Layers panel, or Command-clicking (macOS) or Ctrl-clicking (Windows) content within the group.

5 To show distance measurements between objects, with content selected, press the Option key (macOS) or Alt key (Windows) and position the pointer on other content.

6 WORKING WITH ASSETS AND CC LIBRARIES

Lesson overview

In this lesson, you'll learn how to do the following:

- Understand the Assets panel.
- Add colors to the Assets panel to reuse and edit.
- Save and edit character styles.
- Work with components.
- Work with Creative Cloud Libraries.

 This lesson will take about 60 minutes to complete. To get the lesson files used in this chapter, download them from the web page for this book at www.adobepress.com/XDCIB2020. For more information, see "Accessing the lesson files and Web Edition" in the Getting Started section at the beginning of this book.

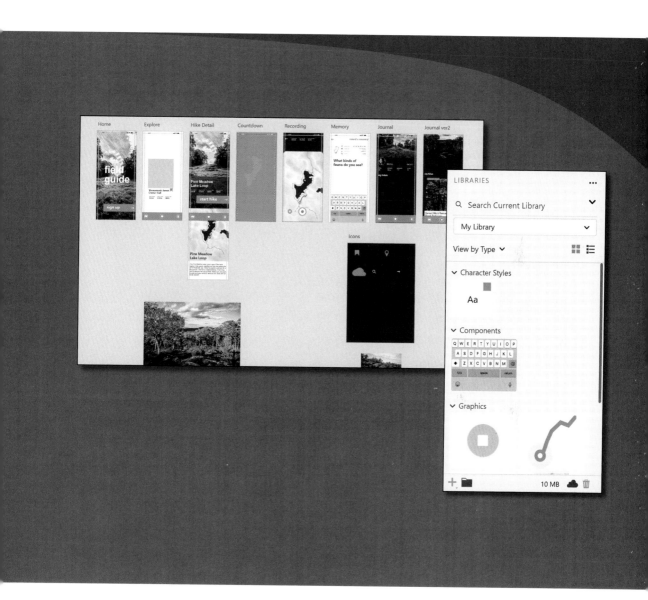

In this lesson, you'll explore useful concepts for working smarter and faster in Adobe XD, including saving colors, character styles, and components in the Assets panel. You'll also explore the use of Creative Cloud Libraries to save and reuse design assets from XD and other Adobe applications in Adobe XD.

Starting the lesson

In this lesson, you'll work smarter by saving content in the Assets panel and working with Creative Cloud Libraries. To start, you'll open a finished lesson file to get an idea of what you will create in this lesson.

● **Note:** If you have not already downloaded the project files for this lesson to your computer from your Account page, make sure to do so now. See the "Getting Started" section at the beginning of the book.

● **Note:** The screen shots for this lesson were taken on Windows. On macOS, you'll see the menus above the application window.

1 Start Adobe XD, if it's not already open.

2 On macOS, choose File > Open From Your Computer. On Windows, click the menu icon (≡) in the upper-left corner of the application window and choose Open From Your Computer. Open the file named L6_end.xd, which is in the Lessons > Lesson06 folder that you copied onto your hard disk.

● **Note:** For either macOS or Windows, if the Home screen is showing with no files open, click Your Computer in the Home screen. Open the file named L6_end.xd, which is in the Lessons > Lesson06 folder that you copied onto your hard disk.

3 If the Assets panel opens on the left and you see a Missing Fonts message, close the panel by clicking Assets panel icon (▭) in the lower left.

4 Press Command+0 (macOS) or Ctrl+0 (Windows) to see all of the content.

This file shows you what you will create by the end of the lesson.

5 Leave the file open for reference, or choose File > Close (macOS) or click the X in the upper-right corner of the open window (Windows) to close the file.

Managing assets with the Assets panel

You can use the Assets panel to save and manage project assets, including colors, text styling (called character styles), and components. Saving content in the Assets panel can save you a lot of time. For instance, when a saved color that's being used in a document is edited, each occurrence of that color will automatically update. Each project file can have its own set of assets that can also be shared between projects. Assets are organized according to type by default.

1   Choose File > Open From Your Computer (macOS) or click the menu icon (≡) in the upper-left corner of the application window and choose Open From Your Computer (Windows). Open the Travel_Design.xd document in the Lessons folder (or wherever you saved it).

2   Press Command+0 (macOS) or Ctrl+0 (Windows) to see all of the content.

3   Click the Assets panel button (▱), in the lower-left corner of the application window, to reveal the Assets panel.

> **Note:** If you are starting from scratch using the jumpstart method described in the section "Getting Started," open L6_start.xd from the Lessons > Lesson06 folder.

> **Tip:** You can toggle the Assets panel open and closed by pressing Command+Shift+Y (macOS) or Ctrl+Shift+Y (Windows).

By default, the Assets panel is empty, but you can add your own colors, type styling (called character styles), and components from selected content or from the entire document by selecting all artboards. (You may see the Missing Fonts section if your system does not have fonts used in the document installed.) As you go through this section, you'll learn about each of these types of assets and see how you can use them to save time and effort later.

Saving colors

To begin working with the Assets panel, you'll save custom colors you've created. Saving colors in the Assets panel is similar to saving colors as swatches in a document in other Adobe applications, like Adobe Illustrator, and they live within the current document only. Once you save a color in the Assets panel and apply it to design content, if you edit the color later, any content that the color is applied to is updated. Saving colors in the Assets panel can be useful for a few reasons, including maintaining color accuracy and consistency and also for saving you time.

1   With the Assets panel showing, press Command+Y (macOS) or Ctrl+Y (Windows) to show the Layers panel.

2   Double-click the artboard icon (▱) to the left of the artboard name Icons in the Layers panel to fit the artboard in the document window.

3 With the Select tool (▶) selected, right-click the cloud icon on the Icons artboard and choose Add Color To Assets from the menu.

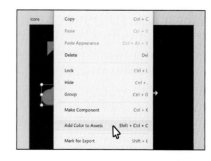

This is one method for saving color associated with content in the Assets panel.

▶ **Tip:** You can double-click the name of a color when the Assets panel is in List view (the default view) and change it. You'll learn about changing views at the end of this section.

4 Click the Assets panel button (◲), in the lower-left corner of the application window, to reveal the Assets panel, if it isn't showing already, and you'll see the orange-red color saved in the Colors section.

Aside from saving an individual color, you can also select a series of objects and save all of the colors from those selected objects at once.

5 Press Command+0 (macOS) or Ctrl+0 (Windows) to see all of the design content.

6 Press Command+A (macOS) or Ctrl+A (Windows) to select all of the content in the file.

7 Click the plus (+) in the Colors section of the Assets panel to save any colors applied to the selected content.

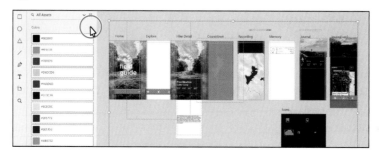

As you can see, this method captures any color from the selected content in your design, including solid color fills, gradients, and fills or gradients with an alpha transparency applied. Gradients saved are always ordered or sorted last in the list.

8 Press Command+Shift+A (macOS) or Ctrl+Shift+A (Windows) to deselect.

9 Click the Grid View button (⊞) at the top of the Assets panel, to view the colors in a grid.

You can view the content in the Assets panel in List view or Grid view.

10 Press Command+S (macOS) or Ctrl+S (Windows) to save the file.

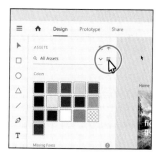

Note: The colors or ordering you see may not be exactly the same, and that's okay.

Editing saved colors

Next, you'll see how to edit a color you saved in the Assets panel and see the effect on the design content in your Travel_Design project.

1 Move the pointer over the green swatch with the tooltip #275454 (90%). When you find that green swatch, click to select it; then right-click it and choose Highlight On Canvas to see where it's being used (the rectangle on the Hike Detail artboard). If the option is dimmed, make sure the green swatch is the only one selected.

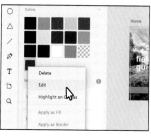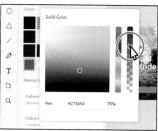
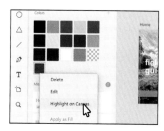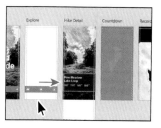

The "(90%)" next to the color name means that it has 90% opacity.

2 Right-click the green color again in the Assets panel and choose Edit. Change Alpha to **70%**. Press the Esc key to hide the color picker.

Note: To delete a swatch or multiple swatches in the Assets panel, select the swatches you want to delete, right-click one of them, and choose Delete. Deleting a color swatch in the Assets panel will not remove the color from the content in the document.

3 Zoom in to the Journal artboard with the picture of Meng.

4 To select the image of Meng in the group, Command-click (macOS) or Ctrl-click (Windows) the image.

To apply a color in the Assets panel to selected content, you can simply click the color swatch. The color is applied as a fill by default. To apply a color to the border of selected content, you can right-click a color in the Assets panel and choose Apply As Border. That's what you'll do next.

5 Right-click the orange swatch with the tooltip #FF491E in the Assets panel and choose Apply As Border to apply the color to the border of the selected image.

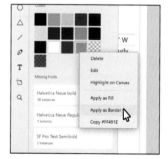

6 Change the border size in the Property Inspector to **3** to more easily see it.

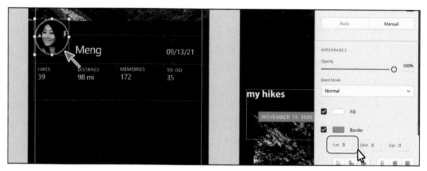

7 Click in a blank area of the pasteboard, away from the image, to deselect.

Saving text formatting as a character style

In the Assets panel, you can also save text formatting as a character style. Character styles allow you to format text consistently and are helpful when text attributes need to be updated globally. Once a style is created, you only need to edit the saved style, and then all text formatted with that style in the document is updated. In this section, you'll save text formatting you applied in a previous lesson as a character style to see how they work.

1 Press Command+0 (macOS) or Ctrl+0 (Windows) to see everything.

2 Zoom in to the bottom half of the Hike Detail artboard.

3 Select the Text tool (T) and move the pointer above the paragraph of text, aligning it with the aqua guide. Drag to make a text area. Type **Pine Meadow Lake Loop**.

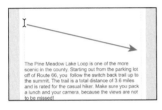 

4 Press the Esc key to select the text object.

5 Change the font size to **36** in the Property Inspector. Ensure that the font is Helvetica Neue (macOS) or Segoe UI (Windows) (or similar) and that the font weight is Bold, and change the Line Spacing (the distance between lines of text—similar to leading) to **40**.

6 Select the Select tool (►) and drag a corner of the text box to show all of the text, if necessary, and so that it wraps like you see in the figure. Then drag it into the position you see in the figure. Make sure to keep the left edge aligned with the guide.

7 Right-click the text object and choose Copy. Navigate to the Memory artboard and right-click anywhere in the Memory artboard. Choose Paste to paste a copy of the text.

8 With the text object on the Memory artboard selected, click the orange-red color swatch with the tooltip that shows #FF491E in the Colors section of the Assets panel to change the color.

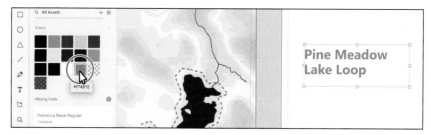

9 Double-click the text to select it. Type **What kinds of fauna do you see?**

The same text formatting (including the color) needs to be applied to the original "Pine Meadow Lake Loop" text on the Hike Detail artboard. To do so, you can save the formatting from the text on the Memory artboard as a character style and apply it to the text on the Hike Detail artboard.

10 With the Select tool (▶) selected, press the Esc key to select the text object, and drag a corner so the text appears on two lines if the text isn't fitting.

11 With the text object selected, click the plus (+) in the Character Styles section of the Assets panel.

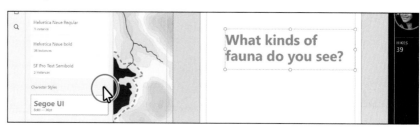

The text formatting is captured and saved as a style in the panel. Notice that the style name shows as the font name. I chose Segoe UI (Windows) for the font, so the style I see is named Segoe UI. If you chose a different font in the previous steps, your style name will be different—that's okay.

12 Navigate to the bottom half of the Hike Detail artboard and click to select the "Pine Meadow Lake Loop" text. Click the character style named Helvetica Neue (macOS) or Segoe UI (Windows), or the character style name you see, to apply the formatting.

▶ **Tip:** Character styles are ordered alphabetically. If you have a lot of styles named Helvetica Neue, for instance, they are sorted by font size—largest at the top.

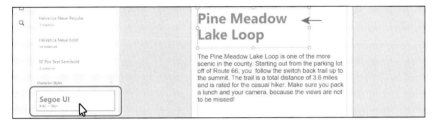

If you plan ahead, you can create a series of character styles before you begin your design or create them from content later, maybe when you need to reuse text formatting. The character styles, colors, and components (you'll learn about components shortly) can also be used as part of an overall design system or as a starting point for a similar project later.

Editing character styles

With a character style created, next you'll edit that style and see how all of the text with the character style applied changes.

1 Press Command+Shift+A (macOS) or Ctrl+Shift+A (Windows) to deselect all.

2 Press Command+0 (macOS) or Ctrl+0 (Windows) to see all of the content.

3 Right-click the character style in the Assets panel and choose Highlight On Canvas to see where it's being used.

To edit a color or character style, you don't need to highlight the content on the canvas. It's just a useful way to see what will be affected when you edit the color or character style.

4 Right-click the style you saved in the Character Styles section of the Assets panel and choose Edit from the menu that appears.

5 Make sure Hex is chosen in the color picker and change the color to **466D6D** in the menu that appears. Press Return or Enter to accept the value. Click away from the menu to close it.

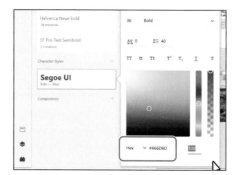

As you edit the character-style formatting, you should see the text in the document changing. Unfortunately, when it comes to applying color to a character style, you can't select a saved color swatch from the Assets panel while editing the character style. You could, however, select the Eyedropper tool in the editing menu and sample (click) a color swatch to copy and apply that color to other text.

6 Save the file by pressing Command+S (macOS) or Ctrl+S (Windows).

Creating components

As you've seen, saving colors and character styles is a great time-saver and a way to maintain design consistency, among other benefits. Being able to save content, like a button you drew or content for a footer you will need to reuse, can also be helpful. Objects you save in the Assets panel can be saved as components.

A *component* is an object that can be reused multiple times across artboards in a document, like a button. When you create a component, it is known as a master component. If you place multiple copies of a component in your design, called *instances*, you can change any properties of the master component and the instances are changed as well because the instances are linked to the master component. Changes you make to an individual instance are specific to that element, but changes you make to the master component affects all of the instances where that specific property hasn't been customized. Next, you'll save button artwork as a component.

1 Zoom in to the Home artboard.

2 Select the Text tool (**T**) and click the orange-red rectangle to add some text. Type **sign up**. Make sure it's lowercase.

3 Press the Esc key to select the text object.

4 With the text object selected, click the white color swatch with the tooltip #FFFFFF in the Colors section of the Assets panel to change the color.

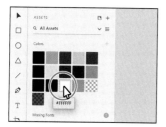 

5 Change the font size to **40** in the Property Inspector. Ensure that the font is Helvetica Neue (macOS) or Segoe UI (Windows) (or similar) and that the font weight is Bold.

6 Select the Select tool (▶) and drag the text into the position you see in the figure. Make sure to keep it *visually* vertically aligned with the orange-red rectangle shape.

7 Shift-click the orange-red button group to select both the text object and the button.

8 Click the plus (+) in the Components section of the Assets panel to save the selected content as a master component.

▶ **Tip:** Because the text box may be taller than the text, it can be tricky to align the text box with the orange-red rectangle.

▶ **Tip:** You can also save content as a component by right-clicking the selected content and choosing Make Component from the menu.

If a message appears, you can close it. Notice that after content is saved as a component, the button content appears in the Components section of the Assets panel. The button on the Home artboard is now a master component. You can tell it's a master component because there is a green filled diamond in the upper-left corner. The border around the component is now also a subtle green—but that shows on master components as well as on instances.

You will also now see COMPONENT (MASTER) in the Property Inspector on the right (shown in the figure). In a later lesson on prototyping, you will learn more about using that area of the Property Inspector.

Adding a component instance to the design

You save content as components for several reasons. One is to be able to reuse content easily; another is to easily update content. Next, you'll reuse the button component on another artboard as an instance.

▶ **Tip:** When the Assets panel is displayed in list view, you can drag colors, character styles, and components to reorder them within each section.

1 Click the List View button (☰) toward the top of the Assets panel. If you scroll down in the Assets panel, you can see the Components section. In List view, you can see the name of the component.

2 Double-click the name of the new component, most likely "Component 1," and type **button**. Press Return or Enter to accept the name.

3 If you don't see the Hike Detail artboard in the document window, you can press Command and − (macOS) or Ctrl and − (Windows) to zoom out until you see it.

Next, you'll drag a copy of the button component (called an *instance*) onto the Hike Detail artboard. First, you'll arrange some of the content to make room for it.

4 Drag across the image and Pine Meadow Lake Loop text to select it. Drag all of it up a bit, matching the figure.

▶ **Tip:** You can also copy and paste a component instance within an artboard or from one artboard to another.

5 Drag the button component from the Components section of the Assets panel onto the Hike Detail artboard.

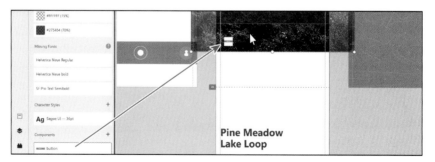

The instance now appears on the Hike Detail artboard. You can tell it's an instance and not the master component because the diamond in the upper-left corner is hollow (circled in the figure).

Editing a master component

Suppose that the button component you created needs to be updated, maybe by changing the color or adding a border. In this next section, you'll edit the appearance of the master component so that every instance will also be updated.

1   With the component instance selected, right-click it and choose Edit Master Component.

Editing the master component, rather than the instance, will update all instances.

2   To edit the content in the master component, double-click the master component (the orange button) on the Home artboard. Click to select the orange-red rectangle if it's not already selected.

> **Note:** If you delete a master component from the canvas, XD generates a master component next to the objects you're currently editing.

> **Note:** Make sure the rectangle is selected; if you were to double-click the "sign up" text in the previous step, the text would be selected.

3   Zoom out so you can see the button instance on the Hike Detail artboard as well.

4   On the Home artboard, drag the left edge of the rectangle to the right to make it narrower.

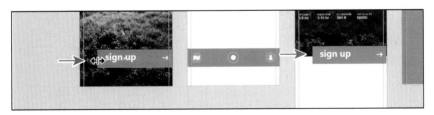

The instance on the Hike Detail artboard should change as well. You can make changes to the style, size, shadow, or position of objects in the master component and see these changes reflected in all linked instances.

5   Click in a blank area away from the artboards to deselect.

6   Press Command+S (macOS) or Ctrl+S (Windows) to save the file.

Editing an instance

There may be times when you need to make an appearance change to a specific component instance. For instance, with the button component you created, maybe you need one of the buttons to be another color. If you change a property of the instance, not the master component, only that instance changes. Every property you change is considered an override. Overridden properties are always preserved, even if you edit the same property from the master component.

Next, you'll edit the button instance without affecting the master component.

1   Press the T key to select the Text tool (**T**).
    Select the text "sign up" on the Hike Detail
    artboard and type **start hike**.

You can edit the text within a component instance, and the other instances or the master component won't update. This can be useful in a project like this one, where we have a series of buttons with the same appearance but different text.

2   Select the Select tool (▶) and click in a blank area of the pasteboard to deselect; then click the "start hike" component instance to select it.

If you look in the upper-left corner of the bounds of the component, you will see that the diamond icon has a dot in the middle. That dot indicates that the instance has an override.

● **Note:** If you do choose Reset To Master State, you can press Command+Z (macOS) or Ctrl+Z (Windows) to undo the command.

3   Right-click the button component instance with the "start hike" text and, in the menu that appears, you'll see the command Reset To Master State. *Don't choose it!*

The Reset To Master State command is useful if you want the selected button instance to look like the master component again. In other words, it will remove all of the changes you just made to that instance.

4   Drag the "start hike" button so its right edge snaps to the right edge of the artboard and is positioned as you see in the figure.

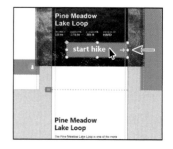

5   Click in a blank area away from the artboards to deselect.

6   Press Command+S (macOS) or Ctrl+S (Windows) to save the file.

Making the footer a component

Now you'll turn the footer group into a component and add it to all of the artboards.

1   With the Select tool (▶) selected, click the footer group on the Explore artboard (see the figure). Press Command+K (macOS) or Ctrl+K (Windows) to save it as a component. Drag the footer component to the bottom of the artboard.

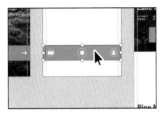 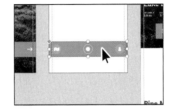 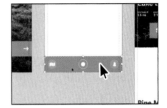

It is faster to save content as a component this way rather than clicking the plus (+) in the Components section of the Assets panel. After converting the content to a component, you should now see the green-filled diamond in the upper-left corner, indicating it's the master component.

2   To copy the new component, press Command+C (macOS) or Ctrl+C (Windows).

3   Deselect everything by clicking in a blank area of the gray pasteboard.

4   Press Command+0 (macOS) or Ctrl+0 (Windows) to see everything. Now you'll paste the component as instances on several artboards.

5   To show the Layers panel, press Command+Y (macOS) or Ctrl+Y (Windows). In the Layers panel, click the Hike Detail artboard name to select it, and while pressing the Command key (macOS) or Control key (Windows), click the Journal name in the Layers panel list to select that artboard as well.

6   To paste the footer on both selected artboards in the same relative position, press Command+V (macOS) or Ctrl+V (Windows).

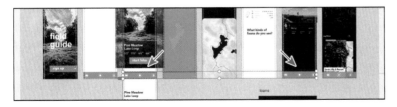

7   Click in an empty area to deselect.

Swapping components

In Adobe XD, you can also replace or swap components in your document. Maybe you need to swap out a button on one of your artboards with a different button, for instance. You simply drag a component from the Assets panel on top of the component you'd like to swap it with. Next, you'll make two components from the status bar content in the document that was pasted back in Lesson 3.

1 With the Layers panel showing, double-click Pasteboard in the Layers panel to show the content on the pasteboard in the panel.

   You will create two components from the two Status Bar groups.

2 Click the top Status Bar group name in the list and press Command+K (macOS) or Ctrl+K (Windows) to save it as a component.

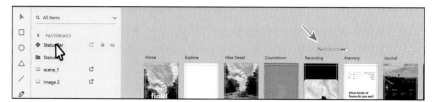

   You can see that the folder icon (▬) in the Layers panel has changed to a diamond icon (◆), which indicates it's a component.

3 Click the other Status Bar group name in the Layers panel and make that a component as well by pressing Command+K (macOS) or Ctrl+K (Windows).

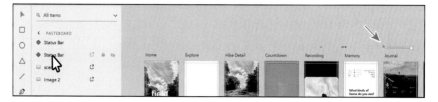

   One of the status bars is white in color and the other is black. Now you'll add the black status bar component to most of the artboards.

4 Open the Assets panel by pressing Command+Shift+Y (macOS) or Ctrl+Shift+Y (Windows). Scroll in the Assets panel to see the Components section, if necessary. Drag the black status bar component instance onto the top of the Home artboard.

5   Zoom in by pressing Command+3 (macOS) or Ctrl+3 (Windows). Drag the component into the horizontal center of the artboard—a magenta alignment guide should appear when it's aligned—and so the bottom of the status bar is aligned with the horizontal guide along the top. You may want to zoom out a little to see the guides.

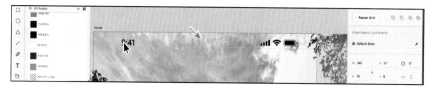

6   Copy the status bar component by pressing Command+C (macOS) or Ctrl+C (Windows).

7   Press Command+0 (macOS) or Ctrl+0 (Windows) to see everything.

8   Drag across the Explore, Hike Detail, Countdown, Recording, Memory, and Journal artboards to select the artboards (not the content on them).

9   Press Command+V (macOS) or Ctrl+V (Windows) to paste the component instance in the same relative position on all of the selected artboards.

10 Click away from the content to deselect it all.

Now you'll replace a few of the dark status bars with the white status bars so they are more readable.

11 Zoom in closer to the Countdown and Recording artboards.

12 From the Assets panel, drag the white status bar on top of the black status bar on the Countdown artboard.

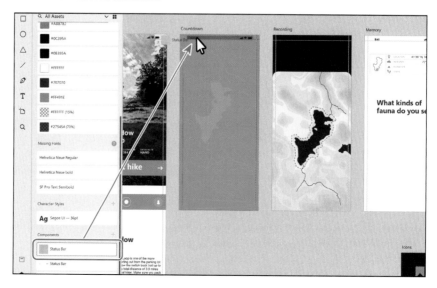

When the black status bar instance is highlighted, release the mouse button to replace that instance of the black status bar with an instance of the white status bar.

13 Drag the white status bar from the Assets panel onto the black status bar at the top of the Recording artboard to replace it as well.

14 Press Command+S (macOS) or Ctrl+S (Windows) to save the file.

Ungrouping components

Sometimes you will need to edit content that is a component instance and you don't want the instance content to be linked at all to the original master component. In that case, you can ungroup a component instance from the master component. That command breaks the link between the instance and the component, so changes made to the component no longer affect the instance.

1 Pan or scroll over to the Home artboard so you can see it, and zoom in a bit to the "sign up" button.

2 To select *part* of the white arrow in the button, Command-click (macOS) or Ctrl-click (Windows) the white arrow. Press the Esc key to select the whole arrow group.

3 To copy the arrow, press Command+C (macOS) or Ctrl+C (Windows).

4 Move to the top of the Hike Detail artboard. Click in the Hike Detail artboard and press Command+V (macOS) or Ctrl+V (Windows) to paste the arrow on the artboard in the same relative position as it was on the Home artboard.

5 Drag the arrow toward the top of the Hike Detail artboard, aligning it with the guide on the left side of the artboard, as you see in the figure. You will most likely need to zoom in.

6 To flip the pasted arrow, click the Flip Horizontally button (▷◁) in the Property Inspector on the right.

Note: Clicking in the artboard is important. The arrow group you copied is deselected. If you don't click in the artboard, the arrow you paste will be a part of the original arrow group.

7 To save the arrow as a component, press Command+K (macOS) or Ctrl+K (Windows).

8 Copy the component instance by pressing Command+C (macOS) or Ctrl+C (Windows). Press Command and – (macOS) or Ctrl and – (Windows) to zoom out a bit so you can see the Hike Detail, Recording, and Memory artboards. You may want to press the spacebar and drag to see them.

9 Click in the Recording artboard and press Command+V (macOS) or Ctrl+V (Windows) to paste the arrow component instance in the same relative position on the artboard. Click in the Memory artboard and press Command+V (macOS) or Ctrl+V (Windows) to paste the arrow on that artboard as well.

The arrow on the Memory artboard needs to be the orange-red color you saved previously so you can see it and other potential changes later. You'll break the link to the master component so you can change anything and it won't be affected by the master.

10 With the component instance selected on the Memory artboard, right-click the instance and choose Ungroup Component.

The content is no longer a component instance and is ungrouped.

11 Click the Assets panel button (▭) in the lower-left corner to see the Assets panel, if it's not already open. In the Colors section of the Assets panel, click the orange-red color to apply it. The arrow on the Memory artboard now has an orange-red border.

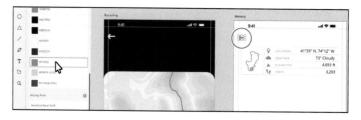

12 To group the arrow content together (if it isn't already), press Command+G (macOS) or Ctrl+G (Windows).

Using components in other documents

In Adobe XD, you can copy a component from one source document to other documents. If you change the original component in the source document, components you pasted into other documents are updated because they are linked. Linked components allow you to create and maintain a style guide, design system, or UI kit or simply use that content in other Adobe XD documents.

When you modify a linked component in the source document, XD shows a notification in other documents telling you that those components have been updated. You can then preview the changes in the original component and choose to accept or reject them.

So far in this lesson, you've been working with *local components*. Local components are components that reside within a document. In the next few sections, you'll explore *linked components*, or saved components copied from a source document to a destination document.

1 Choose File > Open From Your Computer (macOS) or click the menu icon (≡) in the upper-left corner of the application window and choose Open From Your Computer (Windows). Click Your Computer in the dialog box that appears. Open the Icons.xd document in the Lessons > Lesson06 folder.

2 With the Select tool (▶) selected, click to select the text group in the top half of the artboard. Shift-click the group in the bottom half of the artboard to select both.

▶ **Tip:** You can share a source document with linked components. You can invite designers to edit or consume components from the source documents and receive update notifications when those documents are updated.

● **Note:** If you move the linked component source and the target documents to a new location, you need to ensure that the source and target documents are within the same parent folder structure. Otherwise, the links will be broken.

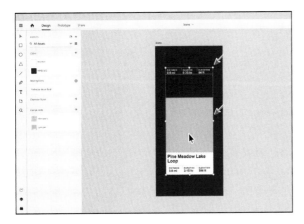

If you look in the Assets panel, you'll see that both groups were saved as components.

3 With both instances selected, right-click either of them and choose Copy.

4 Choose File > Close (macOS) or click the X in the upper-right corner (Windows) to close the Icons.xd document.

5   Back in the Travel_Design.xd document, press Command+0 (macOS) or Ctrl+0 (Windows) to see all of the design content; then zoom in to the Explore artboard (the artboard to the right of Home).

6   Right-click in the Explore artboard and choose Paste.

7   Click in a blank area to deselect; then click one of the component instances you pasted.

● **Note:** If you have multiple XD documents open, to see the Travel_Design.xd document, choose Window > Travel_Design (macOS) or press Command+~ (macOS) or Alt+Tab (Windows) to switch to the Travel_Design.xd document.

With one of the component instances selected, you'll see a green link icon in the upper-left corner. This indicates that the component instance is linked to another document (the source document). The green color also

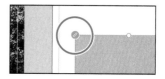

indicates that the component is up to date, meaning that it already reflects the latest saved changes to the component in the source document.

8   In the Assets panel, scroll down to see the Components section, if you don't already see it. Make sure the List View option (≡) is selected toward the top of the panel so you can see the component names.

You should now see components named "hike specs" and "carousel" listed in the Assets panel, along with a gray link icon to the right of each name.

9   In the Assets panel, move the pointer over the link icon (⊘) to the right of the "carousel" component name.

In the tooltip that appears, you'll see "Up-to-date" and the name of the document that the component came from, which is Icons.xd. The link icon for a component in the Assets panel indicates a saved component copied from the source document to the destination document. You'll learn more about working with linked components in the next section.

10 To save the file, press Command+S (macOS) or Ctrl+S (Windows).

Linking assets

With linked assets, you can easily share and consume components—what were formerly known as symbols—as well as colors and character styles. This is useful if you reuse design elements across projects, for instance.

Linked assets complement the workflow of linked components. When you modify a linked asset in the source document, all the consuming documents with those linked assets receive update notifications. From there, you can choose Preview and accept the updates.

To learn more about working with linked assets, visit helpx.adobe.com/xd/help/linked-assets.html.

Updating linked components

When you paste components from another document, a link between the original and the copy is created. You can choose to maintain that link and only edit the original, break the link between the source document and current document (making the component a local component), or maintain the link and apply style overrides to the component.

In the next few sections, you'll explore how to work with linked components.

1   In the Travel_Design document, press Command+0 (macOS) or Ctrl+0 (Windows) to see all content. Zoom in to the Icons artboard.

2   Click the orange-red banner icon on the Icons artboard and press Command+C (macOS) or Ctrl+C (Windows) to copy it.

You'll add the banner to the carousel component in the Icons.xd document to update it.

3   In the Assets panel, right-click the carousel component and choose Edit Master In Source Document.

In the menu that showed, there was also a command for deleting the component. If you delete a component from the Assets panel, any instances in the document are still there; they are just no longer linked to a component.

4   In the Icons.xd document that opens, double-click the gray box at the top of the carousel component on the artboard to edit the content within. Zoom in to it.

5   Right-click the content and choose Paste to paste the orange-red banner icon. Drag it into the position you see in the second part of the following figure. Make it smaller by Shift-dragging a corner.

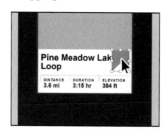

6   To save the file, press Command+S (macOS) or Ctrl+S (Windows). To close the Icons.xd file, choose File > Close (macOS) or click the X in the upper-right corner (Windows).

Back in the Travel_Design document, if you look at the carousel component in the Assets panel, you should now see a blue circle and link icon notification (⊘) indicating that it has been modified in the source document and can now be updated in the Travel_Design document. You may also see a message window appear that you can close, and the Assets panel icon in the lower-left corner of the application windows is now highlighted. All of this indicates that the component has been edited in the source document.

7   To see everything, press Command+0 (macOS) or Ctrl+0 (Windows).

8   Move the pointer over the blue link notification in the Assets panel to see a preview of the update. Move the pointer away from the notification and the update preview will stop.

You may want to zoom in to the Explore artboard to more easily see the change.

9   Click the Update All (1) button at the bottom of the Assets panel to accept the component update and make the change to the carousel component.

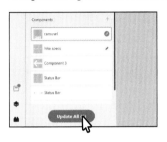 

▶ **Tip:** To accept the component update, you can also click the blue update icon or right-click a component or multiple selected components in the Assets panel list and select Update from the context menu.

The link icon to the right of the name in the Assets panel is now gray, indicating that the component has been updated. For the next step, you may want to zoom in.

10 Double-click directly on the text "Pine Meadow Lake Loop" on the Explore artboard. Change it to **Shunemunk Sweet Clover Trail**.

The carousel component in the source document (Icons.xd) still has the "Pine Meadow Lake Loop" text, and the destination component is still linked to the source component. Any appearance changes you make to the source carousel component will still affect the carousel component in the destination document, if you choose to update.

Breaking the link to a component

There may be times when you no longer want a component in the destination document to update when that source component is changed and the document saved. For instance, the lines in the hike specs component in the source document (Icons.xd) are white. All of the component instances in the Travel_Design.xd document need to be green. The only way to edit the line color in the Travel_Design document component is to convert the destination (linked) component to a local component.

1 Drag the hike specs component instance you pasted onto the Explore artboard to the Recording artboard.

    Since the text in the hike specs component instance is white on a white artboard, it may be challenging to select. You can drag across the area above the carousel component instance to select it.

2 On the Recording artboard, drag the white arrow component and the hike specs component into the position you see in the figure. You may need to zoom in to the artboard to align them.

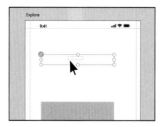 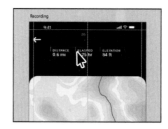 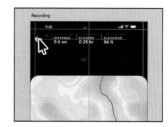

3 In the Assets panel, right-click the hike specs component. Choose Make Local Component from the context menu that appears.

    The link icon disappears to the right of the hike specs name in the Assets panel and also on the component instance(s) in the document. The component in the Travel_Design document is now a local component and will not update if changes are made to the source component in the Icons.xd document.

Working with Creative Cloud Libraries

Creative Cloud Libraries are an easy way to create and share stored content such as images, colors, character styles, XD components, and Adobe Stock assets between Adobe applications like XD, Photoshop, Illustrator, InDesign, and certain Adobe mobile apps.

Creative Cloud Libraries connect to your creative profile, putting the creative assets you care about at your fingertips. When you create content in XD, Illustrator, or Photoshop and then save it to a Creative Cloud Library, that asset is available to use in all of your XD project files. Those assets are automatically synced and can be shared with anyone with a Creative Cloud account. As your creative team works across Adobe desktop and mobile apps, your shared library assets are always updated and ready to use anywhere. In this section, you'll explore Creative Cloud Libraries and use them in your project.

● **Note:** To use Creative Cloud Libraries, you will need to be signed in with your Adobe ID and have an Internet connection.

Adding assets in XD to a Creative Cloud Library

The first thing you'll learn about is how to work with the Creative Cloud Libraries panel in Adobe XD and add assets from an XD document you open into a Creative Cloud Library, then use them in your Travel_Design document.

1   Choose File > Open From Your Computer (macOS) or click the menu icon (≡) in the upper-left corner of the application window and choose Open From Your Computer (Windows). Open the CC_assets.xd document in the Lessons > Lesson06 folder.

2   Choose File > Open CC Libraries (macOS), or click the menu icon (≡) in the upper-left corner of the application window and choose Open CC Libraries (Windows), to open the CC Libraries panel.

When you start working with Creative Cloud Libraries, you have one library to work with, called My Library. You can easily create other libraries in XD, maybe for keeping assets for specific jobs or clients, but in this section you'll focus on using the default library. Toward the top of the panel you'll see a menu for choosing a library, and you may see that the library named My Library is chosen. You can choose a different library you've created from that menu. For this exercise, make sure My Library is chosen or choose another library you have created.

▶ **Tip:** You can also open the CC Libraries panel by clicking the Open CC Libraries button (▣) at the top of the Assets panel.

▶ **Tip:** In the CC Libraries panel, click More Options (...) and choose Create New Library to create a new library.

3   Drag the Creative Cloud Libraries panel so you can see the artwork on the artboards. With the Select tool selected, click the image at the top of Artboard 2.

4   To add it to the library, click the plus (+) at the bottom of the CC Libraries panel and choose Graphic to add the image to the library.

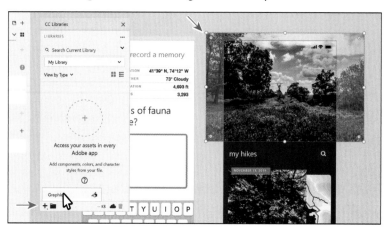

5   Click the keyboard at the bottom of Artboard 1 to select it.

You can tell it's a master component because of the green-filled diamond in the upper-left corner and the green border.

6   Click the plus (+) at the bottom of the CC Libraries panel and choose Component to add the component to the library.

7   Click the text "record a memory" at the top of Artboard 1. You'll save the formatting from the text so you can use it in your document.

8   Click the plus (+) at the bottom of the CC Libraries panel and choose Character Style to add the formatting to the library.

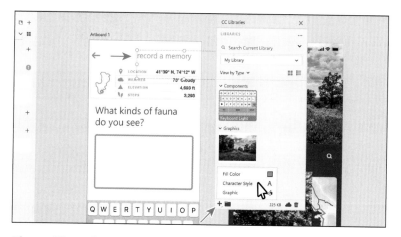

9 Choose File > Close (macOS) or click the X in the upper-right corner (Windows) without saving the file.

Adding Illustrator assets to the library

Now you'll open Illustrator and add vector artwork to the same library that you can then use in XD. You could add content from other applications as well, like InDesign or Photoshop, but in this section, we'll focus on one.

1 Open Adobe Illustrator.

2 In Adobe Illustrator, choose File > Open. In the Open dialog box, navigate to the Lessons > Lesson06 folder, and select the AI_Libraries.ai file on your hard disk. Click Open.

Note: If you see a color profile warning, you can ignore it for now and click Continue or OK.

   The file contains a few elements for the login screen of your app design in XD.

3 Choose Window > Workspace > Essentials, if it's not already chosen, and then choose Window > Workspace > Reset Essentials.

4 Choose View > Fit All In Window to see the two artboards in the document.

5 Choose Window > Libraries to open the Libraries panel, if it isn't open already. Choose My Library, or the library name you chose in the previous section, from the library menu.

6 Click View By Group and choose View By Type to see the assets organized by type.

   Next, you'll drag some of the artwork from Illustrator into the library.

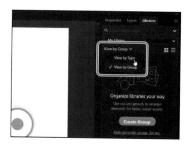

7   Select the Selection tool (▶) in the toolbar on the left. Drag the large map into the Libraries panel. When a plus sign (+) appears in the panel, release to add the artwork to the library.

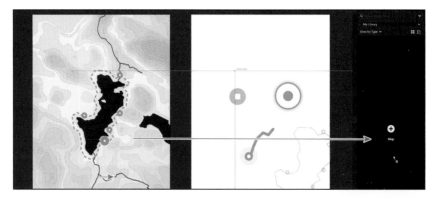

8   Drag each of the icons from the artboard, one at a time, into the Libraries panel to save them.

9   Choose File > Close, without saving, and leave Illustrator open.

10 Return to Adobe XD.

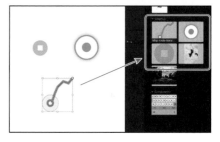

Using CC Library character styles in XD

You can now use the CC Library assets in your Adobe XD projects. In this section, you'll apply the character-style text formatting from the CC Libraries panel.

1   Back in XD, in the Travel_Design document, zoom in to the Memory and Journal artboards.

● **Note:** If a font from a character style is not present on the local computer, a warning icon is displayed to the right of the character style in the CC Libraries panel.

2   Select the Text tool (**T**) and click in the top part of the Memory artboard. Type **record a memory**; then press the Esc key to select the text object. The text you see may have different formatting, and that's okay.

● **Note:** In the next few sections, on Windows, you may need to press Alt+Tab to show the Creative Cloud Libraries panel again.

3   In the Creative Cloud Libraries panel (you may need to open it again), click the style with the orange, Helvetica Neue (macOS) or Segoe UI (Windows) (or other font), Bold (or other), 24pt font to apply the styling to the text.

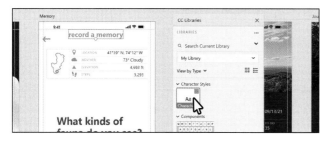

When you apply a character style from a CC Library, it's not added to the Assets panel as a style in the current document. Also, you cannot edit the style found in the Creative Cloud Libraries panel in Adobe XD.

4 Select the Select tool (▶) and drag the content into position as you see in the figure.

5 Option-drag (macOS) or Alt-drag (Windows) the text object to the Journal artboard to the right, below the Meng group of text. Release the mouse button and then the key to make a copy.

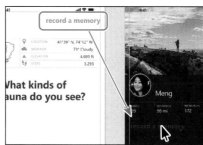

6 Press T to select the Text tool. Click in the copied "record a memory" text to select it. Type **my hikes**. Press Esc to select the text object again.

7 Press the V key to select the Select tool (▶). Click the white color (#FFFFFF) in the Assets panel.

Using graphics from a CC Library

Raster images and vector graphics stored in a CC Library are called *graphics* and can be dragged into an open XD document. Graphics you drag into XD from a library are linked to the original source in the library. If you update the image in Photoshop or the vector graphic in Illustrator, for instance, it will be updated in your XD document. Next, you'll drag the image from the CC Libraries panel into the document, replacing the current image on the Journal artboard.

● **Note:** In Adobe XD, you cannot drag a graphic from the CC Libraries panel onto a locked image to replace it.

1 With the Select tool (▶) selected, click the image at the top of the Journal artboard to select it.

2 Drag the image from the Graphics section of the Creative Cloud Libraries panel on top of the image at the top of the Journal artboard. When it has a blue highlight, release. The new image is placed behind the original.

3 Press Backspace or Delete to remove the original image that is still selected at the top of the Journal artboard.

If you add an image to the library from Photoshop or other applications, it will replace the image you drag it on top of in XD. Since the image you saved from the XD file was a graphic, it won't replace the image.

The image is not linked to the graphic in the library. If it were an image from Photoshop that you saved in the library, then it would be linked. That means that if you edit the image in another application, such as Photoshop, the image on the Journal artboard would update.

4 Drag the keyboard component from the CC Libraries panel onto the bottom of the Memory artboard. It will be positioned and resized in a later lesson.

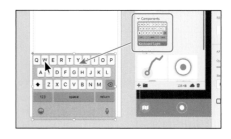

5 Drag the Record button icon, the Stop button icon, and the Map route trace artwork from the Creative Cloud Libraries panel onto the Recording artboard and arrange them as you see in the figure.

● **Note:** It may take a little time for the graphics to appear on the artboard.

▶ **Tip:** You can select multiple objects in the CC Libraries panel with the Shift key or Command key (macOS)/ Ctrl key (Windows). You can then drag all of the selected objects into XD at one time.

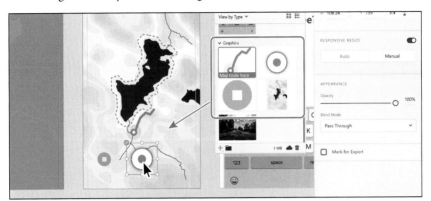

The graphics on the Recording artboard should now have green borders and show a link icon in the upper-left corner. They are each linked to the graphic in the library.

6 Drag the map graphic, the one you saved from Illustrator, from the Graphics section of the CC Libraries panel into an empty area of the Hike Detail artboard.

7 Right-click the map and choose Send To Back (macOS) or Arrange > Send To Back (Windows). Position it, and the other content, as you see in the figure.

Editing library items

You can edit vector artwork and raster images in a Creative Cloud Library from within XD. You can also edit raster and vector graphics stored in Creative Cloud Libraries. Right-click a graphic in the Creative Cloud Libraries panel or on the canvas and click Edit. Raster graphics open in Photoshop and vector graphics open in Illustrator. After you make changes to a graphic, save it. The graphic is updated in the Creative Cloud Library, and the thumbnail in the Creative Cloud Libraries panel in XD is automatically refreshed. The graphic on the canvas is also refreshed with your changes.

1 Click the stop button thumbnail in the Graphics section of the CC Libraries panel to select it, then right-click the same thumbnail and choose Edit.

2 When the asset opens in Illustrator, click the artwork to change the fill color.

3 Choose Window > Properties to open the Properties panel.

4 In the Properties panel on the right, click the Fill color, and in the menu that appears, click the Swatches button (■) and click a gray color to change the fill of the shape.

5 Press Command+S (macOS) or Ctrl+S (Windows) to save the file.

6 Close Illustrator by choosing Illustrator CC > Quit Illustrator (macOS) or File > Exit (Windows).

7 Switch back to Adobe XD, and after the graphic has synced, you'll see it has updated on the Recording artboard.

8 Press Command+S (macOS) or Ctrl+S (Windows) to save the file.

● **Note:** If you started with the L6_start.xd jumpstart file, then keep that file open.

9 If you plan on jumping to the next lesson, you can leave the Travel_Design.xd file open. Otherwise, choose File > Close (macOS) or click the X in the upper-right corner (Windows) for each open document.

Review questions

1. What types of assets can be saved in the Assets panel?
2. How do you edit a character style in the Assets panel?
3. How do you create a component?
4. What property changes made to a master component will reflect in all instances of that same component?
5. What is a Creative Cloud Library?
6. What types of assets can a Creative Cloud Library contain?

Review answers

1. You can use the Assets panel to save and manage colors, character styles, and components.
2. To edit a character style in the Assets panel, right-click the character style and choose Edit. Make edits to the style in the panel that appears, and the text formatting will automatically update wherever the style has been used.
3. To create a component, you will select content in a document and then perform one of the following actions: click the plus (+) in the Components section of the Assets panel, right-click the content and choose Make Component, or press Command+K (macOS) or Ctrl+K (Windows).
4. You can change any properties of a master component to customize all of its instances. Changes you make to an instance only affect that element, but changes you make to the master component applies to all instances where that property hasn't been customized.
5. A Creative Cloud Library is an easy way to create and share stored content such as images, colors, text styles, and more between Adobe applications like XD, Photoshop, Illustrator, InDesign, and certain Adobe mobile apps.
6. A Creative Cloud Library can contain assets such as colors, text styles, graphics, text frames, components, and more.

7 USING EFFECTS, REPEAT GRIDS, AND RESPONSIVE LAYOUT

Lesson overview

In this lesson, you'll learn how to do the following:

- Understand effects.
- Work with background and object blur.
- Work with gradients and transparency.
- Create and edit repeat grids.
- Add padding to objects.
- Understand responsive layout.

This lesson will take about 60 minutes to complete. To get the lesson files used in this chapter, download them from the web page for this book at www.adobepress.com/XDCIB2020. For more information, see "Accessing the lesson files and Web Edition" in the Getting Started section at the beginning of this book.

Adobe XD offers a variety of effects that can add both functionality and pop to your designs, including drop shadows, transparency, and blurs. In this lesson, you'll explore those design features, learn about repeat grids—a feature that is sure to save you time—and explore responsive layout options.

Starting the lesson

In this lesson, you'll explore adding effects like drop shadows to your designs, you'll apply gradients, and you'll work with repeat grids and responsive layout. To start, you'll open a final lesson file to get an idea of what you will create in this lesson.

● **Note:** If you have not already downloaded the project files for this lesson to your computer from your Account page, make sure to do so now. See the "Getting Started" section at the beginning of the book.

● **Note:** The screen shots for this lesson were taken on macOS. On Windows, the menus can be accessed by clicking the hamburger menu.

1 Start Adobe XD, if it's not already open.

2 On macOS, choose File > Open From Your Computer. On Windows, click the menu icon (≡) in the upper-left corner of the application window and choose Open From Your Computer. Open the file named L7_end.xd, which is in the Lessons > Lesson07 folder that you copied onto your hard disk.

   ● **Note:** For either macOS or Windows, if the Home screen is showing with no files open, click Your Computer in the Home screen. Open the file named L7_end.xd, which is in the Lessons > Lesson07 folder that you copied onto your hard disk.

3 If the Assets panel opens on the left and you see a Missing Fonts message, close the panel by clicking Assets panel icon (⊟) in the lower left.

4 Press Command+0 (macOS) or Ctrl+0 (Windows) to see all of the content.

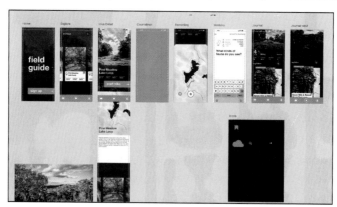

This file shows you what you will create by the end of the lesson.

5 Leave the file open for reference, or choose File > Close (macOS) or click the X in the upper-right corner of the open window (Windows) to close the file.

Applying and editing gradients

A *gradient fill* is a graduated blend of two or more colors, and it always includes a starting color and an ending color. In Adobe XD, you can create a *linear* gradient (the beginning color blends into the ending color along a straight line) or a *radial* gradient (the beginning color defines the center point's fill color, which radiates outward to the ending color).

▶ **Tip:** You can import objects with gradients from other applications, such as Adobe Illustrator. You can then edit the colors in the gradients within Adobe XD.

When you click the Fill color in the Property Inspector, in the color picker that appears, you can choose the type of gradient you want from the menu at the top. The gradient editor appears (labeled B in the figure). The leftmost gradient stop (labeled A) marks the starting color; the rightmost gradient stop marks the ending color (labeled C). A *color stop* is the point at which a gradient changes from one color to the next. You can add more color stops by clicking the gradient editor and changing the color within the color picker.

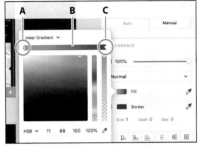

Applying gradients

In this section, you'll explore the options for creating gradients and apply a gradient to several shapes in the design, starting with the Home artboard.

1   Choose File > Open From Your Computer (macOS) or click the menu icon (≡) in the upper-left corner of the application window and choose Open From Your Computer (Windows). Open the Travel_Design.xd document from the Lessons folder (or where you saved it).

2   Zoom in to the Home artboard using any zoom method. Make sure you can see the entire artboard.

3   Select the Rectangle tool (☐) in the toolbar. Starting in the upper-left corner of the Home artboard, drag to the lower-right corner of the artboard to create a rectangle that covers the artboard.

● **Note:** If you are starting from scratch using the jumpstart method described in the section "Getting Started," open L7_start.xd from the Lessons > Lesson07 folder.

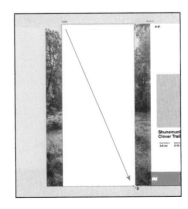

4 With the rectangle selected, click the Fill color box in the Property Inspector to show the color picker. Click Solid Color at the top of the color picker and choose Linear Gradient from the menu that appears.

By default, a white-to-gray gradient is now applied to the fill of the shape. Notice the bar that appears on the shape (an arrow is pointing to it in the following figure).

This is called the on-canvas gradient editor, and it helps you change the direction and duration of the gradient.

● Note: You can tell when a color stop is selected because it has a thicker border and a hollow center.

5 Click to select the leftmost color stop on the gradient editor in the color picker (circled in the following figure). Drag in the color spectrum to select any red. You'll change this color later, so it doesn't have to be an exact match to what you see in the figure.

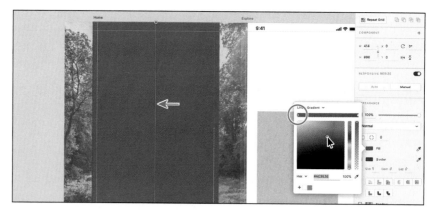

6 Click to select the rightmost color stop on the gradient slider (circled in the following figure). Make sure HSB is chosen from the color mode menu and change the HSB color values to a blue: H=**205**, S=**88**, B=**35**, A=**80**. Press Return or Enter after the last value is entered.

7 Deselect the Border option in the Property Inspector to remove it.

8 To open the Layers panel if it isn't open, press Command+Y (macOS) or Ctrl+Y (Windows). In the Layers panel, drag the selected rectangle down so it's on *top* of the image but beneath everything else.

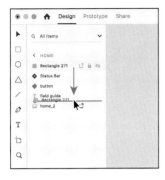 

Next, you'll save the gradient color so that you can easily edit it across more than one object.

9 Right-click the rectangle on the artboard and choose Add Color To Assets.

The gradient color is now saved in the Assets panel and can be used elsewhere.

10 To show the Assets panel, press Command+Shift+Y (macOS) or Ctrl+Shift+Y (Windows). You may need to scroll in the Assets panel. The gradient color should be highlighted in the panel. Your color values may be different and that's okay.

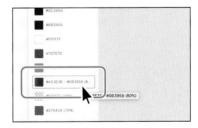

Tip: To see the gradient color in the Assets panel, if the panel is already open, you can right-click an object and choose Reveal Color In Assets.

11 With the rectangle still selected on the Home artboard, copy it by pressing Command+C (macOS) or Ctrl+C (Windows), right-click in the Explore artboard to the right, and choose Paste.

12 Right-click the rectangle copy on the Explore artboard and choose Send To Back (macOS) or Arrange > Send To Back (Windows) so it's behind all of the other content. Leave the rectangle selected.

13 Press Command+S (macOS) or Ctrl+S (Windows) to save the file.

Editing gradient colors

Gradients can have more than the default two colors and can be adjusted directly on the artwork to give you more control over their appearance. In this section, you'll edit the linear gradient you just created and saved in the Assets panel.

1 In the Assets panel, right-click the gradient you saved in the previous section and choose Edit.

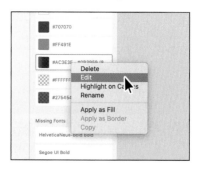

2 Click to select the leftmost (red) color stop on the gradient slider (circled in the figure). Make sure that HSB is chosen from the color mode menu and change the HSB color values to this green: H=**180**, S=**54**, B=**33**, A=**90**. Press Return or Enter after the last value is entered.

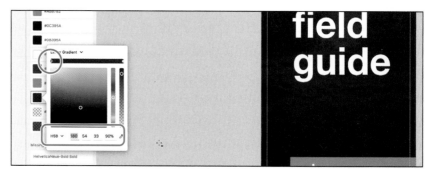

3   Move the pointer over the middle of the Gradient slider and click to add
    another color stop. Change the new color to a red.

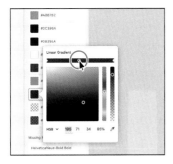 

4   Drag the new red color stop on the Gradient slider to the left and then to the
    right and watch what happens to the gradient in the shape.

5   To remove the new red color, drag it away from the slider and release. There
    should be only two colors in the gradient again.

 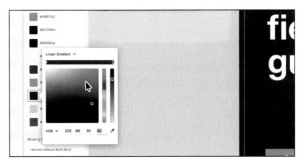

Dragging a color stop along the slider changes the duration of the gradient (the
distance it takes for one color to transition to another).

6   Click away from the color picker to hide it.

Adjusting the direction and length of a gradient

Not only can you adjust the colors in the color picker, but you can also adjust them
on the art using the on-canvas gradient editor, which is what you'll do next. Note
that edits to the gradient made on the art affect only the selected object.

1   With the gradient-filled rectangle on the Explore artboard still selected, select
    the Select tool (▶), and then Shift-click the rectangle on the Home artboard to
    select it as well.

    Adjusting the direction and length of a gradient can only be done to selected
    objects. You want the gradients on these artboards to look the same, which is
    why you selected both.

▶ **Tip:** When editing
on-canvas, to remove
a color stop you can
also click to select
it and press Delete
or Backspace.

2 Click the Fill color in the Property Inspector.

You should now see the on-canvas gradient editor on the rectangle on the Explore artboard. When you select multiple shapes, the on-canvas gradient editor appears on the first selected shape.

● **Note:** The on-canvas gradient editor will not appear unless the color picker is showing in the Property Inspector.

3 Drag the bottom color stop of the on-canvas gradient editor up to make the gradient shorter within the shape.

▶ **Tip:** You can move the end of the on-canvas gradient editor segment by using the arrow keys. You can move an inner color stop along the segment by using the arrow keys as well.

You can change the direction and length of the gradient by dragging the color stops, so try exploring a bit. If you do explore, your gradient may not look like you see in the figures going forward, and that's okay.

▶ **Tip:** When editing on-canvas, you can also press Tab to select and change color stops along the on-canvas gradient editor.

4 Click the top color stop (circled in the following figure) and change the alpha in the color picker (to the right) to **80**.

▶ **Tip:** If you move the pointer over the Gradient slider on the art, a plus (+) will appear next to the pointer, indicating that if you click, you will add a color stop.

5 Press the Esc key to hide the color picker; then press Command+S (macOS) or Ctrl+S (Windows) to save.

Understanding effects

In Adobe XD there are several types of effects we can apply to content, including drop shadows, transparency, and blur effects. Drop shadows can be used to show depth, transparency can be used for design effect and overlays, and blur effects can be used to show focus for overlays, for instance.

In this section, you'll add a few of these effects to your design.

Working with background blur

Background blur uses an object as an overlay (the orange rectangle in the figure) to blur content that is behind it (the image of the surfer). Most of the time, the overlay object that is used to blur content is a shape, and the color fill and border of the shape have no effect on the result.

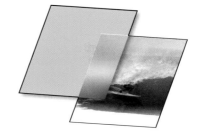

Note: You currently cannot apply a blur to a group.

Next, you'll apply a background blur to existing content.

1 Zoom in to the Hike Detail artboard using any method you've learned.

2 With the Select tool (▶) selected, Command-click (macOS) or Ctrl-click (Windows) the green rectangle behind the Pine Meadow Lake Loop text to select it.

Since the rectangle is part of a group, Command/Ctrl-clicking will select just that object within the group.

3 Make sure the Border option is deselected to remove the border if there is one.

4 Select the Background Blur option in the Property Inspector, and change the following options:

- Blur Amount (◢): 7 (Determines how much blur is applied.)
- Brightness (☀): −30 (How dark or light the overall effect is. 0 is neutral, negative is darker, and positive is lighter.)
- Effect Opacity (▨): 50 (How opaque the effect is. Lower the value to make it more transparent.)

Notice that the color of the overlay shape is reduced and any content that it overlays (the image) is blurred. Feel free to adjust the background blur settings to get a better feel for how it works.

5 Press Command+S (macOS) or Ctrl+S (Windows) to save the file.

Working with object blur

Object blur is a method for blurring content such as a shape or an image. You can use object blur to indicate things like a state for a button or a hero image on a web page with overlay text, or maybe to move the focus to content above the blurred object, like a small pop-up form. Unlike with background blur, you select the content to be blurred. Next, you'll blur artwork on the Recording artboard.

1 Press Command+0 (macOS) or Ctrl+0 (Windows) to fit all design content in the document window.

2 Right-click the image scene_1, which is on the gray pasteboard, and choose Copy to copy it.

3 Right-click in the Explore artboard and choose Paste to paste a copy.

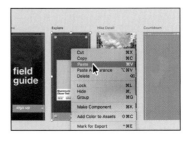

4 To make the image larger from its center and maintain the proportions, Option+Shift-drag (macOS) or Alt+Shift-drag (Windows) a bounding point away from the center. Make sure the image covers the artboard.

● **Note:** You don't need to press the Shift key if the Lock Aspect option (🔒) is selected to the right of the Width and Height fields in the Property Inspector.

5 Right-click the image and choose Send To Back (macOS) or Arrange > Send To Back (Windows) so the image is behind all other content on the artboard.

6 Click the Background Blur option in the Property Inspector on the right and choose Object Blur from the menu to turn it on. Change Blur Amount (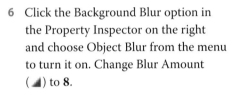) to **8**.

Adjusting the blur and opacity of objects is a great way to layer effects, make text readable on an image, and much more.

7 Drag the selected image so it is positioned something like you see in the figure.

8 Click away in a blank area to deselect all.

9 Press Command+S (macOS) or Ctrl+S (Windows) to save the file.

Applying a drop shadow

Drop shadows are another effect that can add a nice design touch to content, give a sense of depth, indicate the state of a button, and much more. In this section, you'll see how to add a drop shadow to an image. First, you'll add more content to the Journal artboard.

1 Press Command+0 (macOS) or Ctrl+0 (Windows) to fit all design content in the document window. Zoom in to the Journal ver2 artboard on the far right.

2 With the Select tool (▶) selected, drag across the content on the Journal ver2 artboard you see in the first part of the following figure—making sure not to select the orange footer. Shift-click the "my hikes" text and the blue background shape to deselect them.

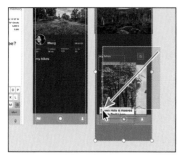 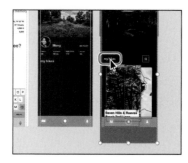 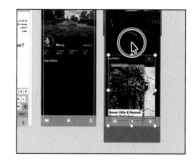

3 Press Command+C (macOS) or Ctrl+C (Windows) to copy the content. Right-click in the Journal artboard and choose Paste.

4 Press Command+3 (macOS) or Ctrl+3 (Windows) to zoom in to the selected content.

5 Drag the content so it's horizontally centered on the artboard and the search eyeglass icon is aligned with the "my hikes" text.

6 Right-click the content and choose Send To Back (macOS) or Arrange > Send To Back (Windows) so that it's behind the footer component.

For the next step, you'll most likely need to zoom out or pan in the window.

7 Click in the gray pasteboard area to deselect, and then Command-click (macOS) or Ctrl-click (Windows) the image of Meng in the group toward the top of the same Journal artboard.

8 Select the Shadow option in the Property Inspector and change the following options:

- X (Distance along the X axis [horizontal]): **0**
- Y (Distance along the Y axis [vertical]): **0**
- B (Blur of the shadow): **10**

9 Click the Shadow color box (to the left of the word Shadow in the Property Inspector), and with black selected, change the alpha to **70**. Press Return or Enter to accept the new value if you typed it in.

10 Press Command+S (macOS) or Ctrl+S (Windows) to save the file.

Applying blend modes

Blend modes are a way to blend the color of one object into content beneath it and are found in a lot of other Adobe applications, like Illustrator, Photoshop, and InDesign. You can use them to do things like apply a color cast to an image or to make text more readable over an image. In this short section, you'll blend one object into another using a blend mode.

1 Press Command+0 (macOS) or Ctrl+0 (Windows) to fit all design content in the document window. Zoom in to the Home artboard.

2 Click to select the gradient-filled rectangle behind the text on the Home artboard.

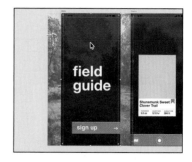

3 In the Property Inspector, click the Blend Mode menu, which shows Normal as the default blend mode. Try choosing any of the blend modes to see the effect on the selected image.

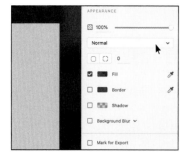
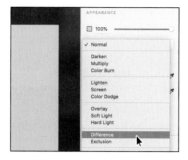
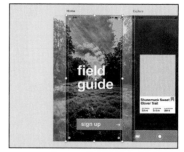

The blend modes blend the color of the selected object into the content beneath it in different ways. They are grouped according to their overall effect, though. For instance, the Darken, Multiple, and Color Burn blend modes will usually make the resulting blend darker overall. The Lighten, Screen, and Color Dodge blend modes will make the resulting blend lighter.

4 Choose a blend mode you like from the Blend Mode menu.

I chose Darken so it looks something like it did before the blend mode was applied, but the grass and trees show more contrast.

Using repeat grids

When designing for mobile apps or websites, you may create repeating elements or lists, such as a series of employee profiles or a list of entrées available at a restaurant. The repeating elements share a common design and general elements, but the images and text may be different. It can be cumbersome to create a grid of elements, especially when you need to easily adjust the spacing between them or rearrange common elements.

In Adobe XD, you can select an object or group of objects and apply a repeat grid to easily repeat the content. With a repeat grid applied to content, you can simply pull a handle at the bottom or right side of the content, and the content repeats

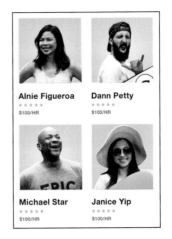

An example of a repeat grid

in the direction you pull. When you modify any style of an element, the change is replicated in all elements of the grid. For example, if you round the corners of an image in one of the elements, the corners of all images in the grid are affected.

If you have a text element in the grid, only the style of the text element is replicated and not the content. So you can style text elements quickly while keeping the content different in the grid elements. You can replace placeholder text in a repeat grid by dragging a text file onto the grid. The repeat grid in Adobe XD has to be my favorite feature.

Adding content for a repeat grid

Next, you'll add some content and set up your document so that you can create a repeat grid.

1. Press Command+0 (macOS) or Ctrl+0 (Windows) to zoom out.

2. With the Explore artboard showing, drag the component instance that contains the text "Shunemunk Sweet Clover Trail" below the Home artboard.

   This content is a description for a local hike.

Note: If you started with the L7_start.xd jumpstart file, then the green icon in the upper-left corner (◇) will look different since the component was embedded in the file.

3. Click in the gray pasteboard to deselect, and then zoom in to the hike description content you just dragged below the Home artboard.

4   Right-click the selected content and
choose Unlink Component. Leave the
hike description content selected.

You can make a repeat grid from
a component, but when the hike
description content is repeated, the
gray rectangle in each will need to be
a different image. As a component, it
will be the same image. Unlinking the
component instance from the original
means it's no longer a component
instance and it's now just a group
of content.

5   Press Command+S (macOS) or Ctrl+S (Windows) to save the file.

Creating a repeat grid

Now that you have some content ready, you'll create a repeat grid from it. The Hike
Detail artboard will show a series of hikes. Instead of copying and pasting, you will
take the group of content from the previous section and apply a repeat grid to it.

1   With the hike description group selected, click the Repeat Grid button in the
Property Inspector to convert the selected content into a repeat grid.

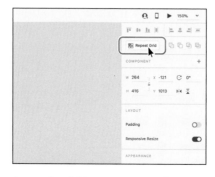

A couple of things to notice when you convert content to a repeat grid:

*   First, there is now a subtle dotted green border around the content,
    indicating it's a repeat grid.

*   Second, there are now two handles: one on the bottom and one on the right
    side. You drag the handles to create copies of the original content vertically
    (the bottom handle) or horizontally (the handle on the right side). The
    original content and the copies become cells in the repeat grid. You can then
    edit the cell and adjust the gap between rows, columns, or both.

For the next step, you may want to zoom out a bit or scroll down to see below
the artboard.

2 Drag the bottom green handle down until you see two copies of the content.

The content is repeated vertically, and the entire repeat grid acts like a group of the repeating elements. Later in this lesson, you'll learn how to adjust the gap between the repeated elements. To make it so you can scroll the content vertically in your prototype, you'll make the artboard taller.

3 Drag the handle on the right side of the repeat grid to the right until you see a total of six hike descriptions.

▶ **Tip:** Pressing the Option (macOS) or Alt (Windows) key while dragging a grid handle resizes the repeat grid on the opposite side as well, from the center. Pressing the Shift key while dragging a grid handle resizes both handles proportionally, from the center.

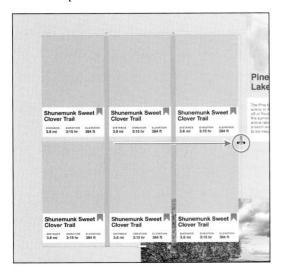

This adds columns containing more duplicates of the hike description.

4 Drag the bottom green handle back up until you see only one row of hike descriptions.

The content is repeated horizontally, and the entire repeat grid acts like a group of the repeating elements. When it's finished, you'll add this repeat grid content to the Hike Detail artboard. To create room for it, next you'll resize the Hike Detail artboard and arrange some of the content.

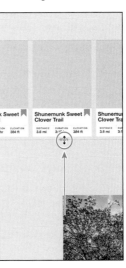

5 If there's an image below the Hike Detail artboard, move it out of the way so you can make the Hike Detail artboard taller.

6 Press Command+0 (macOS) or Ctrl+0 (Windows) to zoom out.

7 Click the Hike Detail artboard name (above the artboard) to select it. Drag the bottom-middle handle down until you see an approximate height of 2300 in the Property Inspector to the right.

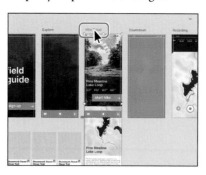 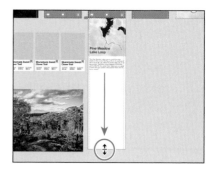

Editing content in a repeat grid

One of the benefits of a repeat grid, aside from being an easy way to duplicate content, is the ability to change the content in the grid. If there are repeating images in the grid, you can replace as many images as you like. You can also edit text independently, but styling remains applied to all copies of the object in the grid. Next, you'll change some of the content in the repeat grid you created.

1 Zoom in to the repeat grid content below the Home artboard.

2 Click any content in the repeat grid to select the entire repeat grid. Double-click the first large gray rectangle on the left to select it.

When you double-click an object within a repeat grid, you enter into the repeat grid's edit mode. The dashed green border around the repeat grid turns into a thicker solid-green border to indicate that you are in edit mode and can edit content within.

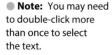
Note: You may need to double-click more than once to select the text.

3 Double-click the middle Shunemunk Sweet Clover Trail text to select it, and type **Pine Meadow Lake Loop** to replace the text.

Notice that the other text objects did not change. You can edit the *content* of each of the copies in a repeat grid separately.

4 Double-click the Shunemunk Sweet Clover Trail text in the hike description on the right to select it, and type **Seven Hills & Reeves Brook Trail Loop** to replace the text.

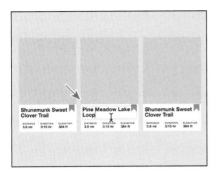 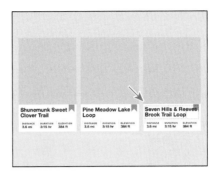

5 Click in a blank area away from the repeat grid to deselect it. You may need to click a few times.

6 Click the image below the repeat grid and press Command+C (macOS) or Ctrl+C (Windows) to copy it.

7 Command-click (macOS) or Ctrl-click (Windows) any of the large gray rectangles in the repeat grid to select it. Right-click the same gray rectangle and choose Paste Appearance.

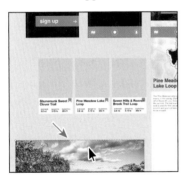 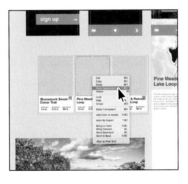 

The image is pasted into all of the gray rectangles as a fill. In a repeat grid, if you change the appearance of any of the content, the rest of the copies in the repeat grid reflect that change.

▶ **Tip:** Images are placed in the cells in alphanumeric order. You'll notice I added a "_1," "_2," and so on, to the names of the images. That helped me control the ordering of the images as they were placed in the repeat grid.

8 Go to the Finder (macOS) or File Explorer (Windows), open the Lessons > Lesson07 > repeat_grid folder, and leave the folder open in a Finder window (macOS) or File Explorer (Windows). With XD and the folder showing, click the image named hike_1.jpg and Shift-click the image named hike_4.jpg. Drag any of the selected images on top of any of the repeating images in the repeat grid. When it shows a blue highlight, release the mouse button to replace the images.

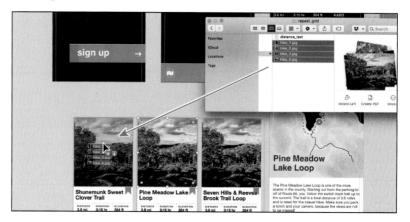

You can easily change the content of a repeat grid, either by changing an individual object or by dragging in images or a plain text file. Order in a repeat grid is defined in left-to-right reading order (left to right, then top to bottom). In this case, the repeat grid shows only the first three images since only three of the gray rectangles are showing. If you were to select the entire repeat grid and drag the right handle to show a few more of the hike descriptions, you'd see the fourth image, and when it came to the fifth description, the first image would appear again.

You can also drag a text file into a repeat grid to replace text in a repeating pattern. See the sidebar on the next page for specifics on how to set up a text file for import.

9   With both XD and the repeat_grid folder still showing, click the text file named distance_text.txt. Drag it on top of any of the "3.6 mi" text blocks in the repeat grid. When it shows a blue highlight, release the mouse button to replace the text.

● **Note:** The data is imported and not linked, so any changes you make to the source file won't affect the data you've already placed in your XD file.

The first occurrence of the 3.6 mi text (on the left in the repeat grid) is replaced with the first paragraph in the text file, and so on.

10 Press Command+S (macOS) or Ctrl+S (Windows) to save the file.

Setting up a text file for a repeat grid

Text files you drag into a repeat grid must have the extension .txt. You can create this using TextEdit in macOS (choose Format > Make Plain Text), Notepad in Windows (save as .txt), or any text editor you prefer.

Within the text file, make each piece of data a separate paragraph. In the example in the previous section, you dragged the bottom of the repeat grid to reveal a total of three repeated elements. If the text file had four paragraphs (with returns between each), the first four repeated text elements would be replaced and then the pattern would start again.

Editing content appearance in a repeat grid

With content in the repeat grid, next you'll adjust the distance between the rows, as well as some of the formatting within.

Tip: You can drag to change the distance between rows or columns in the repeat grid. You can even drag so that rows or columns overlap. This will show as a negative value in the row or column indicator.

1 Click away from the repeat grid to deselect it. Click any content within the repeat grid to select the entire repeat grid.

2 Move the pointer between the first two hike descriptions. When the magenta column indicators show, drag right and then left to see the distance between the columns change. A small distance value will appear above each pink column indicator. Drag until you see a value of approximately 30.

3 If the right side of the rightmost hike description content is being covered, drag the handle on the right side of the repeat grid to the right.

If you drag far enough, a repeat of the column will be revealed to the right. If you don't drag far enough, the content in the third description may be cut off.

4 Press Command+S (macOS) or Ctrl+S (Windows) to save the file.

Adding content to a repeat grid

After you create a repeat grid, you can always add content to or remove content from it later using a variety of methods. Next, you'll add content to the repeat grid.

1 Zoom out or pan over so you can see the Icons artboard, if necessary.

2 With the Select tool (▶) selected, right-click the orange-red map pin icon and choose Cut.

3 Click back on the repeat grid below the Home artboard, and to zoom in, press Command+3 (macOS) or Ctrl+3 (Windows).

4 With the repeat grid selected, double-click one of the images in the repeat grid. This enters repeat grid edit context mode.

5   Press Command+V (macOS) or Ctrl+V (Windows) to paste the icon into the
center of each object.

Now you'll adjust some of the content to position the map pin icon.

6   Click the text Shunemunk Sweet Clover Trail to select the type object.

7   Change the font size to **20** in the Property Inspector to make it smaller.

8   Drag the right edge of the type object to the
left to make it narrower.

9   Drag the type object to the right to make
room for the icon. See the first part of the
following figure.

10 Drag the map pin icon to the left of the
Shunemunk Sweet Clover Trail text.

11 Shift-drag a corner of the map pin to make it smaller so it fits. Drag it just to the
left of the Shunemunk Sweet Clover Trail text.

> **Tip:** To move
> the icon in 1-pixel
> increments, you can
> press an arrow key.

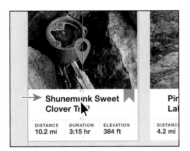  

You can draw any element or add text to a repeat grid, even after you've created
it. Since a repeat grid automatically repeats every element, this allows us the
flexibility to play with design in a new way.

12 Press Command+S (macOS) or Ctrl+S (Windows) to save the file.

Finishing the repeat grid

In this last section on repeat grids, you'll drag copies of the repeat grid into place on the Hike Detail and Explore artboards. You'll also add a few finishing touches to those same artboards.

1 Press Command+0 (macOS) or Ctrl+0 (Windows) to see all of the artboards.

● **Note:** You may need to click in the gray pasteboard more than once to deselect.

2 Click in the gray pasteboard area to deselect. Drag the repeat grid into the middle of the Explore artboard.

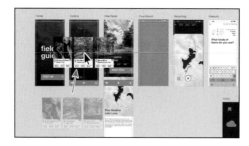

You may find that the content of the repeat grid isn't exactly centered on the artboard even though the repeat grid is. That's because there may be space off the right edge of the rightmost object. You can either drag the right handle of the repeat grid to the edge of the content or press the arrow keys right or left to align it visually. Now you'll drag a copy of it to the Hike Detail artboard.

3 Option-drag (macOS) or Alt-drag (Windows) the repeat grid to the bottom of the Hike Detail artboard. Release the mouse button and then the key.

Now you'll add a rectangle behind the repeat grid on the Hike Detail artboard.

4 Select the Rectangle tool and drag to create a rectangle that covers the bottom part of the Hike Detail artboard.

5 Open the Assets panel by clicking the Assets panel button (▢) in the lower-left corner of the application window, if you don't already see it. Click the green color with the name #265353 to apply it to the fill of the rectangle.

6 Right-click in the green rectangle on the Hike Detail artboard and choose Send To Back (macOS) or Arrange > Send To Back (Windows).

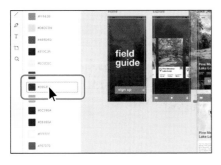 

Now you'll add some of the final content to the Explore artboard so users can navigate when you add interactivity.

7 Zoom in to the Journal artboard, making sure you can see the whole artboard.

Note: If you select any other content when you drag across, Shift-click the content you don't want selected.

8   On the Journal artboard, select the Select tool (▶) and drag across the "my hikes" text and the search icon to the right of it. To make it a component, press Command+K (macOS) or Ctrl+K (Windows). As a component, it'll be easier to make edits across the copies.

9   Copy the component by pressing Command+C (macOS) or Ctrl+C (Windows).

10 Click in the Explore artboard and press Command+V (macOS) or Ctrl+V (Windows) to paste it in the same relative position.

11 Drag the component instance up toward the top of the artboard, making sure it is aligned horizontally in the center. An alignment guide will appear when it is.

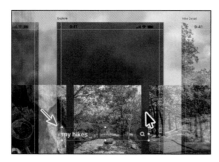 

12 Press Command+S (macOS) or Ctrl+S (Windows) to save the file.

Responsive content and layouts

When designing a website in Adobe XD, it's important to consider how content acts across the wide variety of screen sizes available across mobile and tablet devices, as well as for desktops. Designers have long created multiple artboards at different sizes for each page in a web design, for instance. That meant copying and resizing an artboard, and then resizing all of the content on the new artboard manually. To solve this problem, Adobe XD has several layout features.

The first feature, content-aware layout, allows you to set padding values on groups or components and automatically scale the background when content changes are made. This can be useful if you have versions of buttons, drop-downs, tool tips, or even dialogs that need to be resized.

The other feature is called responsive resize. With responsive resize, XD automatically predicts which constraints you are likely to apply and then automatically applies those constraints as objects are resized. Unlike responsive resize that acts when you resize an entire group, padding acts when you change the content within a group.

Responsive padding with content-aware layout

In this first section, you'll explore setting fixed padding values on content to make resizing easier.

1 Choose File > Open From Your Computer (macOS) or click the menu icon (≡) in the upper-left corner of the application window and choose Open From Your Computer (Windows). Open the Responsive_content.xd document in the Lessons > Lesson 07 folder.

▶ **Tip:** To see the final version of Responsive_content.xd, you can open Responsive_content_final.xd in the Lessons > Lesson 07 folder.

2 Press Command+0 (macOS) or Ctrl+0 (Windows) to see all of the artboards.

3 Zoom into the Journal – padding artboard at the top.

4 With the Select tool selected, drag across the red "start hike" button to select the content.

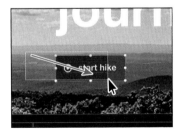

5 To group the selected content, press Command+G (macOS) or Ctrl+G (Windows).

In order to make it so that the button body (the orange-red rectangle) will resize if you edit the text, for instance, you need to group the content. If you have multiple instances of a single button component and need to make text changes to them, this could save you time.

6 With the button group selected, in the Property Inspector, turn on the Padding option in the Layout section.

By default, the amount of space between the background and the edge of the content within, on each side, is the amount of default padding. You have two options when editing padding, having the same padding for all edges (▣) or different padding for each edge (▥). By default, different padding is typically chosen.

● **Note:** The Different Padding For Each Edge icon will look different, depending on which value you have selected (top, right, bottom, or left).

7 With the Different Padding For Each Edge (▥) selected, click in the first field value (the padding value for the top).

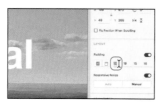

You will see the top padding value in the button appear as a magenta color the value to the left of the button. You may want to zoom in further to the button.

8 Select the second value from the left—which is the right padding value—and change it to **20**.

9 Select the fourth value from the left—which is the left padding value—and change it to **20** to match the padding on the right.

When you increase the padding values, XD creates an invisible padding that acts as a safe-space around logos or in a larger tap area for buttons when prototyping.

10 Press the letter T to select the Text tool and double-click the "start hike" text to select it. Change it to **explore hiking**.

You can see that the red button body (the rectangle) resizes, keeping the same padding value between the right edge of the text and the rectangle. This is the idea behind padding. If content changes within a group or component, the background resizes, keeping the padding on all sides consistent.

Padding examples

To see other examples of working with padding in Adobe XD and to see the latest features, check out the video "Working with padding," which is a part of the Web Edition of this book. For more information, see the "Web Edition" section of "Getting Started" at the beginning of the book.

Getting started with responsive resize

In this section, you'll explore responsive resize to begin creating a tablet design from a phone design. You'll explore how to turn on responsive resize and see how it affects different artboards.

1 Press Command+0 (macOS) or Ctrl+0 (Windows) to see all of the artboards.

Below the padding artboard, there are two sizes for a single page in a website—a mobile design and a desktop design. You'll make a copy of the mobile-sized artboard, turn on responsive resize, and then resize the artboard to be a tablet-sized version of the design.

2 With the Select tool (▶) selected, click the Journal – phone artboard name to select the artboard.

3 To duplicate the artboard, press Command+D (macOS) or Ctrl+D (Windows). The new artboard, named "Journal – phone – 1," is selected.

4 Double-click the new artboard name and change it to **Journal – tablet**.

5 Press Command+3 (macOS) or Ctrl+3 (Windows) to zoom in to the artboard.

6 Drag the right-middle point of the selected Journal – tablet artboard to the right to make it wider. When you see a width of approximately 850 in the Property Inspector, stop dragging.

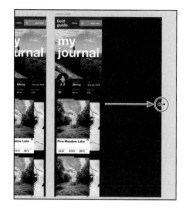

The content on the artboard doesn't resize or move by default. By default, the responsive resize option is turned off for artboards, but you can turn it on for selected artboards. Turning it on for an artboard will allow the content on that artboard to resize.

● **Note:** You could just drag the right-middle point of the artboard to the left to make it narrower, but using the undo command puts it back to the same size every time more easily.

7 Press Command+Z (macOS) or Ctrl+Z (Windows) to undo the artboard resizing.

8 With the artboard still selected, in the Property Inspector click the Responsive Resize toggle to turn it on.

The content on the artboard is now set to resize as the artboard is resized.

9 Drag the right-middle point of the Journal – tablet artboard to the right until you see a width of approximately 800 in the Property Inspector.

You can see that the header image resizes, the button content is separated, the repeat grid adds columns, and more. Notice that the HIKES, DISTANCE, and MEMORIES text, along with the numbers below it, is not staying together.

With responsive resize turned on for the artboard, Adobe XD analyzes the objects on the artboard, their grouping structure, their proximity to the edges of the parent group (such as the artboard), and the layout information when resizing. When resizing either objects on the artboard or the artboard itself, pink crosshairs appear on the content that is being resized. These crosshairs indicate what constraint rules are applied to a group. Constraint rules are used to determine how objects behave when you resize them. You'll explore constraint rules in the next section.

10 Press Command+Z (macOS) or Ctrl+Z (Windows) to undo the artboard resizing.

Grouping content

When you resize an artboard with the responsive resize option enabled, Adobe XD does its best to recreate the placement of your elements on a larger or smaller artboard. Before resizing content, you can group similar objects to establish relationships between them. When resized, grouped objects stay together by default and allow you to establish a hierarchy in your projects.

Next, you'll group content to keep it together when it's resized and also set manual constraint rules. This will make more sense when you see it in action.

1   Zoom in to the top half of the Journal – tablet artboard.

2   With the Select tool (▶) selected, drag across the text "MEMORIES, 172" and the short vertical line just to the left of the text and number to select it all.

3   To group them together, press Command+G (macOS) or Ctrl+G (Windows).

4   Drag across the text "DISTANCE, 98 mi" and the short vertical line just to the left of the text and number to select it all.

5   To group them together, press Command+G (macOS) or Ctrl+G (Windows).

6   Click the Journal – tablet artboard name to select it. Drag the right-middle point of the artboard to the right. You can see that grouped content now stays together.

7   Press Command+Z (macOS) or Ctrl+Z (Windows) to undo the artboard resizing.

Next, you'll group the content for the orange start hike button so it stays together when the artboard is resized.

8   Click the orange start hike button at the top of the artboard. The green border and hollow diamond in the upper-left corner indicate that it's a component instance.

9 With the component instance selected, Shift-click the white double-circle on the button and the menu text. To group them together, press Command+G (macOS) or Ctrl+G (Windows).

10 Click the Journal – tablet artboard name to select it. Drag the right-middle point of the artboard to the right. You can see that all of the content in the orange button group now stays together.

11 Press Command+Z (macOS) or Ctrl+Z (Windows) to undo the artboard resizing.

Setting manual constraints

If you're not happy with the content resizing when you resize an artboard, you can also edit constraint rules manually, which enables you to determine how objects behave when you resize the component, artboard, or group. Manual constraints you apply will always override automatic constraints placed by XD.

1 Click the orange "start hike" button group at the top of the artboard.

In the Layout section of the Property Inspector, there are two buttons below Responsive Resize: Auto and Manual. By default, the content in an artboard with responsive resize turned on is set to Automatic. For selected content, you can set the constraints manually by clicking the Manual button and setting which edges of the artboard you want it to stick to and whether you want to keep its height or width fixed.

2 Click the Manual button to set constraints for the button group manually.

With Manual selected, you can now see position and size options. The position options are used to fix the position relative to the parent. In this case, the parent of the button group is the artboard. The

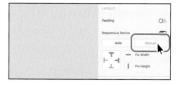

Fix Width and Fix Height options can be used to ensure that the content does not resize horizontally, vertically, or both.

By default, the position of the button is set to be fixed to the top and right edges of the artboard. In this case, the button needs to stay in the same relative position it is currently in. To do that, you can set the position to Fix Left and Fix Top.

3 Click Fix Left (⊢).

With Fix Left selected, Fix Right is disabled. The button group will now stay the same distance from the left edge of the artboard no matter how wide the artboard becomes.

4 Deselect Fix Width (−).

 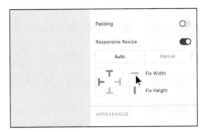

Tip: If content within a group has the Fix Width content turned off, you can choose Fix Left *and* Fix Right for that group.

Tip: Undoing by pressing Command+Z (macOS) or Ctrl+Z (Windows) can be used to undo constraint options you set.

The width of the button group will now resize horizontally. That doesn't mean each object will get wider. It means that the content within the button will spread out to match a changing button width.

5 Click the Journal – tablet artboard name to select it. Drag the right-middle point of the artboard to the right a little. As you drag, you should see a faint pink line from the left edge of the orange button group to the left edge of the artboard. This is the constraint rule applied to the group—fixed left.

You can see that the left edge of the button stays the same relative distance from the left edge of the artboard. It is now fixed to the left side of the artboard. The white

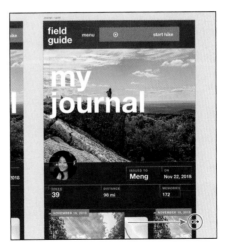

double-circle moves and also the orange button stretches because you turned Fix Width off for the button group.

6 Press Command+Z (macOS) or Ctrl+Z (Windows) to undo the artboard resizing.

7 Click the orange "start hike" button group at the top of the artboard again.

8 With the Manual option still selected in the Property Inspector, make sure the following are set:

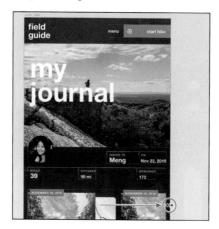

- Fix Top (**T**): selected
- Fix Right (**⊣**): selected, so the selected button stays fixed to the right edge of the artboard (in this case)
- Fix Left (**⊢**): deselected
- Fix Width (**−**): selected, so the button content doesn't resize anymore
- Fix Height (**ǀ**): deselected

Setting the Fix Width option on the group overrides an individual object in the group which has the Fix Width option turned off. In other words, if the group can't resize (it has a fixed width), the content within can't either.

9 Click the Journal – tablet artboard name to select it. Drag the right-middle point of the artboard to the right. You can see that the orange button shape no longer resizes.

Finishing the design

When it comes to resizing artboards, responsive resize will only get you most of the way there, but it may not always get it right. To finish the design, you'll set the artboard to a specific width and resize or move some of the content.

1 With the artboard still selected, change the Width value in the Property Inspector to **834**. Press Return or Enter.

The content should resize like it did at the end of the previous section.

2   Click the repeat grid object. For the next step you may need to zoom out or scroll down. Move the pointer between the columns, and when the magenta column indicators show, drag to the right until you see a distance value above the pink column indicator of approximately 80.

3   Drag the handle on the right to the left so that only two columns show.

Note: If you don't see an alignment guide, you can also just drag it so it's visually aligned on the artboard.

4 Drag the grid so it's visually centered horizontally on the artboard. If you need to, you can also press the right or left arrow keys on your keyboard to nudge it in either direction.

5 Click in a blank area of the pasteboard to deselect.

6 To see everything, press Command+0 (macOS) or Ctrl+0 (Windows).

7 Press Command+S (macOS) or Ctrl+S (Windows) to save the file.

8 Choose File > Close (macOS) or click the X in the upper-right corner of the open window (Windows) to close the Responsive_content file.

Note: If you started with the L7_start.xd jumpstart file, then keep that file open.

9 If you plan on jumping to the next lesson, you can leave the Travel_Design.xd file open. Otherwise, choose File > Close (macOS) or click the X in the upper-right corner (Windows) for each open document.

Review questions

1 What is the difference between object blur and background blur?

2 How do you apply a gradient to content?

3 What is a repeat grid?

4 How do you replace a series of images in a repeat grid?

5 What are two ways to add content to a repeat grid?

Review answers

1 Background blur uses an object as an overlay to blur content that is behind it. Most of the time, the overlay object that is used to blur content is a shape, and the color fill and border of the shape have no effect on the result. Object blur is a method for blurring selected content such as a shape or an image.

2 You apply a gradient to the fill of content by clicking the Fill color in the Property Inspector and choosing Linear Gradient or Radial Gradient from the menu at the top of the color picker.

3 In Adobe XD, you can select an object or group of objects and apply a repeat grid to easily repeat the content. With a repeat grid applied to content, you can simply pull a handle at the bottom or right side of the content and the content repeats in the direction you pull. When you modify any style of an element, the change is replicated in all the elements of the grid. For example, if you round the corners of an image in one of the elements, the corners of all images in the grid are affected.

4 To replace images in a repeat grid, go to the Finder (macOS) or Windows Explorer (Windows) and open a folder. With XD and the folder showing, drag the image(s) on top of any image in the repeat grid. When a blue highlight appears, release the mouse button to replace the image(s).

5 Enter into edit content mode by double-clicking content within a repeat grid or by Command-clicking (macOS) or Ctrl-clicking (Windows) content within a repeat grid. Then you can either create content within the repeat grid or paste content into it.

8 CREATING A PROTOTYPE

Lesson overview

In this lesson, you'll learn how to do the following:

- Explore Design mode versus Prototype mode.
- Set the home screen, link and unlink content.
- Add a connection to a component master.
- Adding multiple states to components.
- Integrate auto-animation.
- Work with a drag trigger.
- Applying multiple interactions to a single object.
- Preserve scroll position.
- Work with fixed positioning.
- Create overlays.
- Add timed transitions ▆◣.
- Use voice triggers and speech ▆◣.

 This lesson will take about 75 minutes to complete. To get the lesson files used in this chapter, download them from the web page for this book at www.adobepress.com/XDCIB2020. For more information, see "Accessing the lesson files and Web Edition" in the Getting Started section at the beginning of this book.

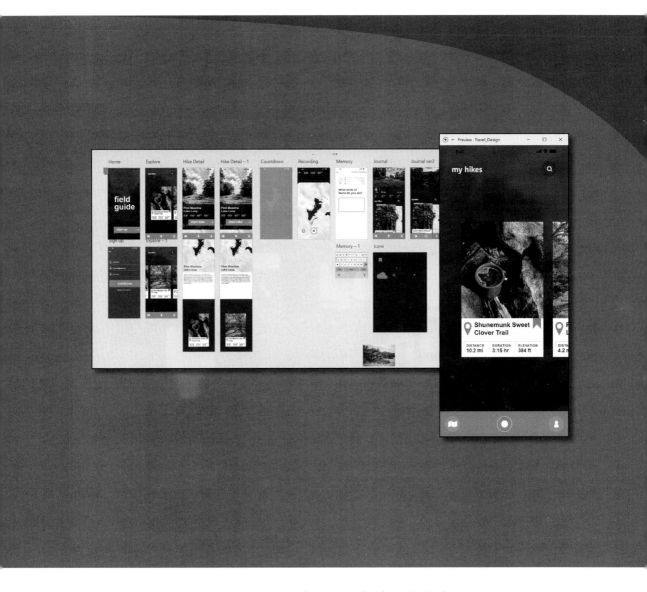

A prototype lets you visualize the navigation between artboards (screens). It's useful for gathering feedback on the feasibility and usability of designs, which saves time on development. In this lesson, you'll create a working prototype from your design and preview it locally in Adobe XD.

Starting the lesson

In this lesson, you'll create a working prototype from your app design and test it locally in XD. To start, you'll open a final lesson file to get an idea for what you will create in this lesson.

1   Start Adobe XD, if it's not already open.

2   On macOS, choose File > Open From Your Computer. On Windows, click the menu icon (≡) in the upper-left corner of the application window and choose Open From Your Computer. Open the file named L8_end.xd, which is in the Lessons > Lesson08 folder that you copied onto your hard disk.

> ● **Note:** For either macOS or Windows, if the Home screen is showing with no files open, click Your Computer in the Home screen. Open the file named L8_end.xd, which is in the Lessons > Lesson08 folder that you copied onto your hard disk.

3   If the Assets panel opens on the left and you see a Missing Fonts message, close the panel by clicking Assets panel icon (⬒) in the lower left.

4   Press Command+0 (macOS) or Ctrl+0 (Windows) to see all of the content.

This file shows you what you will create by the end of the lesson.

5   Leave the file open for reference, or choose File > Close (macOS) or click the X in the upper-right corner of the open window (Windows) to close the file.

● **Note:** If you have not already downloaded the project files for this lesson to your computer from your Account page, make sure to do so now. See the "Getting Started" section at the beginning of the book.

● **Note:** The figures in the lesson were taken on Windows. On macOS, certain parts of the XD interface will be a little different.

Starting with prototypes

Creating an interactive prototype of your design allows you to test the user experience by visualizing the navigation between screens. You can generate prototypes at any point in the design process. Using prototypes, you can also gather critical feedback on the feasibility and usability of designs, which can save time on development. For instance, to test the checkout (purchasing) process for an app design, you could generate a prototype that allows users to tap or click a button and proceed to the next screen. This would allow everyone to experience how the final app might work.

In Adobe XD, you link interactive elements to create connections between screens. That means we create links (also called connections) between artboards or objects and other artboards using several methods.

Note: Going forward, the terms "link" and "connection" will be used interchangeably, as well as "artboards" and "screens."

Note: The figures on this page are just examples of connections in an interactive prototype.

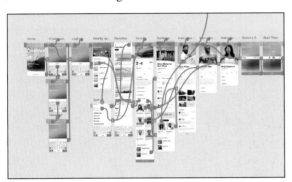

In the following figure, the thin blue border surrounding the Create Account button represents a hotspot, or interactive area. An arrow is pointing to it in the figure. The blue connector (also called a wire) coming from the right edge of the button indicates the connection (link) between the hotspot and the resulting screen (artboard).

While testing a prototype, if you tap or click the Create Account button, a transition you choose, such as a dissolve or slide, will occur to show the next artboard.

Design mode vs. Prototype mode

When you open a file in Adobe XD, the program starts out in Design mode. In Design mode, you have access to all of the design tools and panels necessary to create and edit. When you're ready to begin prototyping, you need to switch to Prototype mode and create any necessary interactive connections.

In this short section, you'll explore switching between the two modes.

Note: If you are starting from scratch using the jumpstart method described in the section "Getting Started," open L8_start.xd from the Lessons > Lesson08 folder.

1   Choose File > Open From Your Computer (macOS) or click the menu icon (≡) in the upper-left corner of the application window and choose Open From Your Computer (Windows). Open the Travel_Design.xd document in the Lessons folder (or where you saved it).

2   If the Layers panel or Assets panel is showing, click its icon in the lower-left corner of the workspace to close it.

3   Press Command+0 (macOS) or Ctrl+0 (Windows) to see all of the design content.

    Notice that two of the three modes, Design and Prototype, are listed near the upper-left corner of the application window. By default, Design mode is selected.

4   Click Prototype, to the right of Design, to switch to Prototype mode.

    Notice that the toolbar shows only the Select and Zoom tools now, and the Property Inspector shows Interaction at the top. While in Prototype mode, you can still import or paste content into your design; copy and paste content or artboards; access the Assets, Layers, and Plugins panels; and even drag components into the design from the Assets panel. Other design changes, such as creating content or making text formatting changes, are not allowed. To do so, you would need to switch back to Design mode.

5   Press Control+Tab (macOS) or Ctrl+Tab (Windows) a few times to switch between Design, Prototype, and Share modes. Press Control+Tab (macOS) or Ctrl+Tab (Windows) and make sure that Prototype mode is showing before proceeding.

Setting the home screen

One of the first things you may do in Prototype mode is set the home screen. The home screen is the first screen that users encounter when they view your prototype, and you can set any artboard as the home screen. If you don't set a home screen, by default the home screen is the topmost, leftmost artboard (in that order). Suppose you want to send a prototype to a colleague for feedback on a specific part of the design, such as the checkout (purchasing) process of an app. Instead of having your colleague start at the default home screen (the Home artboard in the Travel_Design file), you can set as the home screen the artboard on which the checkout process begins. That way, the first artboard users will see when they open the prototype is the start of the checkout process.

Note: Don't confuse the home screen with the artboard named Home in the Travel_Design.xd file.

In this section, you'll ensure that the home screen is set to the artboard named Home—which will be the first screen users see.

1   In Prototype mode, with the Select tool (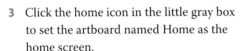) selected, click the name "Home" above the artboard to select the entire artboard.

2   Press Command+3 (macOS) or Ctrl+3 (Windows) to zoom in to the artboard.

With the artboard selected, you should see a small gray shape with a little white house in it, called the home screen indicator, off the upper-left corner of the artboard. If a selected artboard is the home screen, the home screen indicator will be blue with a little white house icon in it.

Note: If you don't see the white house icon in the small gray shape off the upper-left corner of the artboard, you most likely need to zoom in further.

3   Click the home icon in the little gray box to set the artboard named Home as the home screen.

The artboard named Home will be the home screen by default anyway, because it's the topmost, leftmost artboard. In this case, you are explicitly setting the Home artboard as the home screen in case you add another artboard later that becomes the topmost, leftmost artboard.

4   Click away from the artboards in a blank area of the pasteboard to deselect all.

Linking artboards

Now you'll test the user experience of your design by creating an interactive prototype. That way, you, as well as others, can interact with the prototype by testing the links between screens. A designer could use it as a way to visually describe an interaction between screens to a developer, and much more. In this section, you'll explore how to create links (connections) and, later, test those links.

1 Press Command and – (macOS) or Ctrl and – (Windows) a few times to zoom out of the Home artboard.

   Make sure you can see a few of the artboards to the right of the Home artboard. You may want to press the spacebar and drag in the document window, or two-finger drag, so you can see more artboards.

2 Click the name "Home" above the Home artboard (or, with the Layers panel showing, you could click "Home" to select the artboard).

   In Prototype mode, when you select an artboard, you'll see a small white arrow in a circle ( ) on the right side of the artboard. It's circled in the previous figure. This is called the *connecting handle* and is what you use to make a connection.

3 Drag the connecting handle away from the artboard and you'll see a connector (blue line). Drag the connector within the bounds of the Explore artboard. When a subtle blue highlight appears around the Explore artboard, release the mouse button to connect the Home artboard to the Explore artboard.

   When you test the prototype, either in the Desktop preview in XD or in the Adobe XD mobile app on your device, tapping anywhere on the home screen will transition to the Explore screen. Now you're tasked with setting the options for the interaction.

4   In the Property Inspector panel on the right, change the following:

- Trigger: **Tap** (the default setting) (Trigger is an interaction you set that triggers or causes the transition from one screen to the next.)

- Action: **Transition** (the default setting) (The action is what happens when a connection or link is triggered.)

- Preserve Scroll Position: **unselected** (For maintaining the vertical scroll position when you transition to another artboard.)

- Destination: **Explore** (The destination is the screen [artboard] that appears when a user taps or clicks an artboard or object that has a connection.)

- Animation: **Slide Left** (Choose Slide Left from Animation menu. Animations occur when one screen [artboard] replaces another.)

- Easing: **Ease Out** (the default setting) (Easing makes transitions feel more natural. Ease Out, for instance, means the transition starts quickly and decelerates toward the end.)

- Duration: **0.3s** (the default setting) (Duration is the length of time it takes to transition from one screen [artboard] to the next.)

5   Click in a blank area of the pasteboard to deselect the artboard.

Notice that the connector line is now hidden. To see connectors in Prototype mode, you need to select content or artboards.

▶ **Tip:** You can also press the Esc key to deselect an artboard.

6   Click the name of either the Home or Explore artboard (above each artboard) to see the connector again.

On the right end of the blue connector line (on the left edge of the Explore screen), you'll see an arrow in the connecting handle (). The arrow indicates the direction and end of the connection. The original connecting handle you dragged from the Home artboard now shows as a plus (⊕). You can combine multiple triggers to create advanced interactions without distributing the triggers across different objects on an artboard. You'll learn more about that in the section "Taking prototypes further."

7 Press Command+S (macOS) or Ctrl+S (Windows) to save the file.

Previewing links locally

As you begin to add connections and create your prototype, you'll want to preview and test those connections. You can do this using several methods, including a desktop preview and the Adobe XD mobile app. In this section, you'll be introduced to the Preview window for testing. In Lesson 9, "Previewing a Prototype," you'll learn more about the different methods for previewing.

▶ **Tip:** You can also press Command+Return (macOS) or Ctrl+Enter (Windows) to open the Preview window.

1 Click Desktop Preview (▶) in the upper-right corner of the application window.

The Preview window is opened at the size of the artboard currently in focus. You can edit the design and interactions in your prototype while previewing in the Preview window. The changes are instantaneously available for preview.

2 Drag the Preview window by the bar at the top so you can see most of the artboards, if necessary.

3   Click any content in the Home artboard to select it, and then click to select content in the Explore artboard. Whichever artboard is the focus (the one you are working on) will show in the Preview window. Make sure the Home artboard is showing in the Preview window before moving on.

● **Note:** In the next few sections, on Windows, you may need to press Alt+Tab to show the Preview window after clicking in the document window.

▶ **Tip:** You can preview design changes you make to content on your artboards in real time in the Preview window, without having to save.

4   Move the pointer over the Home screen in the Preview window. The pointer changes to a hand (🖑), indicating that there is a connection (link) in that area. Click anywhere in the screen and the Explore screen appears after a default transition.

5   Press the left arrow key to return to the previous (Home) screen in the Preview window.

You can easily navigate between screens in the Preview window by pressing the left or right arrow keys.

6   Close the Preview window.

● **Note:** The Preview window must be in focus (selected) to use the arrows for navigating.

Editing links

At times, you will want to remove connections, reroute connections, or change the connection options. Next, you'll edit the options for the connection you created in the previous section. You'll then remove that connection and, instead, create a connection from an object on the Home artboard to an artboard you copy and paste from another document.

▶ **Tip:** You can set the duration for a connection to 2 or 3 seconds and test the prototype to really see the difference between a push and a slide transition. You'll see how to test the prototype shortly.

1 Click the name of either the Home or Explore artboard (above each artboard) to see the connector you created and the settings for it in the Property Inspector. Choose Push Left from the Animation menu to change the animation type.

When you preview a prototype, you'll see the difference between transitions like slide and push. A slide transition slides the artboard you're linking over the top of the current artboard. A push transition pushes the current artboard out of the way as the new artboard slides (animates) in.

▶ **Tip:** You can choose None from the Destination menu in the Property Inspector to unlink the artboard.

2 Move the pointer anywhere over the connector ends or line and drag away from the artboard into a blank area of the pasteboard. Release the mouse button to remove the connection.

Now you'll add a sign-up form to the design so that you can create a connection from the Sign Up button on the Home screen to the form you add on a new artboard.

▶ **Tip:** You can also drag a connecting handle directly to another artboard to change the link.

3 Choose File > Open From Your Computer (macOS) or click the menu icon (≡) in the upper-left corner of the application window and choose Open From Your Computer (Windows). Open the Sign_up.xd document in the Lessons > Lesson08 folder.

4 With the Select tool selected, click the artboard name "Sign up" to select the artboard. To copy it, press Command+C (macOS) or Ctrl+C (Windows).

5 To close the Sign_up.xd file, choose File > Close (macOS) or, on Windows, click the X in the upper-right corner with the Sign_up.xd document showing.

6 Back in the Travel_Design file, click the Home artboard name above the artboard to select it. Paste the Sign up artboard by pressing Command+V (macOS) or Ctrl+V (Windows).

The Sign up artboard should appear beneath the Home artboard or to the right of the Journal ver2 artboard. If the artboard is pasted to the right of the Journal ver2 artboard, zoom out and drag the Sign up artboard by the artboard name to below the Home artboard.

7 If the large image that was below the Home artboard is added to the Sign up artboard you pasted, you can select the image and press Backspace or Delete to remove it.

Now you'll add the status bar and back arrow components from the Recording artboard to the Sign up artboard. You'll copy and paste the component instances from an existing artboard so you can paste them in the same location on the Sign up artboard.

8 Click the white status bar at the top of the Recording artboard. You'll probably have to pan or zoom in the document to see the Recording artboard. Shift-click the white arrow component beneath it. To copy the content, press Command+C (macOS) or Ctrl+C (Windows).

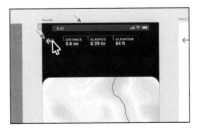

9 Back in the Sign up artboard, right-click and choose Paste.

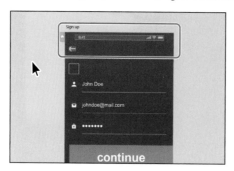

Now that the Sign up artboard has all of the necessary content, you'll create a connection from the sign up button on the Home artboard to the Sign up artboard.

10 Click the "sign up" button on the Home artboard.

When you select content on an artboard in Prototype mode, it will have a blue highlight and you'll see a connecting handle with an arrow on the right side of the content, similar to selecting an artboard in Prototype mode. You can drag the connecting handle to another artboard, but not to another object.

11 Drag the connecting handle to the Sign up artboard beneath it. When the Sign up artboard has a blue border, release the mouse button.

12 In the Property Inspector, ensure that the following are set:

- Trigger: **Tap** (the default setting)
- Action: **Transition** (the default setting)
- Preserve Scroll Position: **unselected**
- Destination: **Sign up**
- Animation: **Dissolve**
- Easing: **Ease Out** (the default setting)
- Duration: **0.5** (You will need to type in the value, since 0.5 does not appear in the menu, and press Enter or Return to accept the change.)
- Fix Position When Scrolling: **unselected**

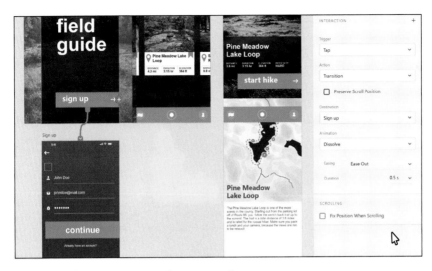

You'll test this interaction in the next section.

13 Click in a blank area of the pasteboard to deselect.

Adding a connection to a component master

In Preview mode, when you apply a connection to a component master, the instances inherit the same connection. If need be, you can override the connection in an instance. Next, you'll apply an action called "previous artboard" to an arrow component so a user can tap or click and return to the previous artboard.

1 Press Control+Tab (macOS) or Ctrl+Tab (Windows) as many times as necessary to switch back to Design mode.

2 Zoom in to the top half of the Hike Detail artboard and click the small white arrow component at the top of the artboard to select it.

Next, you'll add a connection from the left-pointing arrow at the top of the Hike Detail artboard. The problem is that the area that users will tap or click will be very small—the size of the arrow. You can add padding or even a transparent rectangle (or other shape) to use as a hotspot (larger area to click or tap).

3 Select the Padding option in the Property Inspector to turn it on. With the Same Padding For All Edges option (⬚) selected, change the padding value to **10** and press Return or Enter to accept it.

4 Press Control+Tab (macOS) or Ctrl+Tab (Windows) to switch back to Prototype mode.

5 With the arrow component selected, click (don't drag) the connecting handle (the small arrow on the right edge). In the Property Inspector change the following:

- Action: **Previous Artboard** (This creates a connection from the Hike Detail artboard to whichever artboard was last viewed.)

With Previous Artboard selected, the short connecting handle now shows as connecting with a line to a curved arrow (↻).

6 Click in the Explore artboard so that artboard will show in the Preview window when you open it. Click Desktop Preview (▶) in the upper-right corner of the application window.

7   In the Preview window that opens, press the right arrow to show the Hike Detail artboard in the window. On the Hike Detail artboard, click the white arrow to return to the previous artboard.

8   Close the Preview window.

9   Press Command+S (macOS) or Ctrl+S (Windows) to save the file.

Copying and pasting connections

In Preview mode (not in Design mode), when you copy artboards or make a copy of content that has a connection associated with it, the connection is preserved in the copy. You can also copy and paste an interaction, and not the content, from one object or artboard to another object or artboard. This is a real time-saver when you have content that has the same connections, such as footers, across multiple artboards.

Full-screen desktop preview

You can also preview and test your design in full-screen mode. This is useful if you need to present the prototype or design to a client, for instance.

•   Click the green full-screen button in the upper-left corner of the Preview window (macOS), or click the Maximize button (Windows).

    The prototype window expands to fill the entire screen. This is a great way to focus on the prototype without the distraction of the application.

•   Press Esc (macOS) or click the Restore Down button (Windows) to exit full-screen mode.

Taking prototypes further

Prototypes allow you to visualize designs and test ideas. As you dig into creating prototypes in Adobe XD, you see just how many options there are. You can set connections to animate content between artboards, trigger connections with speech, add multiple connections to a single object, add states to components, use a drag gesture to simulate user experiences like dragging between images in a slideshow, and much more.

In this section, you'll explore some of these options and see how some of them can be used in combination to bring your design concept to life.

Adding a hover state to components

▶ **Tip:** For a refresher on high-fidelity vs. other types of prototypes, see Lesson 1.

Components that change appearance based on user interactions are invaluable for creating high-fidelity prototypes. You can create a component, add multiple variations (states) to it, and wire it to mimic real-world user behavior (without having to copy your components multiple times).

Having components with states also makes it easier to manage assets and create interactive design systems (part of which is a collection of reusable components). Common examples of components with states are buttons, checkboxes, and animated toggle buttons. These components need to change when users interact with them by tapping or hovering over them.

1 Click the orange "sign up" button on the Home artboard.

2 Press Control+Tab (macOS) or Ctrl+Tab (Windows) a few times to switch to Design mode.

In the Property Inspector you will see Component (Master). A component can have multiple states. The initial state that appears for every component is the default state. You can add two types of states for your components—New State and Hover State. A new state is for showing variations of a component such as a disabled or clicked version of a component. Add a hover state if you want your component to change appearance, for instance, when a user hovers over the component. The figure shows a hover state, but you won't see one yet.

Next you'll add a hover state to change the appearance of the button when a user moves the pointer over it.

3   Click the plus (+) to the right of the Default State name in the Property Inspector (circled in the first part of the following figure). Choose Hover State from the menu. Leave the state name as Hover State and press Return or Enter to accept it.

Did you notice the little lightning bolt to the right of the Hover State name in the menu? That indicates that the hover state has an interaction automatically wired to switch the state appearance when a user interacts with the button.

4   With Hover State selected in the Property Inspector, Command-click (macOS) or Ctrl-click (Windows) the orange button shape to select it within the component.

5   Click the Fill color box in the Property Inspector to open the color picker. Change the Opacity of the color to approximately **50%**.

● **Note:** When you have an instance selected on canvas and you want to edit existing states or add new states to the master component, you can right-click the component instance and select Edit Master Component.

6   Press Esc to hide the color picker.

7   To select the whole component, press Esc a few more times.

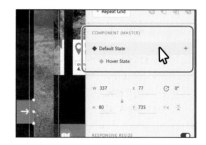

8   In the Property Inspector, click Default State to show the original appearance of the button.

You can preview the states on the component by clicking between them in the Property Inspector.

9   Click Desktop Preview (▶) in the upper-right corner of the application window.

Note: The "sign up"component on the Home artboard is a master component. That means that instances of that component, like you see on the Hike Detail artboard now have the same hover state. The problem with the instance on the Hike Detail artboard is that it has the "sign up" text in the hover state. To fix this, you could select the "start hike" button on the Hike Detail artboard, select Hover State in the Property Inspector and change the text to "start hike."

10   In the Preview window that opens, move the pointer over the "sign up" button to see the hover state change the appearance of it.

11   Close the Preview window.

Adding multiple states to components

Aside from adding a hover state to a component, you can also add other states whose actions and appearance you can control. For instance, you can have a single icon component with three nested icons. You can use the generic New State option to create a different state for each, so any time you want to show one of the icons, you select that state. New State does not have any interactivity by default. You have to wire the interaction in Prototype mode. Next, you'll create the button in the scenario I just described.

1   Zoom in to the Sign up artboard.

2   Make sure that Design mode is showing and the Assets panel is open. Press Command+Shift+Y (macOS) or Ctrl+Shift+Y (Windows) to open the Assets panel if necessary.

If you scroll in the Assets panel, you should see three new components that were pasted in from the Sign_up.xd document: Lock, Mail, and Icon. You will also notice the square higher up on the artboard. That square will become the basis of a new component. You will

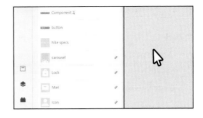

nest all of the icons within the square component, each assigned to a state. This will allow you to choose a different state for a component instance, showing a different icon, depending on your need.

3   Drag the square, by its edge, onto the icon of the person to the left of the text John Doe. Try to align it to the center of the person icon. You may need to zoom in.

4   Shift-click the icon of the person to select both. In the Property Inspector, click the plus (+) to the right of Component to make the shape and icon a new component, nesting the person icon component in the new component. You will now see "Default State" under COMPONENT (MASTER) in the Property Inspector.

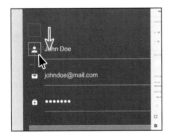

Now you'll create a few states for the component and change the icon for each.

5   With the component selected, click the plus (+) to the right of Default State in the Property Inspector (circled in the figure) to add a new state. Choose New State from the menu. Name the state **Mail** and press Return or Enter.

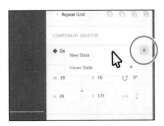

6   With the Mail state selected in the Property Inspector, double-click the person icon on the artboard to select it within the component.

Now you'll swap out the icon for another.

7 Drag the mail icon from the Assets panel onto the icon of the person in the document. Hover over the person icon for a second until the person icon is highlighted in blue, then release the mouse button. You can position the mail icon in the square so it is more centered, if necessary.

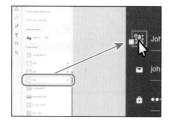  

8 Press Esc to select the main component again. In the Property Inspector, click the plus (+) to the right of Default State in the Property Inspector to add a second new state. Choose New State from the menu. Name the state **Password** and press Return or Enter to accept it.

9 With the Password state selected in the Property Inspector, double-click the mail icon to select it within the component.

10 Drag the lock icon from the Assets panel onto the mail icon in the document to swap it. You can position the Lock icon in the square so it is more centered, if needed.

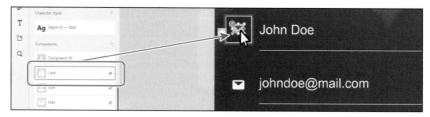

With the component and states set up, now you'll make a few more instances of the component by copying it. Then, you'll change the state for the instance to show the correct icon, depending on where it's used.

11 Click the mail icon to the left of the johndoe@mail.com text and delete it. Do the same for the lock icon to the left of the password dots (·······) on the artboard.

12 To make copies of the component you made, Option-drag (macOS) or Alt-drag (Windows) the component down so it's to the left of the johndoe@mail.com text. Release the mouse button and then the key. Do the same to create a copy to the left of the password dots (·······).

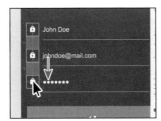

13 Click the component to the left of the John Doe text. In the Property Inspector, select the Default state to show the person icon.

14 Click the component to the left of the johndoe@mail.com text. In the Property Inspector, select the Mail state to show the mail icon.

15 Click the component to the left of the password dots (⋯⋯). In the Property Inspector, select the Password state to show the lock icon, if necessary.

Notice the diamond icon to the left of the state names in the Property Inspector. A solid diamond (◆) indicates that the component is the master. A hollow diamond (◇) indicates it's an instance. A bold, solid diamond (◆) indicates when a state is the chosen for a master component, and a bold, hollow diamond (◈) indicates when a state is the chosen for an instance.

16 Press Command+S (macOS) or Ctrl+S (Windows) to save the file.

Inheritance of component states

Follow these principles while editing states across master components and instances:

- You can override properties (text, bitmap, size, appearance, or structure changes) for states just like you can override a component instance.

- When you edit the state in a master component, that state updates across all instances.

- When you edit the state in an instance, it is treated as a unique override and no longer syncs that property with changes from the master state.

- If you are not happy with the results of your overrides, reset it back to the original master component by right-clicking an instance and selecting Reset To Master State. This clears all overrides on an instance and resets it back to the master component.

—From Adobe XD Help

Auto-animate content

When you create connections between artboards, the default action for a connection is set to Transition. Currently, there are a total of five actions you can set for a connection. The first you'll explore is called *auto-animate*, which allows you to create prototypes where the content between the connected artboards will animate from one to the next. You can duplicate an artboard, modify some properties for the content, such as size and position, and then apply the Auto-Animate action to the connection to create an animated transition when the prototype transitions from one artboard to the next.

In this section you'll create a slideshow that animates—starting with copying the Explore artboard and making a change on the copied artboard.

1 With the Travel_Design.xd document showing, press Command+0 (macOS) or Ctrl+0 (Windows) to see all of the design content.

2   With the Select tool (▶) selected, Option-drag (macOS) or Alt-drag (Windows) the Explore artboard by its name to make a copy beneath the original. When the copy is in place, release the mouse button and then the key.

To use auto-animate, make sure that the objects you are looking to animate have the same name in the Layers panel between each of the artboards. By duplicating the artboard, you're assured that the names of the content between the artboards are the same.

3   Zoom in to the Explore artboard and the new copy beneath it so you can see both.

4   On the original Explore artboard, drag the repeat grid to the right so the first hike description is showing. See the figure. Leave the repeat grid selected.

The idea is to make content or appearance change on either artboard. This could be changing the position of content, opacity, font size, rotation, or a lot more. For a listing of supported properties for auto-animate in XD artboard transitions, visit helpx.adobe.com/xd/kb/supported-auto-animate-features-in-xd.html.

5   Switch over to Prototype mode, and with the repeat grid on the original Explore artboard selected, drag the connecting handle to the Explore – 1 artboard beneath it and release the mouse button to make the connection.

6 In the Property Inspector, after creating the connection, ensure that the following are set:

- Trigger: **Tap** (the default setting)

- Action: **Auto-Animate**

- Destination: **Explore – 1**

- Easing: **Ease In-Out**

- Duration: **0.3**

- Fix Position When Scrolling: **unselected**

7 Click Desktop Preview (▶) in the upper-right corner of the application window.

8 In the Preview window that opens, move the pointer over the repeat grid and click to see the animation from the Explore artboard to the Explore – 1 artboard.

● **Note:** If you add content to both artboards, make sure that the names of the objects in the Layers panel are the same between artboards. Also, if you add something to one artboard, it will either fade out or fade in, depending on which artboard you add it to.

There are so many things you can try with auto-animate. Try moving other content on the Explore – 1 artboard or introducing another object. You could even copy the Explore – 1 artboard, drag the repeat grid on the new artboard to show the last hike description, and make a connection with the Auto-Animate action from the repeat grid on Explore – 1 to the Explore – 2 artboard. You can then preview the connection in the Preview window. Know that if you explore, your design content may look different than what you see going forward.

● **Note:** In order to save on Windows, you may need to click back in the Travel_Design application window before saving.

9 Close the Preview window.

10 Press Command+S (macOS) or Ctrl+S (Windows) to save the file.

Adding a drag trigger

When you create a connection, you can set the trigger to Drag to simulate user actions like dragging to change images in an image slideshow. When you select Drag from the list of triggers, XD automatically switches the Action setting to Auto-Animate. Next, you'll apply a drag to the connection between the Explore and Explore – 1 artboards. That way, instead of clicking to see the animation, you can drag. You can then control the animation speed by how fast you drag.

1 Click the repeat grid on the original Explore artboard to see the connection, if it isn't already selected.

2 In the Property Inspector, choose Drag from the Trigger menu and ensure that None is chosen for Easing.

When you select Drag, the Duration option is no longer visible in the pop-up window. That's because the user controls the duration by how fast they drag.

3 Click Desktop Preview (▶) in the upper-right corner of the application window.

4 In the Preview window that opens, move the pointer over the repeat grid and drag to the left to see the animation happen.

After dragging, your first instinct may be to drag to the right so you see the first hike description again. To accomplish that, you would need to set up another connection from the repeat grid on the Explore – 1 artboard to the Explore artboard.

5 Click the repeat grid on the Explore – 1 artboard to select it.

▶ **Tip:** To try the animation again, you can click in the Explore artboard so it shows in the Preview window.

● **Note:** To transition from the Explore artboard to the Explore – 1 artboard you don't have to drag the entire way. If you drag more than halfway from one artboard to the next, the animation will be completed for you.

6   Drag the connecting handle from the repeat grid to the Explore artboard above it and release the mouse button.

7   In the Property Inspector, the settings should be the same as for the last connection, except for Destination. Ensure that the following are set:

- Trigger: **Drag**

- Action: **Auto-Animate**

- Destination: **Explore**

- Easing: **None**

8   With the Explore – 1 artboard showing in the Preview window, drag to the right to see the Explore artboard. Drag to the left to see the Explore – 1 artboard.

9   Close the Preview window.

Applying multiple interactions to a single object

● **Note:** You can apply Voice and Keys & Gamepad triggers many times per trigger, but you can apply Tap, Drag, Hover, and Time triggers only once.

▶ **Tip:** Hover over the wire to view a tooltip that tells you the number of interactions and their type.

▶ **Tip:** To apply the defined interaction to another object, select the object or the artboard, select copy, click the destination object or artboard, and in the right-click context menu, select Paste Interaction.

To make prototypes more engaging, you can introduce multiple triggers and actions to the same object. This can be useful if, for instance, you want to make it so you can drag an image in a slideshow, like you did in the previous section, and show the next image *or* tap to see more information about that particular image. In this example, you will apply a second interaction to the repeat grid on the Explore – 1 artboard.

1   On the Explore – 1 artboard, double-click the repeat grid to select the Pine Meadow Lake Loop panel in the repeat grid object.

2   Click the arrow on the right edge of the selected content to add an interaction.

3 In the Property Inspector, change the following so the user can tap to go to the Hike Detail page:

- Trigger: **Tap**
- Action: **Transition**
- Preserve Scroll Position: **unselected**
- Destination: **Hike Detail**
- Animation: **Slide Left**
- Easing: **Ease In-Out**
- Duration: **0.3**

4 To add a second interaction, click the plus (+) on the right edge of the repeat grid or click plus (+) to the right of Interaction in the Property Inspector.

A second interaction is set that you will adjust the settings for now.

5 In the Property Inspector, change the following so the user can say a phrase to go to the Hike Detail artboard:

- Trigger: **Voice**
- Command: **Pine Meadow Lake Loop**
- Action: **Transition**
- Preserve Scroll Position: **unselected**
- Destination: **Hike Detail**
- Animation: **Slide Left**
- Easing: **Ease In-Out**
- Duration: **0.3**

Above the interaction settings in the Property Inspector you should now see two interactions listed: Tap and Voice. To change the settings for either, you need to select it in that list first. To remove an interaction, select it in the list and press Delete or Backspace.

You will also see a number 2 on the connection indicating that there are two interactions applied.

● **Note:** When you attempt to say the phrase while pressing the spacebar, you may see a message asking if XD can access your microphone. Click to allow it.

6 Click Desktop Preview (▶) in the upper-right corner of the application window. With the Explore – 1 artboard showing in the Preview window, tap the repeat grid to show the Hike Detail artboard. To show the Explore – 1 artboard in the Preview window again, click in the Explore – 1 artboard. This time, press the spacebar and say "Pine Meadow Lake Loop" to transition to the Hike Detail artboard.

You may see a message at the bottom of the Preview window reminding you to press the spacebar before talking.

7 Close the Preview window.

Setting up content for preserving scroll position

By default, if you scroll through a screen vertically and click an object, like a button, with a connection set to another artboard, the top of the next artboard appears, instead of maintaining your scroll position on the previous screen. When creating connections, you can choose to preserve scroll position, which allows the prototype to transition to the next screen while maintaining the vertical scroll position from the previous screen. In this section, you'll set up the design content to be able to create a connection for preserving scroll position.

1 Drag across the Home, Sign up, Explore, Explore – 1 , and Hike Detail artboards to select them.

2 Drag the selected artboards to the left by dragging any of their names. There needs to be room to add a copy of the Hike Detail artboard to the right of them.

3 Press Control+Tab (macOS) or Ctrl+Tab (Windows) twice to switch back to Design mode.

4 Click the repeat grid at the bottom of the Hike Detail artboard to select it.

5 Press Command+3 (macOS) or Ctrl+3 (Windows) to zoom in to it.

6 Move the pointer between the columns, and when the pink column indicator shows, drag to the right to expand the pink spacing column until the distance above it shows as 100.

7 To drag the repeat grid and constrain its movement to just horizontal, Shift-drag one of the descriptions to the right to show the first hike description. Release the mouse button and then the Shift key when it's visually centered horizontally in the artboard.

Note: You won't see any helpful alignment guides indicating it's centered when dragging the content, because it's part of a repeat grid.

8 Click away from the artboards in the gray pasteboard area to deselect them all.

9 Press Command+0 (macOS) or Ctrl+0 (Windows) to see everything.

10 Click the Hike Detail artboard name and press Command+D (macOS) or Ctrl+D (Windows) to duplicate the artboard.

Next you'll do something similar to the repeat grid at the bottom of the Hike Detail artboard copy (Hike Detail – 1).

11 Shift-drag the repeat grid on the new Hike Detail – 1 artboard to the left to show the second hike description. Release the mouse button and then the Shift key when it's in place.

12 Press Control+Tab (macOS) or Ctrl+Tab (Windows) to switch back to Prototype mode.

Preserving scroll position

Now that you have the content set up, you can create a connection between artboards and learn about preserving scroll position. When you link from one artboard to another or one object to an artboard, the prototype moved you to the top of the next artboard, instead of maintaining your scroll position on the previous artboard. While wiring objects in the prototype mode, you can choose to preserve scroll position, which allows the prototype to transition to the next screen while maintaining the vertical scroll position from the previous screen.

1 Click the repeat grid at the bottom of the original Hike Detail artboard. Drag the connecting handle on the right edge of the selected repeat grid to the Hike Detail – 1 artboard and release the mouse button.

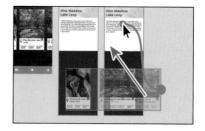

2 In the Property Inspector, the settings should be the same as the last connection. For this connection, you want the user to tap the repeat grid content to dissolve from one artboard to the next. Set the following to achieve that:

- Trigger: **Tap**
- Action: **Transition**
- Preserve Scroll Position: **unselected** (the default setting)
- Destination: **Hike Detail – 1**
- Animation: **Dissolve**

- Easing: **Ease In-Out**

- Duration: **0.3** (the default setting)

- Fix Position When Scrolling: **deselected**

3 Click Desktop Preview (▶) in the upper-right corner of the application window. With the Hike Detail artboard showing in the Preview window, scroll down so you can see the repeat grid at the bottom of the artboard. Click the repeat grid to go to the Hike Detail – 1 artboard.

● **Note:** You may see that some of the content scrolls over the top of the orange footer bar that is set to fixed positioning. If that is the case, you can right-click the orange footer symbol on the Hike Detail artboard and choose Bring To Front (macOS) or Arrange > Bring To Front (Windows). You can do the same for the Hike Detail – 1 artboard.

Notice that the Hike Detail – 1 artboard showed, but it showed the top of the artboard. When using the Tap trigger and Transition action, you can set Preserve Scroll Position so the next artboard that appears will be scrolled to the same position as the artboard you are coming from. Setting a Drag trigger or an Auto-Animate action automatically scrolls to the same position between artboards.

4 Back in the Travel_Design document, with the repeat grid still selected, select Preserve Scroll Position in the Property Inspector.

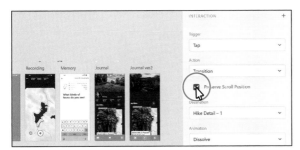

The Preserve Scroll Position property shows in the Property Inspector when either Design mode or Prototype mode is showing.

5   Click in the Hike Detail artboard to show it in the Preview window, if you don't see it already. Back in the Preview window, scroll down to see the repeat grid.

6   Click the repeat grid to see the next hike description on the Hike Detail – 1 artboard. Close the Preview window.

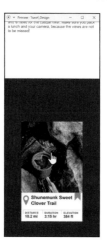 

● **Note:** If the positions of the repeat grid content appear to "jump," here's how to fix it. Back in Design mode, double-click the first image in the Hike Detail artboard repeat grid. Make note of the Width value in the Property Inspector (I see 264) and the X position (I see 75). Then click the repeat grid on the Hide Detail – 1 artboard. The X value should be the X value of the repeat grid on the left – (minus) the sum of the width of the image (264) + 100 (the distance between your images you set earlier by dragging between).

Working with fixed positioning

The footer you created with the map, double-circle, and person icons is intended to go at the bottom of the app screen. If you create an artboard that is set up for vertical scrolling, the footer you create will scroll (move) with the page content. You can set content like the footer to have a fixed position when a user scrolls vertically in an artboard. Fixed-position objects can be above or below other design objects. Next, you'll put the footer into place and set it to a fixed position.

1   Click in the Hike Detail artboard.

2   Click Desktop Preview (▶) in the upper-right corner of the application window.

3   In the Preview window that opens, drag to scroll vertically.

    You can see that the footer is moving along with the rest of the content. To keep it stuck at the bottom of the screen, you'll fix its position.

4   Click to select the footer group on the Hike Detail artboard. In the Property Inspector, select Fix Position When Scrolling.

The footer object on the Hike Detail artboard now shows a pin icon (⬤) in the corner, which is an indicator that the Fix Position When Scrolling options is set for it.

5   Drag in the Preview window again to see that the footer is now fixed to the bottom of the screen and the rest of the content moves beneath it as you scroll.

⬤ **Note:** On Windows, you may need to press Alt+Tab to show the Preview window after clicking in the document window.

If you scroll down far enough, you may notice that the footer goes under some of the content on the artboard. The footer needs to be brought to the front of the content on the artboard, which you'll do shortly.

Also, unfortunately there are other footers on the other artboards that also need to have the Fix Position When Scrolling option set. You cannot apply that to a master component, so you will need to select all of the instances and the master and apply the option at one time.

6   Press Control+Tab (macOS) or Ctrl+Tab (Windows) several times to switch back to Design mode. Click in the gray pasteboard to deselect all.

7   Shift-click the other footer instances in the design and in the Property Inspector select Fix Position When Scrolling. Zoom out if you need.

8   Right-click the selected footers on the Hike Detail artboard and choose Bring To Front (macOS) or Arrange > Bring To Front (Windows).

9   Choose File > Save (macOS) or click the menu icon (☰) in the upper-left corner of the application window and choose Save (Windows).

Setting up content for overlays

Overlays are an exciting type of action in Adobe XD that you can use to create sliding menus, modal overlays, form overlays, and a lot more. In this section, on the Memory artboard, you'll add a field for users to type into. When a user taps (or clicks) in the field, the keyboard will slide in so they can begin typing. The keyboard, as the overlay, needs to be on a separate artboard.

1 In Design mode, zoom out or pan in the Document window so you can see the Memory and Icons artboards.

2 Select the Rectangle tool (▢) in the toolbar. Draw a rectangle above the keyboard and below the "What kinds of fauna do you see?" text.

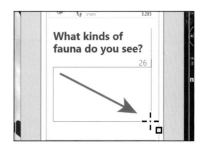

3 Change Border Size to **4** and Corner Radius to **10** in the Property Inspector.

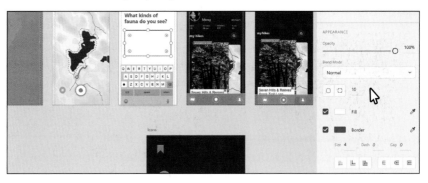

● **Note:** To see the names in the Assets panel, click the List View button (☰) toward the top of the panel. If the Grid View button (▦) is selected, you can move the pointer over a color to see a tooltip with the color name.

4 Press Command+Shift+Y (macOS) or Ctrl+Shift+Y (Windows) to show the Assets panel, if it isn't already showing. Right-click the orange-red color with the name #FF491E, and choose Apply As Border to make the rectangle have an orange-red border.

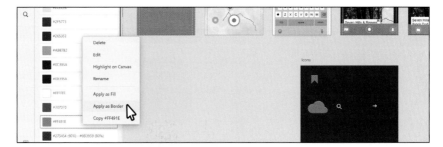

5 To make room for a new artboard below the Memory artboard, drag the Icons artboard by its name to below the Journal artboard.

6 With the Select tool (▶) selected, Option-drag (macOS) or Alt-drag (Windows) the Memory artboard by its name to make a copy beneath the original. Release the mouse button and then the key.

7 Drag across all of the content on the new artboard (Memory – 1), except for the keyboard, to select it. To remove it, press Delete or Backspace. Drag the keyboard to the top of the artboard.

8 To resize the keyboard to fit the width of the artboard, since it's a little narrower, drag the keyboard into the upper-left corner of the artboard. Then Shift-drag the lower-right corner until it's as wide as the artboard.

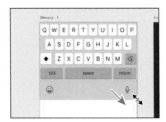

Now you'll resize the artboard to match the size of the keyboard. You could leave the Memory – 1 artboard the same size as the original Memory artboard, but you wouldn't be able to position the keyboard on the Memory artboard. Also, you would need to remove the fill color for the Memory – 1 artboard; otherwise, when the keyboard slides onto the Memory artboard, the Memory – 1 artboard would cover the Memory content since it "overlays," or is on top of, the content.

● **Note:** The artboard
will not snap to the
keyboard content.
You may want to click
the keyboard artwork
to get the Height
value in the Property
Inspector. Then select
the artboard again
and change the Height
value in the Property
Inspector to match.

9 Click the Memory – 1 artboard name to
select the artboard. Drag the bottom-
middle point of the artboard up to
match the height of the keyboard as best
you can.

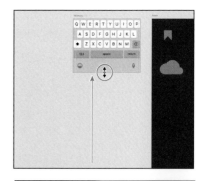

10 Click the keyboard on the Memory
artboard and press Delete or Backspace.

Note that the keyboard you just deleted
was the master component. If you were
to attempt to edit the instance on the
Memory – 1 artboard, XD would create
the master and place it on the canvas.

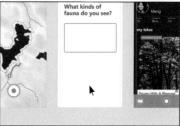

Creating overlays

Now that you have content in place, you'll make it so the keyboard slides into the
Memory artboard from the bottom when someone clicks in the orange box.

1 Press Control+Tab (macOS) or Ctrl+Tab (Windows) to switch back to
Prototype mode.

2 Click the rectangle with the orange-red
border on the Memory artboard, and drag the
connector to the Memory – 1 artboard
beneath it.

3 In the Property Inspector, change the following:

- Trigger: **Tap**
- Action: **Overlay**
- Destination: **Memory – 1**
- Animation: **Slide Up**
- Easing: **Ease In-Out**
- Duration: **0.3**

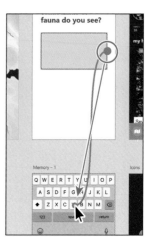

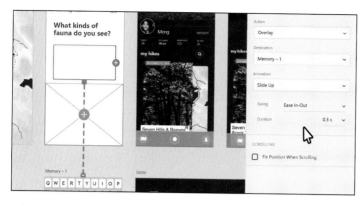

After setting Action to Overlay, you should see a green box with a plus sign (+) in a green circle in the middle on the Memory artboard. This indicates the size and position of the overlay. After selecting Slide Up for the Animation, the green box is positioned at the bottom of the Memory artboard since it will be positioned off the bottom edge of the Memory artboard to start, and then slide up onto the artboard.

4 Press and hold in the middle of the green box on the Memory artboard to see a preview of the keyboard on the artboard. Make sure the green overlay box is at the bottom of the Memory artboard. If it isn't, you can drag the keyboard overlay to position it in the Memory artboard by dragging the green circle in the center of the overlay.

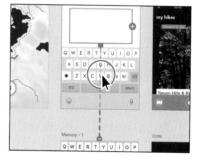

5 Click Desktop Preview (▶) in the upper-right corner of the application window. Click the rectangle in the Preview window to see the keyboard slide onto the Memory artboard from the bottom. When finished previewing, you can close the Preview window.

6 Press Command+S (macOS) or Ctrl+S (Windows) to save the file.

● **Note:** To save on Windows, you may need to click back in the Travel_Design application window before saving.

7 If you plan on jumping to the next lesson or following the videos below, you can leave the Travel_Design.xd file open. Otherwise, choose File > Close (macOS) or click the X in the upper-right corner (Windows) for each open document.

● **Note:** If you started with the L8_start.xd file, then keep that file open.

Setting a timed trigger ■◀

To see how to set a timed trigger in Adobe XD, check out the video "Set a timed trigger," which is a part of the Web Edition of this book. For more information, see the "Web Edition" section of "Getting Started" at the beginning of the book.

Setting timed transition content ■◀

To see how to set timed transitions in Adobe XD, check out the video "Setting timed transitions," which is a part of the Web Edition of this book. For more information, see the "Web Edition" section of "Getting Started" at the beginning of the book.

Adding a voice trigger ■◀

To see how to work with a voice trigger in Adobe XD, check out the video "Setting up a voice trigger," which is a part of the Web Edition of this book. For more information, see the "Web Edition" section of "Getting Started" at the beginning of the book.

Adding speech playback ■◀

To see how to add speech playback in Adobe XD, check out the video "Speech playback," which is a part of the Web Edition of this book. For more information, see the "Web Edition" section of "Getting Started" at the beginning of the book.

Review questions

1 What is meant by the "home screen"?

2 What are the two types of connections you can make in your prototype?

3 How do you edit a connection in Prototype mode?

4 What is a trigger in a prototype?

5 For Auto-Animate to work properly between artboards, what must you ensure when it comes to the content that changes between the artboards?

6 Describe what fixed positioning does.

Review answers

1 The home screen is the first screen that users will encounter when they view your app or website prototype. By default, the home screen is the topmost, leftmost artboard (in that order).

2 The two types of connections you can make in your Adobe XD prototype are a connection between content and an artboard or a connection between an artboard and an artboard.

3 To edit a connection (link) in Prototype mode, you select either the content or artboard that is linked or all of the content. You can then drag a connector away from the linked content and release to remove it or drag a connector away from linked content to another artboard. With a connection selected, you can also edit the properties for the connection in the Property Inspector.

4 In a prototype, a trigger is an interaction you set that triggers or causes the transition from one screen to the next.

5 For Auto-Animate to work, the content that is meant to animate between artboards needs to have the same name in the Layers panel.

6 Fixed positioning allows you to set design objects to a fixed position on an artboard. This is useful for objects, such as a footer, that needs to stay in the same position relative to the viewable area as the page scrolls.

9 PREVIEWING A PROTOTYPE

Lesson overview

In this lesson, you'll learn how to do the following:

- Record prototype interactions.

- Preview on a device via USB.

- Preview a cloud document on a device.

 This lesson will take about 30 minutes to complete. To get the lesson files used in this chapter, download them from the web page for this book at www.adobepress.com/XDCIB2020. For more information, see "Accessing the lesson files and Web Edition" in the Getting Started section at the beginning of this book.

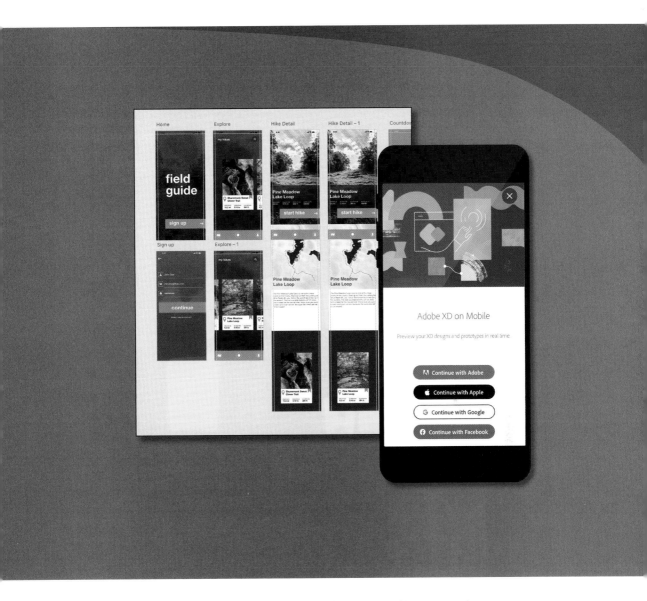

In this lesson, you'll preview a working prototype in Adobe XD, record prototype interactions that you can share with others as a video file, and use the Adobe XD mobile app on a device to preview your prototypes via USB and as a cloud document.

Starting the lesson

In this lesson, you'll test a working prototype from your app design locally as well as on a handheld device. To start, you'll open a final lesson file to get an idea for what you will create in this lesson.

Note: If you have not already downloaded the project files for this lesson to your computer from your Account page, make sure to do so now. See the "Getting Started" section at the beginning of the book.

Note: The screen shots for this lesson were taken on macOS. On Windows, the menus can be accessed by clicking the hamburger menu.

1 Start Adobe XD, if it's not already open.

2 On macOS, choose File > Open From Your Computer. On Windows, click the menu icon (≡) in the upper-left corner of the application window and choose Open From Your Computer. Open the file named L9_end.xd, which is in the Lessons > Lesson09 folder that you copied onto your hard disk.

Note: For either macOS or Windows, if the Home screen is showing with no files open, click Your Computer in the Home screen. Open the file named L9_end.xd, which is in the Lessons > Lesson09 folder that you copied onto your hard disk.

3 If the Assets panel opens on the left and you see a Missing Fonts message, close the panel by clicking Assets panel icon (⬚) in the lower left.

4 Press Command+0 (macOS) or Ctrl+0 (Windows) to see all of the design content. This file shows you what you will create by the end of the lesson.

5 Leave the file open for reference, or choose File > Close (macOS) or click the X in the upper-right corner of the open window (Windows) to close the file.

Recording a prototype

In Lesson 8, "Creating a Prototype," you were introduced to previewing a prototype within Adobe XD using the Preview window. At some point in the design process, you may also want to share your prototype with others. One way to share a prototype is to record prototype interactions and create a video in the MP4 format. In this section, you'll record a video of the prototype interactions in your Travel_Design file.

There are separate instructions for recording on macOS and Windows, so you only need to pay attention to the instructions that pertain to the operating system you are using.

1   Choose File > Open From Your Computer (macOS) or click the menu icon (≡) in the upper-left corner of the application window and choose Open From Your Computer (Windows). Open the Travel_Design.xd document in the Lessons folder (or where you saved it).

2   Click in the gray pasteboard to make sure everything is deselected.

    When you open the Preview window in the next section, with nothing selected, the Home artboard will show in the window.

● **Note:** If you are starting from scratch using the jumpstart method described in the section "Getting Started," open L9_start.xd from the Lessons > Lesson09 folder.

Recording on macOS

To start, macOS users will explore how to create a prototype recording. Windows users can jump to the next section, "Recording on Windows."

1   Click Desktop Preview (▶) in the upper-right corner of the application window to open the Preview window.

▶ **Tip:** You can also press Command+Return (macOS) or Ctrl+Enter (Windows) to open the Preview window.

2   Move the pointer into the Preview window and click the arrow to the right of the time-code (00:00) in the upper-right corner.

    By default, only video—not audio—is recorded. You can select Enable Microphone if you also want to record audio. Leave the microphone option deselected.

3   Press Esc to hide the options, then click the time-code (00:00) to start recording.

A message may appear, asking for permission to record. If you see this message, you will need to follow the instructions in the message window and grant access in the OS system preferences to allow XD to record. This process usually requires that you quit and restart XD.

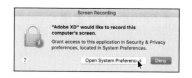

4 While recording, click the "sign up" button to transition to the Sign up screen.

When in the Preview window, while recording, the pointer shows as a circle, which makes it easier to see and follow along with in the video. Notice that the timer in the upper-right corner of the Preview window is changing, indicating that it's recording.

● **Note:** On macOS, recording also stops when you switch away from the application.

5 Press Esc to stop recording. In the dialog box that appears, make sure the filename is Travel_Design, navigate to the Lessons > Lesson09 folder (if you aren't there already), and click Save.

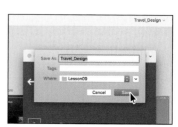

Recording prototype interactivity is easy using this method, which can make this a great way to share that interactivity with someone else. Once the video file is saved, you can share it via email and many other available options.

6 Close the Preview window.

macOS users can skip to the section "Previewing on a mobile device."

Recording on Windows

Recording prototypes is not directly supported in Adobe XD on Windows. However, there's a workaround using the native recorder to record what you do in the Preview window.

Note: To complete this section on Windows, you'll need to have the Game Bar app installed, which is available via the Microsoft Store.

1   Click Desktop Preview (▶) in the upper-right corner of the application window to open the Preview window.

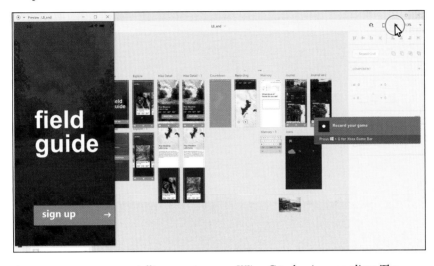

A message may appear, telling you to press Win+G to begin recording. The Windows Game Bar app, installed by default, will be used.

2   Move the pointer over the button in the upper-left corner of the Preview window and a tooltip appears. Press Win+G (Windows) to begin recording.

3   In the Game Bar that opens, click the Record From Now button (the black circle) to begin recording. The display should disappear, and a small toolbar with a timer and Stop button appear in the operating system. You can control the recording from there.

Tip: You can also enable the microphone in the Game Bar if you want to record the audio.

4 Move the pointer into the XD Preview window and click the "sign up" button to transition to the Sign up screen.

● **Note:** On Windows, recording doesn't automatically stop when you switch away from the application or when the Preview window does not have focus anymore.

5 Click Stop in the small floating toolbar to stop recording (an arrow is pointing to the toolbar in the following figure). You can also press Win+G and click the Stop button in the Game Bar that opens.

6 If you want to access the video that was created, you can press Win+G to show the Game Bar, if it isn't showing. You can then click Show All Captures to show your video captures in the Gallery.

Previewing on a mobile device

Previewing locally in Adobe XD using the Preview window can be an effective way to test links and get an idea of what your design will look like. To truly experience your prototype, you should test on a device such as an iPhone. The free Adobe XD mobile app lets you preview designs you create in Adobe XD on iOS and Android devices (see the note to the right).

There are two methods for testing on devices using the mobile app:

- **Real-time preview via USB:** You can connect multiple devices via USB to a computer that is running Adobe XD, make changes to your designs and prototypes on the desktop, and preview them in real time on all connected mobile devices.

- **Loading cloud documents from Creative Cloud** (available for documents created in Adobe XD on macOS or Windows 10+): If you save your XD documents as cloud documents, you can load them onto your devices using Adobe XD on mobile.

● **Note:** To learn more about system requirements for Adobe XD on mobile devices, check out this page: helpx.adobe.com/xd/system-requirements.html.

● **Note:** Real-time preview is supported between macOS and iOS or Android or between Windows 10+ and iOS (currently not Android).

Setting up the XD mobile app

In this section, you'll set up the Adobe XD mobile app on your device. There are a few things you will need in order to proceed:

- Internet access to download and sign in to the Adobe XD mobile app

- A free (trial) or paid Creative Cloud account (preferably the same Creative Cloud account you are using in Adobe XD)

- The free Adobe XD app from the iOS App Store for iOS (iPhones and iPads) or Google Play store (Android phones and tablets)

1   With the Adobe XD mobile app installed on your device, launch the app.

2   Use one of these methods to sign in to the Adobe XD app:

- If you have a free (trial) or paid Creative Cloud account, or if you want to create a free Adobe ID, click Continue with Adobe and log in with your usual Adobe ID.

- If you don't have a Creative Cloud account, click Continue with Apple, Continue with Google, or Continue with Facebook (to use an account you already have with one of those services).

After signing in, you will see the app home screen. By default, on the home screen, you'll see all of your cloud documents saved to Creative Cloud. If you haven't saved any cloud documents, the screen will resemble the figure to the right. You'll learn more about saving a document as a cloud document in Lesson 10, "Sharing Your Designs."

At the bottom of the screen (circled in the figure) you'll see options for Cloud Documents (which is selected by default), Shared with You, Live Preview, and Settings. The Live Preview option is for previewing a file on your device that's open in the Adobe XD desktop (when connected via USB), and the Settings option is where you can log out, check storage usage, and more.

Setting up preview via USB

Previewing via USB, or Live Preview, is available on macOS and Windows (currently, if your device is running Adobe XD on Windows 10, real-time preview through USB is not supported on Android). In this section, you'll test the Travel_Design.xd prototype that is open in Adobe XD on your device.

1 Connect your mobile device to the USB port of the computer running Adobe XD on the desktop.

   Make sure the copy of Adobe XD on your desktop machine is up to date by checking the Creative Cloud desktop app.

2 Tap the Live Preview option at the bottom of the screen.

   The Live Preview screen opens, and instructions may appear in the center of the screen telling you to connect the device to your desktop and/or open an XD document in XD on desktop.

3 Ensure that Adobe XD is showing on your desktop computer and that the Travel_Design.xd file is also showing. The home screen (or currently selected screen) should appear in the mobile app on your device.

4 A message may appear on screen telling you to triple tap to access a menu. Tap the device screen to close the message.

Note: In the figures in this section, the design prototype has black borders when previewing in the mobile app on a device. That's because the artboard size in the design file is set to iPhone X/XS and I'm previewing the prototype on an iPhone 8 Plus.

If the open document in XD on the desktop doesn't appear on your device, you can disconnect and reconnect to the USB port on your machine. You can also close and then launch the Adobe XD app on your mobile device.

An iPhone connected to my laptop via a USB cable

Note: If you are testing on an Android device with macOS, make sure it is set to transfer data through the USB port, not just to transfer power (charging mode). Visit this page to learn more: helpx.adobe.com/xd/help/adobe-xd-on-mobile-faq.html#Android.

Note: In Adobe XD on the desktop, you may see a notification explaining that fonts will be sent to your device(s) when you preview on mobile. If you see this message, click OK. Please be aware that certain font vendors do not allow for the transfer, display, and distribution of their fonts. You are responsible for ensuring that you respect the font license agreement you have with the font vendor.

5   You may also see a message about missing fonts. To see the fonts that are missing, tap SHOW. The missing font or fonts will appear in a list. Since I am previewing an XD file that was originally created on Windows, on my Mac, Segoe UI is missing. Any missing fonts are substituted with available fonts.

6   In Adobe XD on the desktop, you can close the Preview window if it's still open. Click Device Preview (▢) in the upper-right corner of the application window to see a list of connected devices.

macOS   Windows

If there are multiple devices connected via USB to your desktop machine and they're set up to transfer data, they will all appear in the Preview On Device window.

Navigating the XD mobile app

With the XD mobile app set up and your Travel_Design.xd project file showing in the app, next you'll navigate the app and explore some of the features available.

1   With the Home screen of your prototype showing on your device, tap an area of the screen where there are no links to see blue hotspot hints appear. You may need to tap a few times at first to clear a message about tapping with three fingers to show the menu. An arrow is pointing to the hotspot hint in the following figure.

2   Tap the "sign up" button on the Home screen to go to the sign up form.

    By default, blue hotspot hints appear where you created connections in your prototype in Adobe XD. You can turn off hotspot hints in the mobile app settings.

3   Back in your Travel_Design file in Adobe XD on the desktop, zoom in to the Home artboard a bit. With the Select tool (▶) selected, drag

▶ **Tip:** You can easily turn off the blue hotspot hints you saw in the previous section by triple tapping (to show options), and then tapping the Hotspot Hints toggle.

● **Note:** If you rotate your device, the screens will scale to fit, with letterboxing (black bars) around them, if necessary.

the "sign up" button on the Home artboard down a little, to see the mobile app preview change in real time.

4   Save the document in XD by pressing Command+S (macOS) or Ctrl+S (Windows).

5   Back on your device in the Adobe XD mobile app, tap three times (triple tap) on the device screen to open the menu.

The Adobe XD mobile app has a series of settings available in a menu that appears. These settings can make navigating a larger prototype easier, allow you to take screen shots, toggle options, and more.

6   Tap Browse artboards to see all of the artboards. This is a way to jump around in the document when previewing it.

7   Tap the Explore artboard to open it in the app.

8   Triple tap on the device screen again to open the menu. Tap Exit Prototype to return to the app home screen.

At this point, you can resume the preview by tapping Resume Preview or navigate elsewhere.

9 Disconnect the USB cable from the device.

Since you will load a cloud file in the next section, you won't need to have the cable connected. If you want to return to a live preview of an open XD document, you will need to reconnect the USB cable.

You can unplug the USB cable and continue viewing and testing a cached version of the prototype. Without a connection, however, there will no longer be real-time updating if changes are made in Adobe XD on the desktop. If you reconnect the cable while in the same session and with the design file still open in Adobe XD, the app screen will refresh on your device.

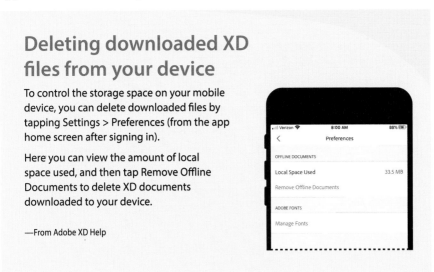

Deleting downloaded XD files from your device

To control the storage space on your mobile device, you can delete downloaded files by tapping Settings > Preferences (from the app home screen after signing in).

Here you can view the amount of local space used, and then tap Remove Offline Documents to delete XD documents downloaded to your device.

—From Adobe XD Help

Previewing cloud documents

In the Adobe XD mobile app, you can also view a cloud document stored on Creative Cloud. To open a cloud document in the mobile app, that cloud document needs to be shared with you or you need to save a document as a cloud document in Adobe XD on the desktop, which is what you'll do next.

● **Note:** To perform this step, you will need access to the storage that comes with your Creative Cloud membership.

1 In Adobe XD on the desktop, with the Travel_Design file open, choose File > Save As (macOS) or click the menu icon (≡) in the upper-left corner of the application window and choose Save As (Windows). In the menu of options that appears, change the name to **Travel_Design_cloud**.

2 Select Cloud Documents in the Save To section, and then click Save.

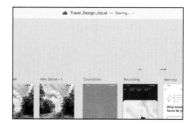

In the title bar above the document, a cloud icon (☁) appears to the left of the name above the document, indicating that it's a cloud document. You may see "Saving..." to the right of the filename in the title bar above the document. When a document has finished saving to Creative Cloud (which may take some time), "Saving" will disappear. The file won't show in the XD mobile app until it has finished saving in Adobe XD on the desktop.

By saving an XD document as a cloud document, you are saving it to a destination called Cloud Documents, which is hosted on Creative Cloud. To view a cloud design file saved in Creative Cloud, you do not need to have your mobile device connected to the USB port of the computer running Adobe XD on the desktop. All you need is an active Internet connection on the device.

● **Note:** Saving the document as a cloud document may take some time, depending on your Internet speed.

3 In the Adobe XD mobile app on your device, with the main app screen showing, tap Cloud Documents (☁) at the bottom of the screen (circled in the first part of the following figure).

Files saved as cloud documents cannot be viewed if there is no Internet connection on the device.

4 In the file list that appears, tap Travel_Design_cloud to load the document.

Note: The list of files you see may be different from those in the figure.

Tip: To refresh the list of XD cloud documents synced with Creative Cloud or to update documents already in the list that you've edited and saved in Adobe XD, pull the XD Documents screen down and release.

5 Triple tap your device screen to open the Adobe XD menu. Tap Exit Prototype to return to the mobile app home screen, where you will see the list of cloud documents again.

Now you'll explore what happens when you update the XD file in Adobe XD.

6 In your Travel_Design_cloud file in Adobe XD on the desktop, with the Select tool (▶) selected, make a simple change to the Home artboard. Maybe move the "sign up" button on the Home artboard, as you did previously.

Note: You may see a message telling you that you can tap three times to see a menu. You can tap the screen with one finger to dismiss it, if necessary.

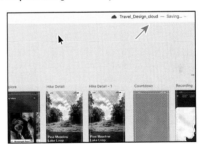

After making the change, you'll see an asterisk (*) to the right of the name in the title bar above the document, indicating that you made a change. If you make a change to the design file in Adobe XD on the desktop, cloud documents are auto-saved. After a short time, you should see "Saving" to the right of the document name in the title bar. The file will update in the app, assuming you have an Internet connection and aren't currently viewing it. You can also make a cloud document available offline. That means it will download in its current state and you can view it whether or not you have an active Internet connection.

Note: The list of cloud documents will update automatically without you having to pull to refresh the screen, but that may take some time, depending on your Internet connection.

7 Back on your device, in the XD app, with the cloud document list showing, drag the screen down to refresh the list. This is a faster way to get the list to update with the latest version of the file.

As stated earlier in this section, you will need to be connected to the Internet to view the cloud documents and update them. What happens if you need to view a cloud document and you know you won't have an active Internet connection when you need to view it? You can set cloud documents in the app to download to the device for offline viewing later.

8 Tap the ellipsis (...) to the right of the Travel_Design_cloud name in the app (circled in the following figure).

9 Tap Available Offline to turn the option on. The document is downloaded in the current state and will be available for offline viewing. Tap in a blank area of the screen to hide the menu at the bottom of the screen.

Note: If you are viewing the cloud document in the XD mobile app and the document has been updated in Adobe XD on the desktop, a message may appear, when you have an Internet connection, asking if you would like to update the file on your device.

The Travel_Design_cloud document is downloaded to the device, and a blue circle with a white arrow now appears on the filename in the app. When Available Offline is set for a cloud document, any further changes made to the document in Adobe XD will be applied as long as there is an Internet connection. When the Internet connection is unavailable, the document remains in its last saved state before losing Internet. As soon as an Internet connection is available again, the cloud document can be updated, even though it's still set to Available Offline.

Note: Using the Adobe XD mobile app, you can also view files shared with you.

10 Close the app on your device and return to Adobe XD on your desktop.

Document history

As you work with cloud documents (not locally saved documents) you can see a history of the changes made to the document. Document history lets you open previous versions of that document so you can copy elements to the current document or save out a previous version and pick up your work from there. Your document's history is available for up to 30 days and you can "mark" specific versions to save those history states indefinitely. You can also name versions to keep track of important milestones throughout a design project.

1   With the Travel_Design_cloud document still open, click the image below the Icons artboard and press Delete or Backspace to remove it.

Note: The figures show working in Design mode. You can also perform the steps in this section in Prototype mode.

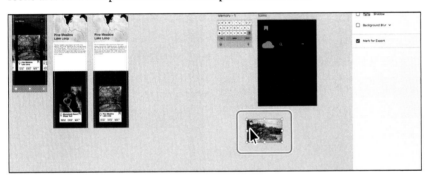

2   Click the artboard name "Journal ver2" in the document window and press Delete or Backspace to remove it. The cloud document will automatically save the changes for you.

3   To see the history for the document, above the document click the arrow to the right of the document name "Travel_Design_cloud."

A menu appears showing versions of history states that you have marked or saved for longer than 30 days, the history states that are saved automatically, and

Note: You may see different history states and that's okay.

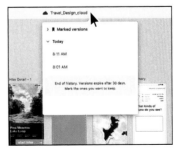

a message. In order to go back in time and see what a previous version of the document looks like, you can choose to open one of the history states in a new window.

4 To see a previous version of the document, move the pointer over the earliest time stamp in the list. I see "8:01 am" because that was the time when XD first auto-saved the document. Click the ellipses (···) and choose Open In A New Window.

The saved version of the document opens in a new window and is a separate cloud document that will have its own history if you begin editing it.

5 Close the version that opened to return to the Travel_Design_cloud document.

6 Click the arrow to the right of the document name "Travel_Design_cloud" again. This time, to save one of the history states so you can access it for more than 30 days, you can mark it. Move the pointer over the earliest time stamp and click the Mark Version icon (▌). Change the name to "Image and Journal Ver 2 artboard" and press Return or Enter to accept the name.

7 Click the arrow to the left of the Marked Versions in the drop down to show the marked history state.

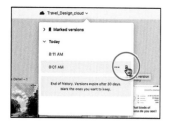  

To open the marked history state in a separate document, you could click the ellipses (···) and you'll see the same options as before.

8 Choose File > Close (macOS) or click the X in the upper-right corner (Windows) for each open document.

Review questions

1   How do you record interactivity in your prototype in Adobe XD on the desktop?

2   What file format does Adobe XD create when recording interactivity in your prototype?

3   What are the two ways you can preview an XD document in the Adobe XD mobile app?

4   Which method of previewing in the mobile app, via USB or viewing a Creative Cloud file, allows for real-time updates?

5   What is a cloud document?

6   With what type of document can you view document history (cloud or local)?

Review answers

1   To record interactivity in Adobe XD on desktop, click Desktop Preview in the upper-right corner of the application. On macOS, click the time code (00:00) to begin recording. After having tested the prototype, press Esc to stop recording. In the dialog that appears, name the video file and click Save. On Windows, after the Preview window is open, press Win+G to begin recording. You can start recording in the Game Bar that appears. After you have finished recording, press Win+G again and click Stop.

2   When recording prototypes, the video file format is MP4.

3   When previewing an XD document in the XD mobile app, either you can view documents saved as cloud documents or you can view an open document in Adobe XD on the desktop using Live Preview.

4   Only previewing via USB in the mobile app allows for real-time updates.

5   A cloud document is an XD document that is saved in Creative Cloud from the Adobe XD desktop app.

6   In order to see the history of a document, the document must be a cloud document.

10 SHARING YOUR DESIGNS

Lesson overview

In this lesson, you'll learn how to do the following:

- Understand the different methods of sharing.

- Share your cloud documents.

- Share your prototype for review.

- Update a shared prototype.

- Comment on a shared prototype.

- Share design specs.

- Update design specs.

- Manage shared links.

 This lesson will take about 60 minutes to complete. To get the lesson files used in this chapter, download them from the web page for this book at www.adobepress.com/XDCIB2020. For more information, see "Accessing the lesson files and Web Edition" in the Getting Started section at the beginning of this book.

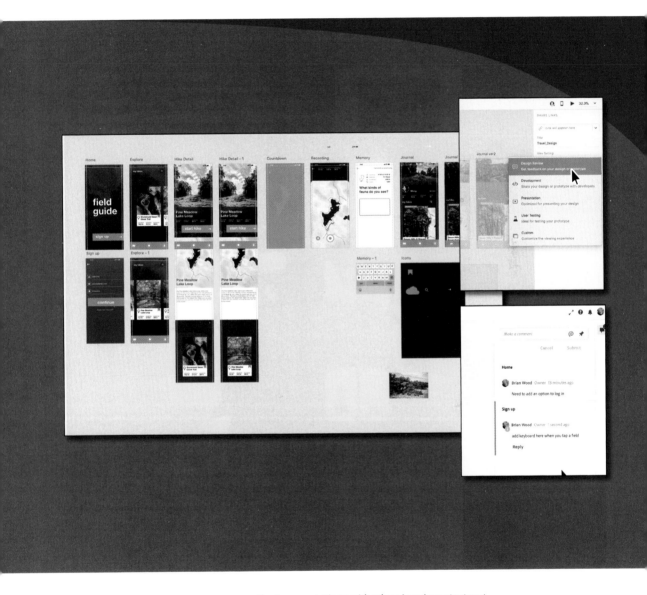

Sharing your projects with others is an important part of the design cycle because it allows for collaborative editing, gathering feedback through comments, sharing design specifications, and more. In this lesson, you'll learn how to share your documents in different ways, depending on your needs.

Starting the lesson

In this lesson, you'll learn about different methods for sharing your prototype, learn how to work with comments, and manage your shared prototypes.

● **Note:** If you have not already downloaded the project files for this lesson to your computer from your Account page, make sure to do so now. See the "Getting Started" section at the beginning of the book.

1 Start Adobe XD, if it's not already open.

2 On macOS, choose File > Open From Your Computer. On Windows, click the menu icon (≡) in the upper-left corner of the application window and choose Open From Your Computer. Open the non-cloud document from Lesson 9, Travel_Design.xd, in the Lessons folder (or where you saved it).

● **Note:** For either macOS or Windows, if the Home screen is showing with no files open, click Your Computer in the Home screen. Open the non-cloud document Travel_Design.xd in the Lessons folder (or where you saved it).

● **Note:** If you are starting from scratch using the jumpstart method described in the section "Getting Started," open L10_start.xd from the Lessons > Lesson10 folder.

3 If the Assets panel opens on the left and you see a Missing Fonts message, close the panel by clicking Assets panel icon (▢) in the lower left.

4 Press Command+0 (macOS) or Ctrl+0 (Windows) to see all of the design content. Leave the file open.

● **Note:** The screen shots for this lesson were taken on macOS. On Windows, the menus can be accessed by clicking the hamburger menu.

Methods of sharing

If you need to share designs and prototypes with others—to invite collaborators to edit a cloud document, gather feedback on a design or prototype, create a presentation, or share design specifications with a developer—you can use Share mode from within the desktop version of Adobe XD. You may choose to share at any point during the design process, from an in-progress design with no interactivity to a fully interactive prototype.

Adobe XD has several default sharing presets that you can use, including:

- **Design Review:** Get feedback on your design or prototype. By default, when viewing in-browser, commenting is enabled and the prototype is not in fullscreen mode.

- **Development:** Share your design or prototype with developers. By default, when viewing in-browser, commenting is enabled and the prototype is not in fullscreen mode. Specs mode is also available in browser for viewing project specifications.

- **Presentation:** Optimized for presenting your design.

- **User Testing:** Ideal for testing your prototype. By default, when viewing in-browser, commenting is NOT enabled and the prototype is in fullscreen mode.

- **Custom**: Customize the viewing experience.

The following table represents the features available in each of the presets:

Design Review	Development	Presentation	User Testing	Custom
✓ Commenting	✓ Commenting	✓ Hotspot hints	✓ Full screen	✓ Commenting
✓ Hotspot hints	✓ Hotspot hints	✓ Navigation controls	✕ Commenting	✓ Hotspot hints
✓ Navigation controls	✓ Navigation controls	✓ Full screen	✕ Hotspot hints	✓ Navigation controls
✕ Full screen	✓ Design specs	✕ Commenting	✕ Navigation controls	✓ Full screen
	✕ Full screen			

As a designer, you can share your designs or prototypes using any of the available sample presets. As a reviewer, you can access the review invite from the Creative Cloud application or email and comment on shared designs or prototypes. A final method for sharing is called sharing a cloud document, which you'll explore first.

Sharing a cloud document

In Lesson 2, "Setting Up a Project," you learned what cloud documents are. In Lesson 9, "Previewing a Prototype," you learned how to save an XD document as a cloud document. In this section, you'll save another document as a cloud document and share it with a user. In order to follow along in this section, you will need to have another XD user that you can send the file to. That way, they can make edits and you will see how the process works. If you don't, you can simply read along.

Cloud documents are XD's cloud-native document type, providing users with a fast and convenient method to manage, share, and retain up-to-date documents. You can save your XD designs as cloud documents to ensure that they are up to date and accessible even when you're offline. You can then share them with other Creative Cloud users and invite those users to collaborate. To share the Travel_Design document with someone else so that they can make edits, the document must first be saved as a cloud document.

Note: To access the sharing window, it doesn't matter which mode is showing, Design, Prototype, or Share. Design mode appears in the figures.

1 Click the Invite To Document icon (⊕) in the upper-right corner of the application window.

   In the window that appears, you will most likely see a message that tells you that the document needs to be saved to the cloud first.

2 Click Continue in the window.

Note: On Windows, the Save options window will appear in the center of the document window.

3 In the Save options window that opens, change the name to **Travel_Design_share**. With the Cloud Documents option selected, click Save.

After the document is saved to Creative Cloud, you can share it with others. In the Share window, after the document has been saved, you will see a place where you can add people to share it with. Type an email address for each person you would like to share the document with. Add a comma (,) between each email address if you want to send it to more than one person.

4 Enter an email address in the field.

If you enter an email address that you've previously entered, you may see it appear below the field. You may not see it now since it may be the first time you are sharing a document.

Once you share a document, collaborators receive a notification from the Creative Cloud desktop application as well as via email. Your recipient will only receive a notification in the Creative Cloud desktop application if you enter the email address that serves as their username for their Creative Cloud membership.

5   Add a message in the Message field.

The message is optional, and the user will see the message in an email that he or she receives.

6   Click Invite.

After XD sends the invite, you, as the initiator, will see a message indicating that it has sent.

7   Click the Invite To Document icon () in the upper-right corner of the application window again. In the window, you'll now see a listing of users you've shared the cloud document with, including the owner (most likely you).

This is one place where you can track who has access to the document. You can also remove invited collaborators from the shared cloud document. To do so, you would move the pointer over an email address in the list (not the owner) and click Remove. You would then need to click Save to remove them.

8 Press the Esc key to hide the window.

If an invited collaborator opens the Creative Cloud desktop app, that user will see a notification and can click to open the file. That collaborator can also open the cloud document from the email he or she receives.

In the upper-right corner, near the Invite To Document icon ( ), if another user has the document open at the same time, you will see an icon. If you move the pointer over the icon, you will see the name of that user.

All invited collaborators can edit your document and save changes to the original file. If a collaborator makes a change to the shared document and the file is saved, the owner will receive a message indicating that there's a newer version of the document available, and vice versa.

If more than one collaborator has simultaneously opened the document, the changes, made by the first collaborator are updated to the cloud document, and the second collaborator is given an option to save as a separate document.

The changes can be accepted to reload the document with the new changes or a copy of the document with their changes can be saved.

9 Choose File > Close (macOS) or click the X in the upper-right corner (Windows) to close the Travel_Design_share document and open to the Travel_Design.xd file again.

Coediting (beta)

Coediting allows multiple users to work on a single project file at the same time without worrying about duplicating work or maintaining redundant documents. As of this writing, the feature is in beta, which means it may not be feature complete.

Coediting is available when working on cloud documents in XD. With coediting enabled for a document, you can invite others to edit the document.

You can see when other users are active in the document and which artboards and objects they're currently editing.

Coediting ▰◀

To see how coediting works in Adobe XD, check out the video "Coediting," which is a part of the Web Edition of this book. For more information, see the "Web Edition" section of "Getting Started" at the beginning of the book.

Sharing a prototype or design for review

In this section, you'll share the Travel_Design.xd prototype to gather feedback about the design and user experience. You can share a document that is either a cloud document or saved locally. To share a prototype that is local, you will enter Share mode. Share mode in XD consolidates different sharing capabilities into the Property Inspector on the right. There are a few things to consider before sharing your document:

- First, set the Home artboard in Prototype mode if you want only artboards with direct or indirect connections to the Home artboard shared.

- Wire the artboards in the order that you want users to navigate them. Artboards that are wired and not connected to the Home artboard will be dimmed in Share mode.

● **Note:** For artboards that aren't wired, the navigation sequence defaults from left to right or top to bottom. If you want to change the navigation sequence, go back to Prototype mode and wire them again.

● **Note:** To share prototypes using the Adobe XD Share feature, you must be signed in with an Adobe account to the Adobe Creative Cloud app or any other Adobe application.

▶ **Tip:** If you don't set the Home artboard, all artboards will be shared.

1   With the Travel_Design.xd document open, click Share in the upper-left corner of the application window to show Share mode.

For the Travel_Design.xd document, there are a series of connections (wires) between the artboards, but there is currently only one artboard, the Sign up artboard, that is connected to the Home artboard. That is why the artboards besides the Home and Sign up are dimmed. They will not be shared. Any artboards that have direct or indirect connections to the artboard set as Home are a part of the shared prototype and can be viewed in the browser. Next, you'll make a connection from the Sign up artboard to the Explore artboard.

2   Click Prototype in the upper-left corner to enter Prototype mode.

3   Click the continue button on the Sign up artboard. Drag the connecting handle (◉) to the Explore artboard and release.

4 In the Property Inspector, ensure that the following are set:

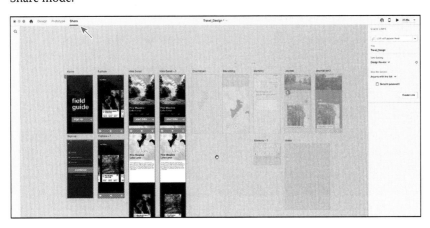

- Trigger: **Tap** (the default setting)
- Action: **Transition**
- Preserve Scroll Position: **unselected**
- Destination: **Explore**
- Animation: **Slide Left**
- Easing: **Ease Out**
- Duration: **0.3**
- Fix Position When Scrolling: **unselected**

With the Sign up artboard connected to the Explore artboard, more artboards should be available for sharing now.

5 Click Share in the upper-left corner of the application window to enter Share mode.

You should now see more artboards that are not dimmed since the Explore artboard was already connected to the Explore – 1 artboard, which was connected to the Hike Detail artboard, and so on.

6 In the Property Inspector on the right, set the following options:

- Choose **Design Review** from the View Setting menu since the main reason for sharing in this example is to gather design feedback. The options in the menu are those that were discussed at the beginning of this lesson. See the introductory paragraphs of the section "Methods of sharing."

- Ensure that **Anyone With The Link** is chosen from the Who Has Access menu. You can make the shared prototype accessible by anyone who has a browser and Internet connection, or you can choose Only Invited People from the same menu to send an email invite to certain people.

- Title: **Travel_Design app** (The title appears when viewing the shared prototype in a browser as well as when managing your shared links. Naming can be a useful way to distinguish between versions of a shared project, for instance.)

- Require Password: **unselected** (You can restrict access to your prototypes and design specs by adding password protection. You can password-protect new prototypes or design specs only.)

● **Note:** The prototype might take a little while to publish, depending on your Internet speed.

7 Click Create Link to create a shared project.

Once the prototype is created and saved to Creative Cloud, the Create Link button turns into the Update Link button.

To view the prototype in the default browser on your system, you could click the blue link.

To share a link to the prototype with others, you could click the Copy Link icon (⬦). With the link copied, you can paste it into an email, for instance, to share with others.

8 Click the link toward the top of the window to open the prototype in the default browser on your machine.

The prototype opens in the default browser on your machine. The prototype home screen will be centered in the browser window and will be the size of the artboard named "Home" in Adobe XD (in this case).

For a list of supported browsers, visit helpx.adobe.com/xd/system-requirements.html.

In the upper-right corner of the web page, you'll see a way to make the preview fullscreen (⤢). Fullscreen hides all UI elements in the browser window (to exit fullscreen mode, press the Esc key), a help and feedback icon (❷), a notifications icon (🔔), and a place to sign in (or sign out if you're already signed in).

Below the home screen, you'll see left and right arrows for navigating between artboards, a home icon (🏠) to return to the home screen, and an artboard counter, which currently shows 6 (or so). If your design includes connections, only those artboards connected directly or indirectly (through other artboards) to the home artboard are uploaded and shared.

To view this shared project, you don't need to be signed in with an Adobe ID. Anyone with access to the link can view the prototype in a desktop browser or in a browser on their device.

9 Interact with the prototype by clicking anywhere in the home screen to see the hotspot hints available. Click the "sign up" button on the home screen to navigate to the next artboard.

10 Click the home icon (🏠) below the artboard to return to the prototype Home screen.

11 Close the browser window and return to Adobe XD.

Updating a shared prototype

After sharing a prototype, you may decide that you want to make changes to the content or change the home screen to share only a portion of the prototype. After making changes to your project, you can share the project again. You will then be able to either create a new shared prototype or update the existing prototype. Creating a new shared prototype can be a great way to create versions of your prototypes.

Next, you'll update the Travel_Design prototype by changing the dark status bars on the Home and Explore artboards to white status bars so they are more readable.

1 Back in Adobe XD, click Design in the upper-left corner of the application window so you can edit the content.

2   Zoom in to the Home and Explore artboards.

3   With the Assets panel showing (Command+Shift+Y [macOS] or Ctrl+Shift+Y [Windows]), find the white status Bar component in the panel—you may need to scroll. Drag the white status Bar onto the black status bar at the top of the Home artboard. When the status bar highlights, release to replace it.

4   Replace the status bar at the top of the Explore artboard using the same process.

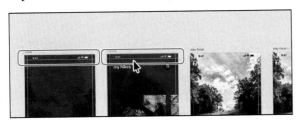

5   Press Command+S (macOS) or Ctrl+S (Windows) to save the file.

    Now that changes have been made, you'll update the link to the prototype.

6   Click Share in the upper-left corner of the application window to return to Share mode.

7   In the Property Inspector on the right, ensure that the title is Travel_Design app and leave the rest of the settings at default. Click the Update Link button.

    The shared prototype has now been updated to reflect the changes. Users you already shared the link with can simply refresh the prototype in the browser.

Note: The prototype might take a little while to publish, depending on your Internet speed.

8 Click the arrow to the right of the Update
   Link button to show some options.

   In the menu that appears, you can choose
   either Copy Link to copy the link or Copy
   Embed code. To learn more about embed
   code, see the sidebar, "Embedding a shared
   prototype in a web page."

9 Click the arrow to the right of the URL link
   toward the top of the window.

   In the menu that appears, you can manage
   your links, create a new link—which would
   create a new prototype link with a different
   title that you could also share with others—
   and see a list of prototype links already
   created that you could click to visit in
   the browser.

10 Press the Esc key to hide the menu and
   click the link toward the top of the Property
   Inspector to view the prototype in your
   default browser. An arrow is pointing to it in the previous figure.

When the prototype opens in the browser, the first screen you'll see is the Home
artboard with the new status bar.

11 Close the browser window and return to Adobe XD.

Embedding a shared prototype in a web page

Prototypes you share in Adobe XD can be embedded in any web page that supports inline frames (iframes). This can be useful if you want to showcase work you've done in Adobe XD in a web portfolio, for instance.

Here's how you copy embed code for a *previously* shared prototype from an open Adobe XD file:

- In Adobe XD, with Share mode showing, click the arrow to the right of the Update Link button. Choose Copy Embed Code from the menu.

When the code for embedding is copied to the clipboard, a message, "Code Copied," appears below the button.

With the code copied, you can paste it in the code of a web page or send it to someone else. Below is an example of embed code:

<iframe width="414" height="896" src="https://xd.adobe.com/embed/e3e6b68d-8ba7-4834-73fe-0ba09a5c4386-95d7/" frameborder="0" allowfullscreen></iframe>

Commenting on a shared prototype

When you share a project in Adobe XD using the Design Review, Development, or Custom settings, the shared prototype is set to allow for commenting. Commenting is done in-browser when the shared prototype is viewed, and guest commenting is allowed, which means anyone can comment because they don't need to be signed in with an Adobe ID. After you receive comments, you can go back to Adobe XD and update your prototype, based on those comments. After making changes to the prototype, you can share it again by updating the existing prototype or creating a new version. In this section, you'll view the shared Travel_Design app prototype in the browser, this time focusing on working with commenting.

1 In Adobe XD, with the Travel_Design app document open and Share mode showing, in the Property Inspector, click the link toward the top to open the prototype in your default browser again.

In the browser you should see a comment icon (💬) in the upper-right corner of the browser window.

● **Note:** If you are not signed in when the page opens, click Sign In and sign in with your Adobe ID. To learn more about guest commenting, see the "Guest commenting" sidebar.

2   If the Comments panel isn't already showing, click the comment icon (💬) on the right to open the Comments panel.

3   Click in the field that shows the text "Make a comment," and type **Need to add an option to log in** and either click the Submit button or press Return or Enter to add the comment. Leave the prototype open in the browser for the next section.

● **Note:** Any users who are currently viewing the prototype will see the comments added without having to refresh the page. If you find that new comments from other users are not showing, you can refresh the web page and show the Comments panel again.

The comment will appear in the Comments panel. If you are signed in with your Adobe ID and you initiated the review, you will see "Owner" next to your name. As the owner, you can add, reply to, delete, and resolve your comments or guest comments.

Guest commenting

When viewing a shared prototype in a browser, with the comments showing, reviewers can either sign in using their Adobe ID or sign in as a guest when commenting on a shared project.

To sign in as a guest, reviewers click Comment As A Guest at the bottom of the Comments panel. They supply a name and select I'm Not A Robot for the Captcha. They can then click Submit.

If, after commenting as a guest, a user ends the session by closing or refreshing the browser, he or she will have no control over the previous guest comments they made. On the other hand, if reviewers sign in using their Adobe ID, they can edit their previous comments.

Pinning comments

Pinning comments is a great way to visually associate a comment with a specific area of an artboard. When you pin a comment, Adobe XD assigns a number to that comment. The comments in the Comments panel show these numbers, so you can easily identify which comment is associated with which number on the artboard. Generic comments, like the first comment you added, are not pinned and do not show a number. Next, you'll add another comment and pin it to an artboard.

1   With the shared prototype still showing in the browser, click the "sign up" button on the prototype Home screen to show the next screen.

The comments from the previous artboard are still showing in the Comments panel because the All Screen Comments option in the Comments panel is selected. The comments are organized by screen, and you can see the name of the screen in the Comments panel list. If you only wanted to see the unique comments for a specific artboard, you could deselect All Screen Comments— but do not do so right now.

> **Tip:** If you click a name, such as Home, in a comment, that screen will show in the browser.

2   Click in the field that shows the text "Make a comment," and type **add keyboard here when you tap a field**.

3   Click the Pin icon (📍) that appears below the comment.

> **Tip:** While pinning a comment, you can press the Esc key to cancel pinning.

4 Move the pointer over the Sign up screen, and click at the bottom to set a comment pin. You can drag the number where you want it on the screen.

5 Click Submit in the Comments panel to accept the comment.

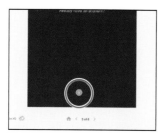 

The number associated with the comment is a visual way to locate the comment in the Comments panel and in the shared project.

6 Click the Pin icon (✦) in the Comments panel, move the pointer onto the screen, and click just above the "John Doe" text to set the comment pin.

7 Type **make text larger** in the comment field of the Comments panel. Click Submit in the Comments panel.

8 Move the pointer over the first comment marker (1) at the bottom of the screen to subtly highlight the associated comment in the Comments panel.

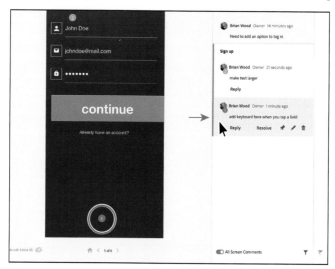

When there are a number of pinned comments, this can help you find the comment associated with a comment pin in the Comments panel.

9 Leave the prototype open in the browser.

Working with comments

With comments added to the artboards in your shared prototype, in this section you'll explore replying to comments and deleting comments in that same prototype.

1 With the prototype still open in the browser and the Comments panel showing, move the pointer over the comment marked "2" in the comments list on the right to see the corresponding pin highlighted in the prototype.

Tip: To view the prototype in the browser without comment pins on the artboards, hide the Comments panel by clicking the comment icon (🗩).

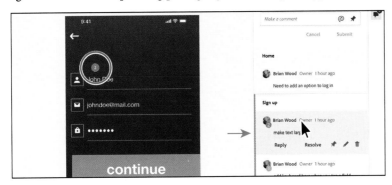

Comments in your shared prototype can be edited, deleted, replied to, and marked as resolved.

2 Move the pointer over the pin icon for comment 2 (next to the John Doe text) and drag it down to the right of the "Already have an account?" text.

This is an easy way to edit the location of a comment pin.

3 Move the pointer over the same comment in the comments list. Click the Edit Comment icon (✏) below the comment to change it. Change the comment from "make text larger" to **"Make text larger and bold."** Click Save.

▶ **Tip:** If you want to delete a comment, you can click the trash can icon (🗑) and verify you want to delete the comment.

Not only can you edit comments, but you and others can reply to comments. Next, you'll add a reply to the same comment, marked "2."

4 Move the pointer over the comment marked "2" in the comments list. Click Reply to add a reply to the original comment. Type **How about changing the text color instead?** and press Return or Enter to add the reply.

5 Click the small arrow to the left of the "1 Reply" text to collapse the comment reply.

Replies to comments appear under initial comments. Comment replies will be collapsed when viewed by other commentators and will need to be expanded to be viewable.

Note: You can't edit other reviewers' comments. The owner can delete guest comments, but guests cannot delete or edit comments by others.

6 Move the pointer over the comment labeled "2" and click Resolve.

Marking a comment as resolved removes it from the list of comments. This method can be used as a way to mark comments as "done," for example. Resolved comments can still be viewed by filtering the comments list, which is what you'll do next.

7 Click the Filter icon (▼) toward the bottom of the Comments panel to see a window with filtering options. Click Resolved in the Status section of the window to see any comments that have been marked as resolved.

▶ **Tip:** When viewing resolved comments, you can also unresolve a resolved comment by moving the pointer over the comment and clicking the Move To Unresolved button in the Comments panel.

There are several useful filtering options in the window that is showing, including filtering by reviewer and time. Notice that the filter icon (▼) now has an indicator that one or more filters have been applied.

8 Click in a blank area of the browser to close the filter window. Move the pointer over the comment in the Comments panel and click Move To Unresolved when it appears.

The comment should now be back in the main comments list. To see those comments, you'll clear the Resolved filter.

9 To clear the Resolved comment filter so you can see other comments, click Clear Filter in the Comments panel.

Comments added by users are stored with the shared prototype. To see comments from a previous version of a shared project, you would need to manage your shared links, which you'll do next.

10 Close the browser window and return to Adobe XD.

Sharing designs or prototypes with developers

As you near the end of the design process and get ready to move to development outside of Adobe XD, you can share the design or prototype by publishing design specs. This creates a public URL that you can share with others. These specs can improve communication by allowing developers to view the sequence and flow of artboards, as well as detailed specs for each artboard, complete with measurements, colors, character styles, relative spacing between elements, and more.

In this section, you'll share design specs and explore the design specs in your default browser. A part of sharing design specs with others is to allow assets to be downloaded with the design specs open in the browser. To allow users to download assets, you need to mark assets for export in the Layers panel, which is what you'll do first. You do not need to mark assets for export to share design specs.

1 Click Design in the upper-left corner of the application window to show Design mode, if it isn't already showing.

2 Open the Layers panel by pressing Command+Y (macOS) or Ctrl+Y (Windows), if it isn't already showing.

3 With the Select tool selected, on the Home artboard, click the gradient-filled rectangle behind the "field guide" text. You should now see the edges of the image behind it. Click the image area outside of the artboard or click the image in the Layers panel list.

4 In the Layers panel, move the pointer over the selected image in the list of layers. You should see that the Mark For Export icon (⏏) is toggled on.

By default, objects will automatically be marked for export when you import images from Photoshop and Illustrator. You can also select an object on your artboard and mark it for export in the Property Inspector. This particular image, because it is marked for export, is available for download to anyone

who views the design specs. With assets marked for export, now you'll share the design specs.

5   Click Share in the upper-left corner to enter Share mode.

6   In the Property Inspector, click the arrow to the right of the URL link toward the top of the window and choose New Link.

Choosing New Link will create a new prototype link with a different title that you could also share with others.

7   In the Property Inspector, now change the following:

- Title: **Travel Design dev** (The title appears when viewing the shared prototype in a browser as well as when managing your shared links.)

- Choose **Development** from the View Setting menu.

- Export For: **iOS** (the default setting) (The units for the shared prototype are based on the artboard size of the home screen. The home screen in this file was set to the iPhone XR/XS Max/11 preset size. Adobe XD recognizes the default artboard for the home screen as being sized for an iPhone [iOS] and sets the units accordingly. The units are important when viewing the design specs in the browser because you can copy and paste the number value along with the unit of measurement—px, dp, or pt—that you need.)

- Downloadable Assets: **selected** (This setting is available because assets were automatically marked for export. If there were no assets marked for export, this option would be dimmed.)

- Require Password: **Unselected**. As with sharing prototypes, when sharing design specs you can make the shared prototype accessible to anyone who has a browser and Internet connection, or you can make it so users must enter a password to see the design specs.

8   Click Create Link.

▶ **Tip:** As with shared prototypes, whichever artboard is set as the home screen will be the first artboard users see in the design specs. Any artboard with a direct or indirect connection to that home screen artboard will be published.

● **Note:** To share prototypes or design specs using the Adobe XD Share feature, you must be signed in with an Adobe ID to either the Adobe Creative Cloud app or any other Adobe application.

● **Note:** The default unit for iOS is pt, the default unit for the web is px, the default unit for Android is dp, and the default unit for custom-sized artboards is px. These default units are not editable.

Understanding the Export For option when sharing design specs

Based on the platform you create the design for, each platform has a separate set of resolution settings. **Web**: Assets are exported at 1x and 2x resolutions. **iOS**: Assets are exported at 1x, 2x, and 3x resolutions. **Android**: Assets are optimized and exported for the following Android screen densities:

- ldpi - Low density (75%)
- mdpi - Medium density (100%)
- hdpi - High density (150%)
- xhdpi - Extra high density (200%)
- xxhdpi - Extra extra high density (300%)
- xxxhdpi - Extra extra extra high density (400%)

—From Adobe XD Help

The design specs are published and saved in Creative Cloud.

● **Note:** With a Home artboard set, unlinked artboards are not published in the design specs. The position of the artboards in the browser when viewing the design specs is identical to the position of the artboards in the design file.

● **Note:** Mobile browsers are not supported or recommended for viewing design specs.

9 Click the URL toward the top of the Property Inspector to open the specs in your default browser.

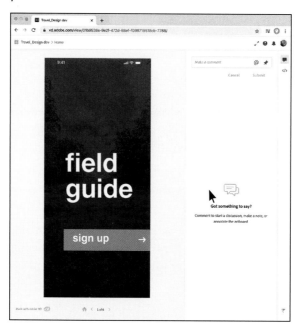

The view initially looks very much like the previous share you did, with the home screen showing and comments on the right. But when you share using the Development preset, there are some specific features useful to developers.

Inspecting design specs

Browser-based design specs allow everyone involved on a project to view the sequence and flow of artboards in what's called the UX Flow view. This view of all the artboards (screens) in the design specs shows the number of artboards that need to be developed (useful for planning the scope of development work), the sequence and flow in the design specs (useful for understanding the end-user workflow), the date when the design specs were last updated, and more.

In order to view design specs, whomever you share the design specs link with will need the following:

● **Note:** For a list of supported browsers, visit helpx.adobe. com/xd/system-requirements.html.

- A link to the design specs (In the previous section, you saw the Copy Link option to copy the link to the design specs in the Property Inspector in Adobe XD. You can paste that link in an email or other method of communication.)

- A supported desktop browser and Internet connection

Next, you'll explore the design specs currently open in the browser.

1   In the upper-left corner of the page in your browser, click the Travel_Design dev name to show different views.

There are two main ways you can view the artboards: Grid view and Flow view. Grid view is the default, and is where you'll see thumbnails of each artboard along with their names.

If you click one of the thumbnails (*don't*), the artboard opens in the window. Click the Linked Screens icon ( ) in the lower-right corner of the Hike Detail artboard, and you can see the artboards that are linked to it.

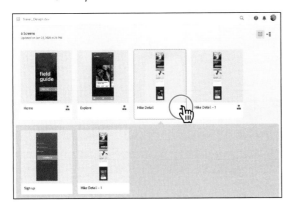

2 In the Upper-right corner, click the Flow View icon (•‖) to show the artboards.

In Flow view, you can communicate the design and layout hierarchy, as well as see any linked artboards when you move the pointer over artboards.

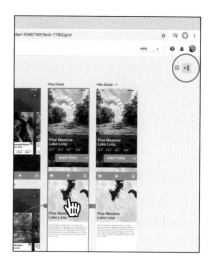

3 Click in the Home artboard to return to the same view you saw when you first opened the design specs in the browser.

In order to see detailed information about content in the prototype, you can view the specs, which is what you'll do next.

4 Click the View Specs button (‹/›) on the right side of the browser window.

To the right of the artboard in the browser window, you can now see all the unique screen details, colors, character styles, and interactions used on that artboard. The colors and character styles you see when viewing an individual artboard in the browser may differ from those found in the Assets panel when the original project file is open in Adobe XD. The design specs show all formatting applied to the content, whether it's been saved in the Assets panel or not.

5   Move the pointer over the white color in the Colors section on the right.
    Objects that have the white fill or border color are highlighted on the artboard.

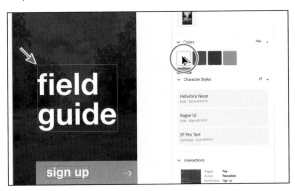

6   Click the orange color in the Colors section on the right side of the page.

Clicking a color or a character style will copy the formatting to the clipboard. For instance, copying a color will copy the Hex value of #FF491E (in this case). If you click to copy a character style, only the name of the font is copied. You can then paste the value into your code or into an email, for example.

Now you'll navigate to the next artboard.

7   Scroll down in the area on the right to see the Interactions section, if you don't already see it.

▶ **Tip:** You can change the color format by clicking Hex above the color swatches and choosing another format, such as HSLA. You can also change the unit that appears in the character styles by clicking the menu to the far right of "Character Styles" (the figure shows "pt"; you may see something different) and choosing another unit, such as px or dp. This change is persistent across the entire session—the same color formats and measurement units are used when you view other screens.

Interactions for a screen are the connections created in Prototype mode. You can see the options set for the connection, and if you click the interaction listed, the connected artboard will appear in the browser window.

8 Move the pointer over the interaction to see the "sign up" button highlight. You may need to scroll in the browser window to see the bottom of the screen. Click the interaction you see to go to the Sign up artboard.

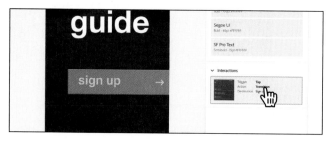

Selecting objects that have a connection set in Prototype mode shows a thumbnail of the target screen (artboard) on the right in the browser. In most cases, you could click the target screen to navigate to it. For some connections, like those set to previous artboard, the target for the selected content won't work if you click it.

9 On the Sign up artboard, click the johndoe@mail text on the artboard.

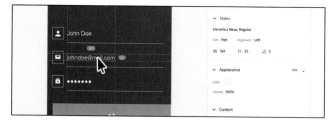

▶ **Tip:** With text formatting showing, you can click certain properties, like the font name (Helvetica Neue, on macOS), to copy them to the clipboard.

After you select an element on the artboard, you can view its height and width coordinates, as well as the properties of the selected content, on the right side of the page. You can also copy the character styles, color values, and content from the design specs.

Adobe XD focuses on the relationships between elements. So for example, if you design an iPhone X/XS artboard at 375x812 units and it uses type with a 10-unit font size, that relationship remains the same, no matter what physical size your design is scaled to.

However, in the design specs in the browser, height and width measurements and X and Y coordinates are displayed in px, pt, or dp. When viewing design specs in a browser, the unit of measurements can be changed from one unit to another. This feature allows you to copy and paste the number value along with the unit of measurement (px, pt, or dp) that you need.

10 Click the Next arrow (>) below the artboard to navigate to the Explore – 1 artboard.

11 Click the text "Pine Meadow Lake Loop." You may need to scroll to see it.

12 In the Content section on the right side of the page, click the text in the Content area to copy it.

The text is copied to the clipboard and can now be pasted wherever you need it. This is great for developers who need content, such as text, to develop the app.

13 Click the image in the middle of the screen, then move the pointer over the image to the right to see the relative distance between the objects.

If you're a developer, this can be useful information as you build the app elsewhere.

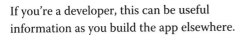
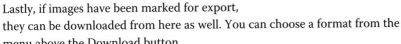
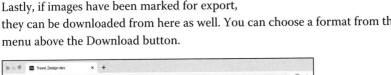

Lastly, if images have been marked for export, they can be downloaded from here as well. You can choose a format from the menu above the Download button.

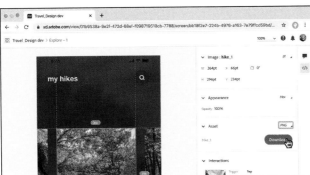

14 Click Travel_Design dev in the upper-left corner to return to Flow view.

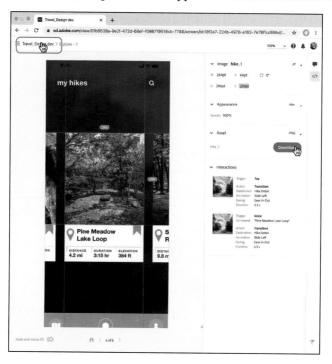

15 Close the browser window and return to Adobe XD.

Managing shared links

You can manage published links of your XD document by navigating to the
Creative Cloud website from XD. In Share mode, in the Property Inspector, click the
arrow to the right of the URL picker at the top of the panel and choose Manage
Links. From the Creative Cloud website, you can copy or delete a published link.

—From Adobe XD Help

Review questions

1 What does the Invite To Document feature allow you to do?

2 When you share a prototype, where are the files stored?

3 How do you embed a shared prototype in a web page?

4 Who can comment on a shared prototype?

5 What is a pinned comment?

6 What is a resolved comment?

Review answers

1 You can use the Invite To Document option to share a cloud document with others. All invited collaborators can edit your document and save changes to the original file.

2 Shared prototypes are associated with the Adobe ID that is associated with Adobe XD, and the prototype is stored in the Creative Cloud account associated with the Adobe ID.

3 To embed a previously shared prototype in a web page, with an Adobe XD file open in Share mode, in the Property Inspector, click the arrow to the right of the Update Link button. Choose Copy Embed Code from the menu and either paste the code into any web page that supports it or share it with others so they may embed the shared prototype in their web page.

4 Commenting is done in a browser by users signed in with an Adobe ID as well as by guests (users without an Adobe ID).

5 When viewing a shared prototype in your default browser, you can pin a comment to a location in an artboard. When a comment is pinned, it is assigned a number. The comments in the Comments panel show these numbers, allowing you to easily identify the context of the pinned comment. Comments that aren't pinned do not show a number.

6 When viewing a shared prototype in your default browser, marking a comment as resolved removes it from the list of comments and can be used as a way to mark comments as "done," for example. Resolved comments can be viewed by clicking the Filter icon (▼) toward the bottom of the Comments panel to see a window with filtering options. Click Resolved in the Status section of the window to see any comments that have been marked as resolved.

11 EXPORTING AND INTEGRATION

Lesson overview

In this lesson, you'll learn how to do the following:

- Export assets.

- Use XD plugins.

 This lesson will take about 30 minutes to complete. To get the lesson files used in this chapter, download them from the web page for this book at www.adobepress.com/XDCIB2020. For more information, see "Accessing the lesson files and Web Edition" in the Getting Started section at the beginning of this book.

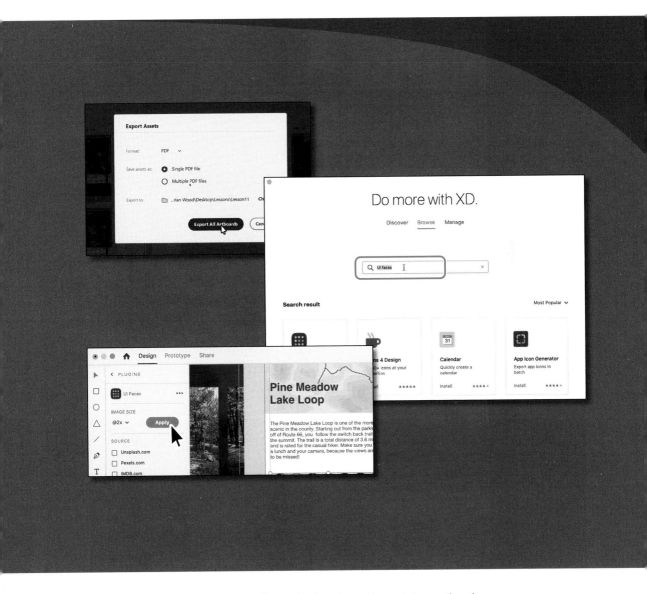

After you've shared a working prototype, gathered feedback, and implemented the suggested changes, you can create production-ready assets for development. In this lesson, you'll export assets in a variety of formats and expand what is possible with XD using plugins.

Starting the lesson

In this lesson, you'll learn how to share design assets by exporting and also how to enhance your design workflow with third-party plugins.

1 Start Adobe XD, if it's not already open.

2 Choose File > Open From Your Computer (macOS) or click the menu icon (☰) in the upper-left corner of the application window and choose Open From Your Computer (Windows). Open the Travel_Design.xd document in the Lessons folder (or where you saved it).

Exporting assets

● **Note:** If you have not already downloaded the project files for this lesson to your computer from your Account page, make sure to do so now. See the "Getting Started" section at the beginning of the book.

● **Note:** The screen shots for this lesson were taken on macOS. On Windows, the menus can be accessed by clicking the hamburger menu.

At any point in the design process, you can create production-ready assets. With Adobe XD, you can export assets for developers and others involved in the project. Assets can be exported in the following formats: PNG, SVG, PDF, and JPG.

- **PNG** (Portable Network Graphic): A raster graphics format best used for raster images such as banners.

- **SVG** (Scalable Vector Graphic): A vector image format that is best used for icons, logos, and page elements.

- **PDF** (Portable Document Format): A format for exchange that retains all vector, image, and text content. This is best for sharing your project designs.

- **JPG** or **JPEG** (Joint Photographic Experts Group): A raster graphics format best used for photographs and other images.

If your XD project was created as a proof of concept, you may want to export artboards to PDF (single PDF or multiple PDFs) or as images. To provide production-ready assets, you can export individual assets from your project in the previously mentioned formats. Given the need for responsive websites and apps, you will likely need to provide raster assets at multiple sizes to enable use on devices with different screen sizes and pixel densities.

When exporting assets, any selected content or artboard in your project is exported. If nothing is selected, all artboards are exported. Exported assets are named according to the name of the asset or artboard in the Layers panel. In the next few sections, you'll export artboards and design content in different formats.

Exporting as PDF

Exporting as PDF allows you to export what you see on the screen (artboards or selected content). Saving as PDF is a great way to share your content for review so the end user doesn't need Adobe XD to view the design. In this section, you'll export all of the artboards as PDF and explore the export options.

1   Make sure that Design mode is showing. Click Design in the upper-left corner if it's not showing.

    You can export content in Design mode, Prototype mode, or Share mode.

2   With the Select tool (▶) selected, click in a blank area away from the artboards to deselect anything that is selected.

3   Choose File > Export > All Artboards (macOS), or click the menu icon (≡) in the upper-left corner of the application window and choose Export > All Artboards (Windows).

    With nothing selected, you will see only two export options: All Artboards and Batch. If you select a series of artboards before exporting, you will see the same All Artboards command as well as the command File > Export > Selected to export only the selected artboards. If you choose File > Export > All Artboards, all artboards are exported, regardless of whether individual artboards are selected.

4   In the Export dialog box, navigate to the Lessons > Lesson11 folder (macOS), or, on Windows, click Choose Destination (or Change) and navigate to the Lessons > Lesson11 folder, and change the following options:

    • Format: **PDF**

    • Save Selected Assets As: **Single PDF File** (the default setting) (If you choose Multiple PDF Files with PDF chosen, each artboard will be saved as a separate PDF.)

Note: If you are starting from scratch using the jumpstart method described in the section "Getting Started," open L11_start.xd from the Lessons > Lesson11 folder.

Note: Content on the pasteboard that is not associated with an artboard will not be included in the PDF.

5 Click Export All Artboards.

The Export dialog box on macOS

The Export dialog box on Windows

A PDF named Travel_Design.pdf will be generated from all of the artboards and placed in the Lesson11 folder. That can be a useful way to share your design with others, and they only need to have a PDF reader to view the PDF.

Exporting as SVG

If your project contains vector graphics, it's best to export them in SVG format. As with all vector graphics, graphics in SVG format are infinitely scalable, so there's no need to export the same graphic at multiple resolutions. As an SVG graphic scales to accommodate various devices with a range of screen sizes, it remains crisp and clean. Icons, logos, and other drawn (rather than painted) page elements are perfect candidates for the SVG format. In this section, you'll export an icon as SVG and explore the export options.

1   Make sure the Layers panel is showing by pressing Command+Y (macOS) or Ctrl+Y (Windows), if necessary.

2   With nothing selected in the document, double-click the Sign up artboard icon (🗋) in the Layers panel to zoom in to it.

3   Click the person icon to the left of the John Doe text on the artboard, to select the icon component.

Looking in the Layers panel, you can see that the asset name is Component 10 – 1 (or something similar). When you export assets on macOS, you can change the name of the asset in the export dialog box. On Windows, the asset name is the same as the name of the content in the Layers panel and can't be changed in the Export dialog box.

● **Note:** As a best practice when naming assets for use on web or app, avoid spaces in names. You can use hyphens (-) or underscores (_) in the names instead.

4   Double-click the highlighted name "Component 10 – 1" in the Layers panel (or whatever you see), change it to **icon-person**, and press Return or Enter to accept the change.

If there was text in the selected content, you might consider converting the text to outlines before saving as SVG. SVG files require the font to be present when viewing the file in browser or an application like Adobe Illustrator. You can convert text to outlines (shapes) by selecting the text object and choosing Object > Path > Convert To Path

▶ **Tip:** The assets you export are named according to the name found in the Layers panel. Naming content according to a final asset naming convention in the Layers panel can make it faster to export assets.

(macOS) or by right-clicking the text object and choosing Path > Convert To Path (Windows).

5 Choose File > Export > Selected (macOS), or, on Windows, click the menu icon (≡) in the upper-left corner of the application window and choose Export > Selected.

6 In the Export dialog box, navigate to the Lessons > Lesson11 folder (macOS), or click Choose Destination (or Change) and navigate to the Lessons > Lesson11 folder (Windows). Change the following options:

- Save As (macOS): **icon-person** (This should already be the name because it uses the name in the Layers panel. As a best practice, we remove spaces in asset names.)

- Format: **SVG**

- Styling: **Presentation Attributes** (the default setting) (With presentation attributes chosen, any formatting, like width and height, will be written inline in the SVG code.)

- Save Images: **Embed** (the default setting) (This option saves any selected raster content directly within the SVG file. If you select Link, selected raster content will be exported as a separate image file that is linked to the SVG file. This results in multiple assets being exported. Linking can be useful if you need to make frequent updates to the raster content and not the SVG content.) We usually embed raster content in SVG to minimize broken links.

- Optimize File Size (Minify) (macOS) or Optimized (Minified) (Windows): **selected** (Minifying SVG will potentially make the file smaller.)

● **Note:** When exporting an SVG to hand off to a developer, for instance, you can ask the developer whether optimizing the SVG is suggested.

The Export dialog box on macOS

The Export dialog box on Windows

7   Click Export.

Exporting as PNG

PNG files are raster files, which means they are composed of pixels and won't scale well when resized. When exporting for websites, best practice is to save multiple versions of each image file: one at the original size in the XD design, and one at twice the size of the original to accommodate different screen sizes and pixel densities. When exporting a PNG asset for iOS apps, you will export three sizes of PNG files. When exporting for Android apps as PNG, you will also need a variety of sizes.

In this section, you'll export content as PNG and explore the export options.

1   Press Command+0 (macOS) or Ctrl+0 (Windows) to see all of the design content.

2   Click the map artwork on the Hike Detail artboard.

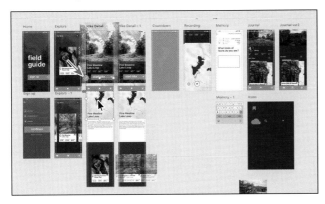

Note: This keyboard shortcut performs the same command as choosing File > Export > Selected (macOS) or clicking the menu icon (≡) in the upper-left corner of the application window and choosing Export > Selected (Windows).

3   Press Command+E (macOS) or Ctrl+E (Windows) to export selected content.

4   In the Export dialog box, for macOS, navigate to the Lessons > Lesson11 folder. On Windows, click Choose Destination (or Change) in the Export To section and navigate to the Lessons > Lesson11 folder.

Change the following options:

- Save As (macOS only): **Map** (XD will automatically add a suffix to each saved asset, depending on the chosen format.)
- Format: **PNG**

After choosing PNG, you will see four Export For options: Design, Web, iOS, and Android. Which option you select will depend on where you will use these images.

Design: This is the default option. Only one image is created, at the original size of the selected content. It is meant to match exactly what is seen on the screen. Design is a great option for sharing individual images and screen designs.

Web creates two sizes for each exported asset: one that is 1x (non-Retina or HiDPI) and another that is 2x, or double the size (Retina or HiDPI).

iOS creates three sizes for each exported asset: one at 1x, a second that is 2x (twice the size of the original), and a third that is 3x (three times the size of the original).

Android creates six sizes for each exported asset: ldpi, mdpi, hdpi, xhdpi, xxhdpi, and xxxhdpi.

- Export For: **iOS** (since this is an app for iOS)
- Designed At: **1x** (the default setting)

With Web, iOS, or Android selected, before exporting, it's important to set the size to the size you've designed at. With the iOS option, you have three choices: 1x (non-Retina or non-HiDPI), 2x, or 3x. By default, artboard sizes (such as iPhone X/XS) and the assets in them are sized at 1x (non-Retina). If you did not change the artboard sizes (the width, we mean, because the height can mean a scrolling screen), then you would leave the Designed At option set at 1x.

For another example, if you choose Web from the Export For option, you are given two choices for the Designed At option: 1x or 2x. You could either create your artboards at twice the default size (2x) and scale down to the smaller size (1x) when exporting, or you could design at smaller, default artboard sizes (1x) and then scale up (2x) when exporting.

5   Click Export.

The Export dialog box on macOS

The Export dialog box on Windows

There are three PNG files generated in this case. The images that are 2x and 3x are named with "@2x" and "@3x," respectively.

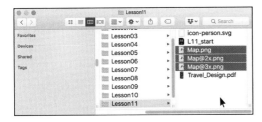

To understand how this sizing works for an iOS app, see the sidebar "Exporting PNG for iOS."

● **Note:** To see a larger version of this infographic, visit helpx .adobe.com/xd/help/ export-design-assets .html.

Exporting PNG for Android

Use the following infographic to understand how your design assets are exported for Android when you design at different resolutions: ldpi - Low density (75%), mdpi - Medium density (100%), hdpi - High density (150%), xhdpi - Extra high density (200%), xxhdpi - Extra extra high density (300%), xxxhdpi - Extra extra extra high density (400%).

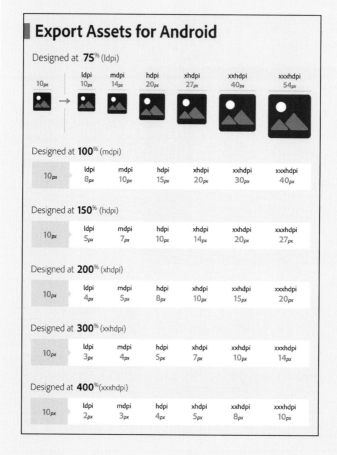

—From Adobe XD Help

Note: If you'd like to see a larger version of this infographic, visit helpx.adobe.com/xd/help/export-design-assets.html.

Exporting PNG for iOS

Use the following infographic to understand how your design assets are exported for iOS when you design at 1x and 2x.

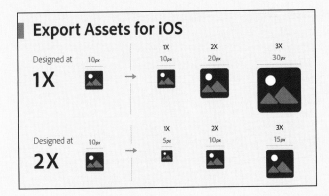

—From Adobe XD Help

Exporting as JPG

The final format we'll discuss is JPG (or JPEG). When you export assets (such as photos) as JPG, you can set the quality level of the exported file according to your needs. You can export as JPG when saving images for a website, when someone asks for a JPG file, and more.

1 Click the image at the top of the Hike Detail artboard.

2 Press Command+E (macOS) or Ctrl+E (Windows) to export it.

3 In the Export dialog box, for macOS, navigate to the Lessons > Lesson11 folder. On Windows, click Choose Destination (or Change) in the Export To section and navigate to the Lessons > Lesson11 folder.

   Change the following options:

   • Save As (macOS only): **HikeDetail-header**

   • Format: **JPG**

   • Quality: **80%**. (The Quality setting determines the file size of the generated asset and the quality. The lower the Quality setting, the smaller the file size, but you sacrifice more and more quality the lower you go.)

   • Export For: **Design** (the default setting) (The Design option will export a single JPG at the original size, whereas the Web option will export two sizes: 1x and 2x. When exporting your own assets, you will need to make a determination as to whether you need one asset or two.)

4 Click Export.

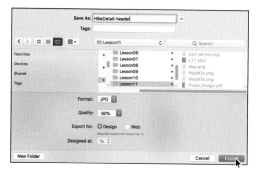

The Export dialog box on macOS

The Export dialog box on Windows

5 Press Command+S (macOS) or Ctrl+S (Windows) to save the file, if necessary.

Exporting to After Effects

If you want to use After Effects to turn your XD designs into custom animations or micro-interactions, do the following:

1 In XD, select the layer or artboard you want to animate in After Effects.

2 Select File > Export > After Effects (macOS) or click the menu icon (☰) in the upper-left corner of the application window and choose Export > After Effects (Windows). If After Effects is not installed on your machine, this option is dimmed. You can also use the Command+Option+F (macOS) or Ctrl+Alt+F (Windows) keyboard shortcut. After Effects launches (if closed) or moves to the foreground (if running in the background).

The selected layers or artboards are transferred as native shapes, texts, assets, and nested compositions in your After Effects project. You can perform multiple asset transfers to the same After Effects project and create animations in stages or from multiple XD files. For a list of supported features, visit helpx.adobe.com/xd/kb/open-after-effects-files-in-xd.html.

—From Adobe XD Help

Using plugins

● **Note:** XD also supports external integrations such as JIRA and in-app extensions to provide a complete solution for designers and stakeholders.

In Adobe XD, you can use plugins and app integrations from Adobe and third-party developers to enhance your design workflow by automating complex and repeat tasks and enabling deep integration with external tools and services. In this section, you'll discover where to find plugins in Adobe XD and use one of them to add a series of user images to artboards.

▶ **Tip:** To see a sampling of the plugins available for XD, visit adobe.com/products/xd/resources.html.

Installing a plugin

▶ **Tip:** XD plugins are saved in the XDX format. If you've downloaded a plugin.xdx file, you can also double-click to install it.

In Adobe XD, you can view and manage available plugins in the Plugins panel. In this first section, you'll explore the Plugins panel and install a plugin.

1   Click the Plugins panel icon (▆) in the lower-left corner of the application window.

▶ **Tip:** To access add-ons, such as UI Kits, plugins, and app integrations, press Command+N (macOS) or Ctrl+N (Windows) to open the Home screen. In the Home screen, click Add-ons on the left side of the dialog box.

In order to use plugins, you will install them. After you have installed at least one plugin, you can manage them in the Plugins panel.

2   In the Plugins panel, click Discover Plugins to get started or click the plus (+) toward the top of the panel.

By default there are no plugins installed. From the Plugin window, you can view, launch, install, and update plugins.

3   In the window that appears, click Browse to search for a specific plugin.
Since new plugins are constantly added, the list of plugins you see will probably be different.

4 In the Search field at the top of the window, type **UI faces**. The UI Faces plugin should appear. If you don't see it, you can clear the search field and try working with another plugin.

5 To learn more about the plugin, click the plugin in the list (circled in the previous figure). You should see a description of the plugin.

6 To install the plugin, click Install.

After a plugin is installed, a success message appears. You can now begin using it.

7 Click Back in the upper-left corner to return to the main options in the window.

8   To see any plugins you've installed, click Manage at the top of the window.

If you move the pointer over a plugin in the list, you'll see an ellipsis (...). If you click the ellipsis, you can either disable the plugin or uninstall it.

9   Close the Plugins window by clicking the red circle in the upper-left corner (macOS) or the X in the upper-right corner (Windows).

Creating plugins

To get started with creating your own plugins, choose Plugins > Development > Create a Plugin (macOS) or click the menu icon (≡) in the upper-left corner of the application window and choose Plugins > Development > Create a Plugin (Windows). The Adobe I/O developer console (https://console.adobe.io/plugins) will open in your default browser, where you can learn what it takes to make your own plugin.

You can also visit adobexdplatform.com for more information on the XD platform, as well as samples, community access, and much more.

—From Adobe XD Help

Using a plugin

After installing a plugin, you can start to use it. In the Travel_Design document you'll insert a series of user images (avatars) with the UI Faces plugin.

1   With the Travel_Design.xd file open, make sure that Design mode is showing. Click Design in the upper-left corner if it's not showing.

2   Zoom in to the bottom half of the Hike Detail and Hike Detail – 1 artboards.

3   Select the Ellipse tool (○) in the toolbar on the left.

4 Shift-drag to create a circle in a blank area of the Hike Detail artboard. When the circle has an approximate height and width of 64 in the Property Inspector, release the mouse button and then the key.

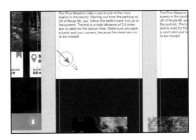

5 Select the Select tool (▶) and drag the circle so its left edge is aligned with the vertical guide on the left.

Now you'll make some copies using the repeat grid.

6 With the circle selected, click the Repeat Grid button in the Property Inspector. A repeat grid handle now shows on the right edge of the circle; drag it to the right to make a total of seven circles.

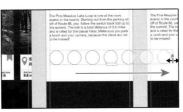

7 Move the pointer between two of the circles, and when the pink column indicator shows, drag left to overlap the circles. Stop dragging when the circles appear to fit width-wise within the bounds of the artboard.

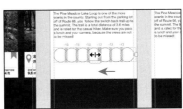

The UI Faces plugin requires separate circles, so next you'll ungroup the repeat grid.

8 Click the Ungroup Grid button in the Property Inspector.

9 With the circles selected, click the UI Faces plugin in the Plugins panel on the left. Any plugins you install will be listed in the Plugins panel.

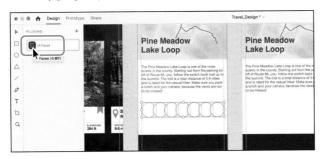

10 In the panel, you can select specific image sources to pull from, as well as age range, gender and more. Click Apply.

11 With all of the circles still selected, group them by pressing Command+G (macOS) or Ctrl+G (Windows).

12 Drag them into position as you see in the figure.

Finishing the design

Next, you'll add some text to finalize the design and then copy the new content to the Hike Detail – 1 artboard.

1 Option-drag (macOS) or Alt-drag (Windows) the green Pine Meadow Lake Loop text down above the avatars. Release the mouse button and then the key.

2 Double-click the text and change it to **Hikers**.

3   With the Select tool (▶) selected, press the Esc key to select the text object and then drag it into position, as in the figure.

With the avatar content finished, now you'll group it all and copy it to the Hike Detail – 1 artboard.

4   Drag across the Hikers text and avatar images to select it all. You may find that the text box above the content is overlapping it. If that is the case, click away from the content to deselect and then click the text box above. Drag the bottom handle up to make it shorter.

5   Drag across the Hikers text and avatar images to select it all again. Group them by pressing Command+G (macOS) or Ctrl+G (Windows).

6   With the new group selected, copy it by pressing Command+C (macOS) or Ctrl+C (Windows).

7   Right-click in the Hiker Detail – 1 artboard and choose Paste to paste the group in the same relative position.

8   Press Command+0 (macOS) or Ctrl+0 (Windows) to see all of the
    design content.

9   Choose File > Close (macOS) or click the X in the upper-right corner
    (Windows) to close all open files.

You did it! You completed a prototype for an app using Adobe XD! I hope you will
continue to learn and explore different ways to work with Adobe XD. The future is
very bright for Adobe XD!

Third-party integration

You can bring your designs into other applications that integrate with XD, such as:
Zeplin, Avocode, Sympli (only on macOS), Kite Compositor, and ProtoPie.

The section below provides a high-level overview of the workflow using the
example of XD running on macOS with Zeplin installed. The procedure works the
same way on XD running on Windows.

1   Select an artboard or layer in your XD file, and choose File > Export > Zeplin.
    Zeplin needs to be installed.

2   In the dialog box that opens, click Import. To replace existing screens in Zeplin
    with the same name, select Replace Screens With The Same Name. Zeplin adds
    it as a new version of that same screen, without losing your notes.

    The artboards are imported into Zeplin.

Note: This procedure varies slightly depending on the application you are using. For
more information, refer to your application's documentation.

—From Adobe XD Help

Review questions

1 In which file formats can you export content from Adobe XD?

2 When exporting PNG, what purpose does the Designed At option serve?

3 Before exporting assets, where can you change the name of the assets to be exported?

4 When exporting as JPG, what does the Quality setting effect?

5 What are some important reasons to use plugins with Adobe XD?

Review answers

1 Currently, you can export assets in the following formats: PNG, SVG, PDF, and JPG.

2 When exporting as PNG for Web, iOS, or Android, Adobe XD makes multiple sizes for each asset it exports as PNG. In order to do that, it has to know what size you designed at (what size the artboards are). In the case of an app you're designing for iOS, you can choose from 1x, 2x, or 3x. If you left the artboard size at the default sizing when setting up a document (for instance, iPhone X/XS at 375 x 812), then you designed at 1x. If you changed the size of your artboards when you started, to 750 x 1624, for example, then you designed at 2x.

3 In the Layers panel in XD, you can change the name of the asset. The asset name given in the Layers panel is the asset name when it is exported.

4 The Quality setting determines the file size and quality of the asset generated from the export. The lower the Quality setting, the smaller the file size, but you sacrifice more and more quality the lower you go.

5 In Adobe XD, you can use plugins and app integrations from Adobe and third-party developers to enhance your design workflow by automating complex and repeat tasks and enabling deep integration with external tools and services.

INDEX

from UI kits, 122
Corner Count values, 94, 95
corner points, 105, 113, 123
Corner Radius values, 94, 100, 101
corner radius widgets, 100
Create Link button, 296
Creative Cloud
    cloud documents stored in, 32
    previewing documents loaded from,
        273, 280–282
    saving XD documents to, 280
    shared prototypes stored in, 317
    working with documents from, 33
Creative Cloud Libraries, 179–186, 187
    adding XD assets to, 179–181
    character styles used from, 182–183
    editing items in, 186
    explanation on using, 179
    graphics used from, 184–185
    Illustrator assets added to, 181–182
    selecting multiple objects in, 185
curves, drawing, 112–114, 123
Custom Size icon, 31

D

Dash values, 107
dashed lines, 107
deleting
    artboards, 35
    character styles, 162
    color swatches, 97, 157
    comments, 306
    downloaded XD files, 279
    guides, 50
    See also removing
Design mode, 13–15
    panels, 14–15
    Property Inspector, 13–14
    toggling Prototype mode and, 15, 230
    tools used in, 13

design review, 289, 295
design specs, 308–316
    inspecting, 311–316
    sharing, 308–310
    viewing, 311–312, 315
designs
    finishing, 336–338
    previewing, 24
    sharing, 25, 27
    workflow for UX, 8–9
Desktop Preview, 24, 234, 240
destination setting, 233
development, sharing for, 289, 308–310
Device Preview option, 276
device previews, 273–282
    cloud documents for, 280–282
    deleting files from, 279
    mobile app setup for, 273–274
    navigating the mobile app for,
        277–279
    USB connection for, 274–279, 285
diamond icon, 168, 248
direction handles, 112
direction lines, 112
    creating, 113, 114, 116
    splitting, 115
direction points, 112
distances
    setting between gaps, 148–149
    viewing with temporary guides, 150
distributing
    artboards, 145
    objects, 143–145
documents
    cloud, 32
    coediting, 293
    creating, 31–32
    panning, 21
    saving, 33
    sharing, 25, 27
    switching between, 26
    zooming in/out of, 17–21, 27

Font menu, 82

fonts

    fixing missing, 84

    formatting, 82, 83–84

    message about missing, 90

    mobile previews and, 275, 276

    used in lesson files, 4

footer components, 167

formatting text, 82–84, 159–162

forums, Adobe, 5

frames

    resizing images within, 64

    support for inline, 301

full-screen mode, 241, 297

G

Game Bar app, 271–272

gaps

    changing in dashed lines, 107

    setting between objects, 148–149

gradient editor, 191, 192

gradient slider, 192, 194, 195, 196

gradients, 191–196

    applying, 191–194, 225

    description of, 191

    direction and length adjustments, 195–196

    editing colors of, 194–195

    linear and radial, 191

grammar check, 86

graphics

    creating and working with, 91

    using from CC Libraries, 184–185

    See also raster images; vector graphics

Grid view, 157, 311

grids, 43–48, 53

    drawing with, 112

    layout, 43, 47–48

    pixel, 107–109

    square, 43–46

    See also repeat grids

groups, 136–138

    creating, 136–137, 219–220

    editing content within, 137–138, 151

guest commenting, 303

guides

    alignment, 92, 111, 145–146

    artboard, 49–50

    deleting, 50

    locking, 50

    temporary, 145–146, 150

Gutter Width values, 48

H

hand pointer, 235

Hand tool, 21, 80, 112

Helvetica Neue font, 4, 79, 82, 161

HEX values, 40, 116, 162, 313

hiding/showing

    content on artboards, 134

    square grids, 93

HiDPI (Retina) sizing, 32, 326

high-fidelity (hi-fi) designs, 9

Highlight On Canvas command, 84, 157, 161

history of cloud documents, 283–284

home icon, 297, 298

Home screen, 10, 31, 231, 265, 309

hotspot hints, 277

hover state, 242–244

HSB color values, 41, 128, 192, 194

I

Illustrator

    adding assets to CC Libraries from, 181–182

    bringing in content from, 71–72

    editing vector graphics in, 186

    exporting artwork from, 72

image icon, 68, 130

working with comments in, 305–307

sharing, 286–317

    cloud documents, 290–293

    design specs, 308–310

    documents, 25, 27

    managing links for, 316

    overview on methods of, 289

    prototypes for review, 294–307

    review questions/answers on, 317

sizing/resizing

    artboards, 37, 53, 217–218

    images, 57, 58, 64

    repeat grids, 205

    See also responsive resize

Sketch files, 70

smooth points, 113, 114, 115, 123

snapping

    avoiding, 94, 112

    disabling, 63, 87

speech playback, 264

spelling check, 86

square grids

    explained, 43

    hiding/showing, 93

    shape creation and, 101

    snapping function and, 94, 103, 112

    turning off, 94

    working with, 43–46

stacking order, 127, 151

Star Ratio option, 94, 95

stars, creating, 95

states added to components

    hover state, 242–244

    multiple states, 244–248

    principles for editing, 248

straight lines, 110–112, 123

styles, text/character, 82–84, 159–162

Subtract option, 105

SVG format

    described, 320

    exporting as, 323–325

swapping components, 168–170

swatches. *See* color swatches

Swatches button, 186

symbols. *See* components

system requirements, 2, 273

T

tap triggers, 233, 238, 250, 253, 256

temporary guides

    aligning with, 145–146

    viewing distances with, 150

text, 78–86

    area, 78, 80–81, 87

    converting, 80

    duplicating, 85–86

    importing, 81

    point, 78–80, 87

    removing, 81

    rotating, 79

    spelling/grammar check, 86

    styling, 82–84, 159–162

text files, for repeat grids, 209

Text tool, 79, 80, 83, 159, 166

third-party integration, 338

timed transitions, 264

timed triggers, 264

toolbar, 11, 12

tools

    Design mode, 13

    Prototype mode, 16

transforming images, 63

transitions, 233, 264

triggers, 233, 265

    drag, 251–252

    tap, 233, 238, 250, 253, 256

    timed, 264

    voice, 253, 264

U

UI Faces plugin, 333, 334, 335
UI kits, 119–122, 123
  copying/pasting from, 122
  downloading, 119–120
  opening content in, 120–122
undo command, 111, 166, 221
Ungroup Grid button, 212, 335
Ungroup Mask command, 76
ungrouping
  components, 171–172
  grouped icons, 147
  repeat grids, 212
units of measurement, 45, 309, 315
Unlink Component option, 204
updating
  cloud documents, 282
  linked components, 175–177
  shared prototypes, 298–300
USB-connected previews, 273, 274–279, 285
user experience (UX) design workflow, 8–9
user testing, sharing for, 289

V

vector graphics
  Adobe XD and, 91
  Illustrator content as, 71
  using from CC Libraries, 184, 186
  working with shapes as, 91–109
versions of cloud documents, 283–284
video recording prototypes, 269–272
videos
  on cloud documents, 33
  on coediting documents, 293
  on exporting Illustrator artwork, 72
  on padding, 217
  on speech playback, 264
  on timed transitions, 264
  on timed triggers, 264
  on voice triggers, 264
view commands, 17–18
View Specs button, 312
viewing
  design specs, 311–312, 315
  distances, 150
virtual pixels, 43
voice triggers, 253, 264

W

Web Edition of book, 3
web pages
  embedding shared prototypes in, 301, 317
  measurement units for, 309
  resolution settings for, 310
widgets, corner, 100
Windows
  native zooming, 19
  prototype recording, 271–272
  system requirements, 2
  workspace, 12
wireframes, low-fidelity, 9, 27
workflow, UX design, 8–9
workspaces, 10
  macOS, 11
  Windows, 12

X

XD program. *See* Adobe XD
XDX file format, 332

Z

Zeplin tool, 338
Zoom tool, 19–21, 108
zooming in/out, 17–21, 27

Contributors

Brian Wood is a web developer and the author of over a dozen training books (Adobe Illustrator, Adobe XD, Adobe InDesign, Adobe Muse, and Adobe DPS), as well as numerous training videos on Dreamweaver & CSS, InDesign, Illustrator, Acrobat, Adobe Muse and others.

In addition to training many clients large and small, Brian speaks regularly at national conferences, such as Adobe MAX and the HOW conference, as well as events hosted by AIGA and other industry organizations. To learn more, check out www.youtube.com/askbrianwood or visit www.brianwoodtraining.com.

Production Notes

The *Adobe XD Classroom in a Book (2020 release)* was created electronically using Adobe InDesign 2020. Art was produced using Adobe InDesign, Adobe Illustrator, and Adobe Photoshop.

References to company names, websites, or addresses in the lessons are for demonstration purposes only and are not intended to refer to any actual organization or person.

Images

Photographic images and illustrations are intended for use with the tutorials.

Typefaces used

Adobe Myriad Pro and Adobe Warnock Pro are used throughout this book. For more information about OpenType and Adobe fonts, visit www.adobe.com/products/type/opentype.html.

Team credits

The following individuals contributed to the development of this edition of the *Adobe XD Classroom in a Book (2020 release)*:

Writer: Brian Wood
Executive Editor: Laura Norman
Senior Production Editor: Tracey Croom
Copyeditor: Scout Festa
Technical Editor(s): Victor Gavenda, Jean-Claude Tremblay
Keystroking: Keith Gilbert, Victor Gavenda, Jean-Claude Tremblay
Compositor: Brian Wood
Proofreader: Becky Winter
Indexer: James Minkin
Cover design: Eddie Yuen
Interior design: Mimi Heft

Lesson project credits

The following individuals created the artwork for the lesson files for this edition of the *Adobe XD Classroom in a Book (2020 release)*:

Dann Petty (http://dannpetty.dribbble.com/, @DannPetty, www.facebook.com/dannpetty)

Meng He (http://www.mynameismeng.com/)

The fastest, easiest, most comprehensive way to learn
Adobe Creative Cloud

Classroom in a Book®, the best-selling series of hands-on software training books, helps you learn the features of Adobe software quickly and easily.

The **Classroom in a Book** series offers what no other book or training program does—an official training series from Adobe Systems, developed with the support of Adobe product experts.

To see a complete list of our Classroom in a Book titles covering the 2020 release of Adobe Creative Cloud go to:

www.adobepress.com/CC2020

Adobe Photoshop Classroom in a Book (2020 release)
ISBN: 9780136447993

Adobe Illustrator Classroom in a Book (2020 release)
ISBN: 9780136412670

Adobe InDesign Classroom in a Book (2020 release)
ISBN: 9780136502678

Adobe Dreamweaver Classroom in a Book (2020 release)
ISBN: 9780136412298

Adobe Premiere Pro Classroom in a Book (2020 release)
ISBN: 9780136602200

Adobe Dimension Classroom in a Book (2020 release)
ISBN: 9780136583936

Adobe XD Classroom in a Book (2020 release)
ISBN: 9780136583806

Adobe Audition CC Classroom in a Book, Second edition
ISBN: 9780135228326

Adobe After Effects Classroom in a Book (2020 release)
ISBN: 9780136411871

Adobe Animate Classroom in a Book (2020 release)
ISBN: 9780136449331

Adobe Photoshop Lightroom Classic Classroom in a Book (2020 release)
ISBN: 9780136623793

Adobe**Press**